VIOLENT ORDER

VIOLENT ORDER

ESSAYS ON THE NATURE OF POLICE

EDITED BY
DAVID CORREIA AND TYLER WALL

FOREWORD BY
RACHEL HERZING

HaymarketBooks
Chicago, Illinois

Published in 2021 by
Haymarket Books
P.O. Box 180165
Chicago, IL 60618
773-583-7884
www.haymarketbooks.org
info@haymarketbooks.org

ISBN: 978-1-64259-466-9

Distributed to the trade in the US through Consortium Book Sales
and Distribution (www.cbsd.com) and internationally through Ingram
Publisher Services International (www.ingramcontent.com).

This book was published with the generous support of
Lannan Foundation and Wallace Action Fund.

Special discounts are available for bulk purchases by organizations and
institutions. Please email info@haymarketbooks.org for more information.

Cover design by Eric Kerl.

Printed in Canada by union labor.

Library of Congress Cataloging-in-Publication data is available.

10 9 8 7 6 5 4 3 2 1

CONTENTS

PART IV: THE MONSTER OF POLICE

THE FANTASY OF POLICE

Rachel Herzing

The summer of 2020 raged onto the calendar with a global pandemic and recession. Midway through this year of deep crisis, Memorial Day marked the beginning of an extended season of protest. The mood was already simmering with quarantine fatigue, economic desperation, and outrage over the murders of Ahmaud Arbery and Breonna Taylor by cops in official and unofficial capacities when Minneapolis police murdered George Floyd on May 25. The response in Minneapolis was explosive, as thousands of people spilled into the streets to challenge the violence of policing and the racism baked into it.[1] No doubt the memories of the murders of Eric Garner, Michael Brown, Sandra Bland, and Freddie Gray, as well as the uprisings following them in 2014 and 2015, were still fresh enough to add to this summer's pain. Protesters in 2020 also reprised the slogan "Black Lives Matter," which had risen to global prominence during the uprisings in 2014. What changed between the summer of 2014 and the summer of 2020? How were 2020's police murders not just more evidence of the long, unbroken pattern of police violence against Black people? Like periods following other rebellions against the violence of policing, 2014 ushered in a rash of newly minted experts offering proposals for the best ways to reform policing in order to make it less lethal to Black people and to "restore" community trust in police. As a result of this expert insight, the public was peddled body cameras, implicit-bias training, community oversight bodies, community policing plans packaged in a range of public relations rhetoric, and similar schemes. With so many recommendations swirling, why didn't all the reforms proposed in 2014 keep George Floyd from being murdered in 2020?

What *was* new in 2020 was a shift in community demands that dispensed with allusions about what policing is good for, instead asserting policing itself as the problem. Summer 2020 saw broad calls to defund policing coming from the grassroots. Minneapolis, the city that sparked the rebellions, went one step further by taking up demands to dismantle its police department, and cities such as Seattle and Portland followed suit.[2] The demands coming from Minneapolis were not the spontaneous outbursts of naive activists. Rather, these demands emerged over years during which organizers applied pressure on city leaders through multiple budget cycles to shift priorities away from logics of containment and control toward health and well-being. Organizations such as Black Visions Collective, MPD 150, and Reclaim the Block translated those years of organizing into clear demands that Minneapolis residents embraced and city leaders committed to moving forward.

Action on the streets played out against a backdrop of a shifting national conversation about policing, racism, and priorities. Corporate media outlets from cable news to the *New York Times* ran stories and published commentary making a case for redirecting resources from policing and toward life-affirming programs, policies, and practices, particularly for Black communities. Tool kits, reports, and opinion pieces demonstrated why and how defunding policing could be done. The issue of defunding policing even found its way into the 2020 presidential election, with each major candidate taking the opportunity to pander to law enforcement agencies and assure voters that they wouldn't support such a "radical" agenda. Organizers, on the other hand, took the opportunity to press further, making a public case for abolishing policing entirely.

The backlash by cops against demands to defund and abolish policing began almost immediately. Bob Kroll, president of the Police Officers Federation of Minneapolis, cast aspersions on George Floyd and on the organizers promoting transformation of policing in the city. Local police forces were joined by federal cops and the National Guard to suppress the rebellions nationwide. Cops across the United States slowed down or stopped responding to calls for service while simultaneously promoting the theory that US cities were suffering under an epidemic of gun violence and spiking crime rates that required an increase in policing. City leaders and the media jumped on the bandwagon, proclaiming the "failure" of the boldest proposals before they were even attempted.[3]

And then, of course, there was Kenosha. On August 23, 2020, Kenosha, Wisconsin, police shot Jacob Blake in the back seven times in front of his children, critically injuring him. The shooting was followed by multiple nights of protest that the Wisconsin National Guard was deployed to quell. On the night of August 25, Kyle Rittenhouse traveled to Kenosha from Antioch, Illinois, in response to a call over Facebook from the far-right group the Kenosha Guard for vigilantes to mobilize to the city to protect property from protestors. Rittenhouse, encouraged by local cops who told him, "We appreciate you guys, we really do,"[4] walked among the protestors, a semiautomatic rifle slung over his shoulder. He went on to shoot two people dead and injure another before the night was over.

Kyle Rittenhouse was recorded on video on the streets of Kenosha with members of the Kenosha Guard and Boogaloo Bois even as cops directed others to leave the streets under a curfew order. Calls similar to the one that brought Rittenhouse to Kenosha also went out across the country as far-right forces mobilized under the pretense of protecting property from the looters and vandals Donald Trump tried to convince the country were putting us all in peril. These groups joined the police project of maintaining order. In doing so they also had free rein to harass, intimidate, provoke, and physically harm protestors.

Kyle Rittenhouse was broadly referred to in the media as a teen or a youth. While his age, seventeen, made that unremarkable, it does stand in stark contrast to the public descriptions of twelve-year-old Tamir Rice, eighteen-year-old Michael Brown, or seventeen-year-old Trayvon Martin, who were respectively referred to as "menacing," "a demon," and "suspicious."[5] Rittenhouse also didn't suffer the character assassinations victims of police violence often experience, with information about any previous law enforcement contact reported as frequently as the details of the violence they experienced.

During the intervening years between the uprisings in Ferguson and Minneapolis, the proposed reforms did not lead to big changes in policing. Black Lives Matter took on unprecedented cultural currency, the Obama administration convened a task force on policing, and a series of consent decrees were implemented in cities including Ferguson and Baltimore. However, the number of people killed by cops did not substantially drop. Nor did the daily indignity of surveillance, harassment, and violence visited on the targets of US state repression, especially Black ones, abate significantly. The Obama task force yielded predictable, stale recommendations. Consent decrees and federal monitoring of police forces across the country merely overlaid the business as usual of policing with a veneer of accountability. Rather than these being the "wrong" reforms, the failure of these reforms rests more properly on a misunderstanding (or willful ignorance) of what policing is and does—*the very nature of policing.* Plainly stated, policing is a set of practices empowered by the state to enforce law and maintain social control and cultural hegemony through the use of force. A misunderstanding of what policing is and does fuels the continued attempts to apply half measures rather than to transform policing or the conditions in which it is legitimated.

We know that any demand to change policing is only as good as the ends to which organizers leverage it. As the demand to defund the police gained momentum across the United States, it was interpreted to mean everything from defund as a means to abolish policing to defund as a way to redistribute policing resources within the institution, for example from new equipment to new training. Liberals declared that the demand to defund the police cost Democrats congressional seats in the 2020 elections and lamented that if only people calling for the police to be defunded didn't ask for what they actually want, but rather repackaged the demand in other language (i.e., made different demands) policing could be fixed. The different purposes to which the demand to defund policing has been put return us to the question of the nature of policing. If we believe policing to be an institution dedicated to promoting safety and security, then we could reasonably assume that improving policing increases safety. If we understand policing as both depending on and generating violence, however, then we understand that the only true way to end the violence of policing is to end policing.

The failure of traditional reforms to address the death-dealing nature of policing requires us to look again and differently at policing. *Violent Order: Essays on the Nature of Police* pulls back the fabrications in which policing is wrapped to lay bare its features and functions. The essays in this collection insist that we not assume some natural or necessary role for policing and reject police being taken for granted. Section by section, the book dissects presumptions about policing from its relationship to order and natural forces to its essential role in maintaining civilization. Throughout, the authors remind us that policing is deeply implicated in shaping our ideas about order and civilization—policing *tells us* what order is and determines what is civilized and then ties itself to the project of maintaining them.

When we look back on 2020, marked as it has been by the structural violence and racism of the response to the SARS-CoV-2 pandemic and the violence of policing and suppression of dissent, we realize that these two fronts of struggle—the "twin plagues" described by David Correia and Tyler Wall in their epilogue—are deeply connected. The current period requires the kind of sober analysis of policing offered in *Violent Order*. We need a new view of policing that disrupts staid perceptions and helps us understand clearly what's at stake if we do not confront the violence of policing, whether that be physical, psychological, or cultural; caught on camera or done in secret. The authors in this collection offer this view via analysis drawn both from the deep well of scholarship on the topic and from organizers and activists waging grassroots campaigns for change. This is not just new scholarship but new ways of making sense of the violence of policing that help us fight in new ways too.

This new view of policing is essential to all the social justice fights of our day, including those for racial and economic justice, health, and well-being and those against climate catastrophe, environmental degradation, displacement, and forced migration. The context for all these fights is deeply shaped by perceptions of order and civilization mediated by a reality shaped directly by police. These struggles are also more effectively waged, as Correia and Wall suggest, through deep solidarity. The year 2020, with all its turmoil, pain, and death, also created openings to think bigger about what we want and need to live healthy, well lives. It set the stage for making bolder demands and pushing the limits. To take the best advantage of these openings, we will need to disabuse ourselves of fantasies about what policing is and remember that the only way to stem the devastation wrought by policing is to abolish it.

ON THE NATURE OF POLICE

David Correia and Tyler Wall

Police violence inaugurates law, and police officers are law's violence workers. It is the violence of police, according to the German social critic Walter Benjamin, that both makes *and* preserves law. This is not the establishment view of police as an institution. Across the political spectrum, cops are called crime fighters who serve and protect our communities. There is an enormous body of critical and radical scholarship on law but less so on police. Why is that? Perhaps police are too obvious or mundane a topic, with nothing available to theorize, so it is law, not police, that gets all the attention. Where and when the institution of police is taken seriously by scholars, it is rarely through a critical, much less radical, analysis. Often the focus centers on explaining racism or gentrification, for example, rather than theorizing how police are central to both race-making and place-making. Reformist approaches predominate, rooted in the premise that the institution of police is integral to democratic society. As a result, the *nature* of police is rarely considered, much less defined or analyzed. And this is because, according to this establishment line of thinking, the institution of police is self-evident. It enforces law, protects and serves, and keeps us safe. What else is there to know?

The idea that the institution of police requires no explanation or, worse still, is essential for democracy is common across the political spectrum. Liberal political thinkers might be more willing to condemn police violence than politically conservative ones, but they rarely understand police violence as systemic. Instead, the killings of people like Breonna Taylor and George Floyd, to name just two, are condemned as unjust aberrations. The solution to the problem of police violence for most political thinkers is thus always more reform, never the abolition of police. The problem—when one is admitted to at all—is rarely considered to be a problem of the institution of policing itself. Since the institution is beyond criticism, it's always a problem of a bad apple cop. The solution is always the same: better training, new and more stringent standards for recruitment, more less-lethal weapons, lessons in cultural sensitivity, and more female officers and officers of color.

But surely the academic field of criminology takes police seriously? Not in our view. This book makes no effort to engage with or contribute to criminological studies of police and policing, a scholarly discipline Michel Foucault dismissed as "so vital for the working of the system that it does not even seek a theoretical justification for itself, or even simply a coherent framework."[1]

Foucault is an important thinker for anyone interested in a radical theory of police. In his January 21, 1976, lecture at the Collège de France, Foucault said,

> War obviously presided over the birth of States: right, peace, and laws were born in the blood and mud of battles. This should not be taken to mean the ideal battles and rivalries dreamed up by philosophers or jurists: we are not talking about some theoretical savagery. The law is not born of nature, . . . the law was born in burning towns and ravaged fields. . . . War is the motor behind institutions and order. In the smallest of its cogs, peace is waging a secret war.[2]

Had Walter Benjamin been in the audience that afternoon, he might have raised a respectful hand during the Q&A and politely asked, "Who is waging this secret war on behalf of so-called law? Who is burning the towns and ravaging the fields?" We suspect Benjamin might have suggested the institution of police was an important part of the answer. In the United States, the slave patrol and the colonial militia served as one model for the modern institution of policing. As Marlese Durr has written, the slave patrol was the "first publicly funded police [department] in the American South."[3] And the policing of Indigenous people has a long history in which, as Sherene Razack has described, the "relationship between police and Indigenous peoples is one of regular, intimate, and violent contact."[4] And this conflict was inaugurated by the colonial militia and continues today via the institution of police. This book offers a view of police less interested in some abstract notion of law and more interested in the everyday, routine policing of our world—in the people and institutions charged with burning the towns and ravaging the fields, those institutions and agents committing the violence that brings law to life.

Law is to police, we might say, as electricity is to the Taser. To say that the nature of police is to enforce the law, and to leave it at that, is like saying the purpose of the Taser is to conduct electrical current along copper wire. The purpose—the *nature*—of police is to inflict pain or to threaten pain in the fabrication of order, just as the purpose of the Taser is to inflict pain in order to control another human being.

The radical view of police we offer in this book is one that begins with a rejection of the notion that the institution of police serves and protects. Police fabricate order.[5] The task is thus to identify whose interests that order serves and how it is brought into the world. The title of this book, *Violent Order: Essays on the Nature of Police*, refers to the multiple meanings of "the nature of police," a phrase we think should be at the heart of any radical theory of police. First, when we talk about the nature of police, we are talking about order. When we refuse to take police for granted, a different view of police comes into focus, one that reveals police as the means through which order is conceived, administered, and fabricated. The bourgeois conception of order is synonymous with police. The *nature* of police is to establish the necessary conditions and relations for the accumulation of capital, as order. Consider it this way: the bourgeois social contract can usefully be thought of as a police conception of history. That which is *human* emerges from a "state of nature," a violent animalistic existence, only because the police powers secure the conditions for civil society—that is, a *human* society based on racial capitalist, colonial, social relations of private property, the wage relation, and accumulation. Humankind in the image of capital, brought to you by police.

Second, if capitalism is anything, it is a way of organizing nature. The nature that capitalism requires is one that must remain forever freely available as a *natural resource*. Capitalism requires a nature that arrives in capital's image—ahistorical, taken-for-granted, abstract, a commodity. The nature that capitalism requires appears as a kind of second nature, one seemingly governed by immutable laws and intrinsically available for capitalist accumulation. Capital seeks a nature ready-made for its own destruction. The police demand for order is an order that requires not only cheap, reliable wage labor but also an equally cheap, equally durable bourgeois claim to nature as a natural resource. Capitalist property relations, after all, require more than racialized and gendered class relations. They require a nature transformed into commodities. It is police and the police powers that secure and harmonize this nature to the needs and dictates of capital. "What is a policeman?" Guy Debord asked. "The cop," he wrote, "is the active servant of the commodity, the man in complete submission to the commodity, whose job it is to ensure that a given product of human labor remains a commodity."[6] Police violence serves as a form of productive labor—it produces the conditions for the conversion of nature and human labor into a commodity for colonial and capitalist exploitation. Make no mistake, this is not some ancillary task or role of police. From the pollution of the atmosphere via the police protecting the interests of large corporations to nature transformed into discrete categories marked by enforced property claims to the police role as the lifeblood of fossil capital to the policing of the environmental movement, policing is the dominant mode in the exploitation of nature. World making, brought to you by police.

Third, if policing plays a key role in the production and exploitation of capitalist nature, then a key aspect of the nature of police is the way police rely on discourses of nature, animality, and monstrosity to *naturalize* unequal, racialized relations of power and violence. Police power defines itself as synonymous with, and the prerequisite of, order through appeals to race and species. Consider the countless examples of cops referring to people who are not cops as animals or savages. A world full of predators and beasts and heathens. Or consider the naturalized discourse of policing as a form of hunting, which is common in police magazine editorials encouraging officers to go on hunting trips for deer and moose to sharpen their skills hunting humans in the urban jungle. The savage monster, subdued by police.

POLICE AS ORDER

It doesn't take much effort to locate the concept of order at the heart of police, if police had a heart. There is an entire stratum of social scientists, theorists, and administrators diligently elaborating and defending the exclusive police claim to order. Their work comes in many forms. Often it comes in the form of so-called scholarly research by criminologists who seek to present police as a self-evident category essential to civilized, democratic society. Theirs is an intellectual mode of police legitimation that takes the nature of police for granted. It is a mode of police legitimation premised on three ideas: (1) the proposition that policing is inherently dangerous (it's not); (2) the idea that the world is dangerous without police (it ain't); and (3) the claim that police officers inhabit some unique, specialized, and professional authority (they don't). According to this mode of legitimation, cops are important, though admittedly minor functionaries, who inhabit a limited administrative realm within a larger, and more important, legal network.[7] Every now and then, however, the central role of police and the pervasive operation of the police powers in the fabrication of order escapes into plain view and requires theorization. Often this happens at crisis moments for police, such as at Standing Rock, in Ferguson, or, more recently, the police murders of George Floyd in Minneapolis and Breonna Taylor in Louisville. These are the moments when the beast in police goes berserk.[8] In these moments, when the *nature* of police comes ruthlessly into focus, it is clear to all that police violence serves no legitimate "legal" purpose. Police murdered George Floyd and Breonna Taylor as part of their role in patrolling a racial and class line essential to bourgeois order.

Outside of these so-called exceptional moments, however, police are, for the most part, of marginal interest to scholars. As a result, reformers see police violence as always aberrant, as always distinct from the nature of police. Pay attention in these moments. You will find two modes of legitimation taking place, two stories reform tells about police. The first, loudest, and easiest to dismiss will be the familiar claim that we should not look at police at all. The problem is found in the criminal nature of the victims of police violence. They and their behavior explain their fate. Claims like this are often made by the police and are then quickly repeated by journalists—for example, the claim that George Floyd had "previous scrapes with the law."[9] This reformist mode is one that invites you to see the world as a cop sees the world. This is the mode that asks, What choice did police have? This is the mode that demands we empathize with police. What else could they have done? This is the mode that celebrates the bravery of police in a dangerous world. And after all, what alternative is there? This is the default mode of police legitimation. In the face of seemingly exceptional violence, however, such as in Ferguson or Standing Rock or Minneapolis, when the very nature of police suddenly and spectacularly splits open for all to see, another mode of legitimation bubbles up from the swamp where it hides. This is the more insidious mode of legitimation that positions police as the beating heart of a *naturalized* social order.

When we understand police as about order, not law, we place police in an older and broader conception of police as an unlimited drive of the modern state to fabricate order through the elimination of threats. The police powers operate ambiguously within the discretionary prerogative of state power and political administration. This is reflected in US constitutional law when the police power is described as "the most essential, the most insistent, and always one of the least limitable of the powers of government."[10] The *nature* of police, then, is a "peculiar nature," as the German philosopher Johann Gottlieb Fichte called it in his *Science of Rights*.[11] Police power has a logic all its own, a logic that operates independently from a purely legal logic. Law only matters, in other words, if police insist it should.

POLICE AS A WAY OF ORGANIZING NATURE

Police fabricate order through terror and murder, and more. Policing is, first and foremost, a mode of world making that relies on claims to nature and the natural in doing so. In the police imagination, ideas of nature provide the central rationale and legal basis for claims to authority. The order that police fabricate is one that police understand as a *natural* order. This is true in two ways. First, it must be understood as a key discursive claim to police authority as a natural authority over human nature. The language of police is one full of naturalized claims about a human nature run amok without police.

Second, and less obvious, is a claim over nature itself. The institution of police serves ruling-class interests and the requirements of capital accumulation via its claimed authority over labor and nature. The alchemy that transforms labor *and* nature into commodities is one that police accomplish, whether by policing the mobility of the working class or by policing environmental movement challenges to capitalist uses of nature.

To say that the institution of police is a way of organizing nature is to say that it secures nature for capitalist accumulation. This idea is often only implicit in radical analyses of capitalist accumulation. The standard version goes something like this: A contradiction emerges when crises in profit realization lead to more and more power by capital over labor. As the rate of exploitation increases (mass layoffs, ever lower wages, longer hours, increased productivity demands, the sacrificing of workers to the factory floor amid a pandemic), so, too, does profit, at least in the short term, until at some future point consumption fails to keep up with production. The despised, immiserated worker is also the cherished, revered consumer. To this contradiction ecological Marxists have added another: nature. Capital stalks the earth for labor and markets, yes, but also nature. Capitalist enterprise impairs not only the social but also the natural relations and conditions on which it depends.

Capitalism, in other words, is a crisis-ridden and crisis-dependent system, designed to degrade and destroy all that it holds sacred. As Karl Polanyi argued, the idea of an unregulated capitalism is absurd, as it "could not exist for any length of time without annihilating the human and natural substance of society."[12] But how does it manage the transformation of nature into commodity, and how does it resolve the resulting crises that the contradictions of treating nature as a commodity provokes? Enter police.

Capitalism is an economic system that requires human labor power and nature. Both must be cheap and reliable, and cheaply and reliably available where and when needed. It turns out, however, that people and nonhuman nature are not all that inclined to make themselves available in this manner. As James O'Connor writes, "Precisely because [labor and nature] are not produced and reproduced capitalistically, yet are bought and sold and utilized as if they were, the conditions of supply (quantity and quality, place and time) *must be regulated by the state or capitals acting as if they are the state.*"[13] We do not have the capitalism we have if we do not have the police we have.

POLICE AS A SYNONYM FOR CIVILIZATION

Civilization is a police invention. Civilization, in the bourgeois imagination, is a synonym for class domination, a way to naturalize an order based on economic and social domination. The primary way ruling-class interests manage the insecurities and anxieties that come with their class privilege is via police. In the logic of bourgeois order, to be policed is to be civilized. To be without police and the order that police bring is to live in a *state of nature*. The institution of police is the "thin blue line" between civilization and savagery. The mandate of police power, then, is a mandate not merely to protect an already existing civilization but to actively fabricate a different one, a "polite society" organized around private property, bourgeois decorum, and classed, gendered, and racial hierarchy. Police will keep you in your place. Consider the progressive reformer Rev. E. H. Chapin, who spoke of police in 1854 as the overseers of cities seized by a fearsome savagery: "And no one needs to be told that there are savages in New York, as well as in the islands of the sea. Savages, not in gloomy forests, but under the strength of gas-light, and the eyes of policeman; with war-whoops and clubs very much the same, and garments as fantastic, and souls as brutal, as any of their kindred at the antipodes."[14] Police forever and everywhere confront a colonial insurgency and out of it make a "civilized" world. You can find the police-as-civilization logic at the heart of former New York Police Department chief William Bratton's 1994 "quality of life" report titled *Reclaiming the Public Spaces of New York*.[15] Bratton, famous for his "broken windows" approach to policing, described policing as the work of civilization building. According to him, "A decent society is a society of civility," and it is the task of the workaday cop to "uphold a uniform standard of civility and mutual respect in all the neighborhoods of the city." Police gift us a "civilized order," defined by bourgeois notions of "civility," "decency," and "politeness." Without police, without the workaday cop, we live in the jungle.

NATURAL POLICE

Without police there is no private property and thus no enforceable claim to labor and nature. China Miéville calls property a form of "everyday sadism."[16] Property, in other words, is central to a sadistic order given life by the cruel violence or threat of violence by police. This is not the accidental violence of a few "bad apples." Police violence, as Mariame Kaba argues, is "inherent to policing."[17] Thus, the radical theory of police elaborated in this book is one rooted in the everyday police violence essential to the fabrication of bourgeois order. It is a theory indebted to the insights, evidence, and arguments of many radical organizers and scholars who understand the police demand for order as a gendered, racialized, and patriarchal order.[18] One of those organizers and scholars to whom we are especially indebted wrote the foreword to this book. We share Rachel Herzing's insistence that we confront the fantasy of police through solidarity, on-the-ground organizing, and political education. This confrontation requires new ways of thinking about police. Police is not the institution many criminologists claim it is. It is not an institution limited to armed individuals enforcing laws in the public interest. Policing is a mode of environment making, of world making, and thus the radical approach we take to police in this book is one that focuses on the role of police in making the world we live in. Police fabricate and defend capitalist order. Police construct and defend relations of environmental injustice. Police don't just patrol the ghetto or the reservations of Native Nations; the thin blue line doesn't just refer to a social order; police announce a general claim to domination—of all human labor and nonhuman nature.

PART I

THE ORDER OF POLICE

CHAPTER ONE

INVENTING HUMANITY, OR THE THIN BLUE LINE AS "PATRONIZING SHIT"

Tyler Wall

Therefore idea that life itself, or at least a life worth living, is impossible without police is a ruling idea of capitalist order. If it were not for police, it is commonly thought, savagery and predation would prevail. This idea is condensed in the *thin blue line* (TBL), a phrase conferring a sort of sacred, mystical character to the "men and women in uniform." In the opening scene of the 2012 Hollywood police drama *End of Watch*, a white male cop played by actor Jake Gyllenhaal provides a concise articulation: "The thin blue line, protecting the prey from the predators, the good from the bad. We are the police." Or consider how the idea was expressed in 1951 by the staunch anticommunist LAPD chief William Parker: "Between the law abiding elements of society and the criminals who prey upon them stands a thin blue line of defense, your police officers."[1] If taken seriously, the TBL forces us to grapple with just how central police—as a specific typology of threat management via administrative violence—are to bourgeois conceptions of "civilized order." If understood as a police conception of humanity, as I argue it should be, the TBL, it becomes clear, aims to rewrite the Brechtian aphorism "first bread, then morality" into a crudely seductive security logic: "first police, then humanity."

TBL aesthetics are seemingly everywhere, whether it's waiting in line for coffee, driving down the interstate, or sifting through social media. Over the last decade or so, there has emerged a fairly visible culture industry, represented by companies like Thin Blue Line USA and Blue Line Beasts that peddle in specialized clothing, flags, hats, bumper stickers, jewelry, coffee mugs, license plates, light bulbs, and home decor. These commodities, to say nothing of DIY memes, are often adorned with melodramatic messages, such as Matthew 5:9, "Blessed are the peacemakers for they shall be called the children of God," or "And maybe remind the few, if ill of us they speak, that we are all that stands between the monsters and the weak." I frequently see students on my university campus wearing TBL bracelets, hats, and T-shirts, and with TBL stickers decorating their laptops. During the Trump presidency, the "thin blue line" flag became closely associated with the administration and the Republican Party, including reactionary street forces like the Proud Boys. What assumptions about the police/society relation are being articulated in these public displays of cop love? How might this mass psychology locate a mythological war against beasts as the ideological lifeblood of police mythology? In what ways does this cult of cop naturalize police prerogative as patriarchal protection? How are racial fantasies and class struggles, if unintentionally forgotten or repressed or actively recalled and remembered, mobilized when a TBL sticker is slapped on the bumper of one's vehicle?

By positioning police as chivalrous defenders of humankind itself, the TBL peddles in a gendered logic of prerogative power—namely, a "logic of masculinist protection" where the security of the nation, often conflated with civilization writ large, is said to be dependent on patriarchal authority.[2] At play here is the construction of a "sovereign manhood" or "national manhood," where it is not, say, the president but the figure of the cop, often imagined as a white man but not reducible to a white man, who promises national security.[3] Yet a nightmarish disfiguration of the body politic is perpetually envisioned, with workaday cops endlessly facing "near impossible odds." Consider an aesthetic increasingly influential in contemporary cop-pop culture: "Old Glory" with one of the stripes colored bright blue, with the rest of the flag rendered in black tones or a black mass.

Endorsed by the Fraternal Order of Police (FOP) in October 2017 as a "symbol of solidarity" amid the reactionary Blue Lives Matter movement,[4] this flag reflects police fantasy as national nightmare with dark, bestial forces threatening to devour the body of the nation, were it not for police "holding the line." If a guiding narrative of the settler state is "white men built this nation, white men are this nation," the TBL rewrites this colonial commonsense as "cops built this nation, cops are this nation." In 1974, at the graduation ceremony for the FBI Academy, an NYPD inspector articulated this in eliminationist terms: "Woven through the fabric of this Nation is a strong, thin, blue thread," which citizens must support in order "to eliminate from society those who seek to subvert the national peace."[5] Or as a cop in 2014 handwrote inside a leaked training manual: "You are the thin line of heroes preserving the fabric of America during these dark and desperate times."[6] To the extent that this political theology splits the world into good and evil while celebrating violence as regenerative, cleansing, and noble, the TBL belongs firmly within the "countersubversive tradition" and "political demonology" that have been fundamental to US settler culture.[7] Just as colonial mythology imagines settlers as always under attack, this police fiction sees savages as launching a perpetual war against cops and the civilization they claim to defend. With this in mind, it is useful to think of the TBL as a fiction of legitimate violence, which Sonja Schillings refers to as a politico-cultural articulation designed to render state violence as always defensive in nature while marking unruly populations as not merely transgressors of positive law but as *hostis humani generis*: "enemies of all humankind."[8]

The TBL, then, articulates the deep-seated belief that police are necessarily a first-order prerequisite for "civilization" to exist in the first place, let alone thrive and flourish. To speak in the name of the TBL is to specifically articulate police as the primary force that secures, or makes possible, all the things said to be at the core of "human" existence: liberty, security, property, accumulation, law, civility, and even happiness. Consider how, at a vigil for "fallen officers" in 1993, Bill Clinton referred to police as "sentinels of liberty," a "thin blue line . . . nothing less than our buffer from chaos . . . a shield that Americans may not always think about, until it's raised in their defense." Taking time to praise the gun-control Brady Bill and "community policing," Clinton mused that "the safety of our citizens in their *homes*, and where they *work* and where they *play* . . . *it all rests on that line.*"[9] It is therefore the duty of individual citizens "to reinforce that line . . . to make it as strong as we can," or in contemporary parlance: "Back the Blue." In 1967, a journalist for the anticommunist John Birch Society expressed the idea in similar terms: "The Thin Blue Line must be supported and preserved—your life and the future of this nation may very well depend upon it."[10] In this sense, the TBL is perhaps the quintessential example of what Christopher Wilson calls "cop knowledge," or a "knowledge economy that has the police—putatively agents of order—at its center."[11] Of course, the issue isn't whether the actual phrase is spoken verbatim or not but how this maxim abbreviates a more generalized police definition of reality: there is no civilization without police, because police is civilization and civilization is police.[12] And while it is true that police don't always speak in a singular voice, as Stuart Schrader argues,[13] the TBL rhetoric at least aims to speak for all police by naturalizing the idea that first there must be police, or there will be no human.

There is nothing innocent about this police melodrama. George Jackson rightly dismissed the TBL as "patronizing shit" for the ways it lays bare the ideological arrogance of police power.[14] To accept the "thin blue line" on its own terms, and I think this was Jackson's point, is to naturalize the violence of racial capitalist order as the necessary and inevitable violence of cops and cages. "The location of the 'thin blue line,'" write Ruth Wilson Gilmore and Craig Gilmore, on the always shifting yet enduring dynamics of the carceral state, "has moved but never disappeared as a prime organizing—or disorganizing—principle of everyday life."[15] To reduce the slogan to sensational catch phrase, then, would miss the vital ways political theater animates political power via melodramatic depictions of predatory evil. The TBL is an exemplar of the broader melodramatization of (in)security that structures the liberal imagination, the point of which is to mark enemies of the state as deserving of violence by rendering them evil incarnate.[16] More than a catch phrase, the TBL marks policing as melodrama of the highest order, a "mythological warfare" between civilization and savagery, good and evil, predator and prey.[17] The effect of this predator/prey formula is a naturalization of police power that renders the police relation a natural relation, as if police prerogative is to "nature" what a wolf's predation is to the untamed wilderness. In this formulation, even the most minor transgressions or unruliness circulate as bestial threats to social order, with police tasked with identifying, containing, and eradicating these threats in ways that reverse the predator/prey relation: police must become predators themselves.[18]

In this chapter, I unpack the TBL as a theoretical object that narrates a story about the police invention of the human through a civilizing and exterminating war against beasts. The project is less a history of the TBL slogan than a conceptually grounded sketch and abolitionist critique of its most basic premises. The idea at the heart of TBL is that the most routine mode of violent state prerogative—the police power—is imagined as always a defense of civilization, which at once means the "human species."[19] TBL, to use a formulation from Sylvia Wynter, is best understood as a defense of a particular genre of the human, or "Man," that "overrepresents itself as if it were the human itself."[20] As I show in this chapter, however, TBL articulates this police project as always incomplete, insecure, and unstable. Of course, it must always be incomplete, because it is through its inability to fully eradicate the bestial trace that police claim a license to endless war in the name of humanity. As a discourse of perpetual crisis, the TBL brings into stark view the failure of civilizational police power to actually secure what Diren Valayden calls the "species-unity" grounding Western bourgeois notions of humanity. At its heart, then, TBL is an expression of what Valayden outlines as "racial feralization," by which he means a strategy of governance that endlessly conjures "the ever present potential that humanity will slip back into and blend with nature."[21] If the historical trajectory of the concept of race has been to determine what it means to be human, feralization encourages a consideration of how fantasies and failures of becoming human animate all things police. And if the project of abolition geography is to imagine and eventually materialize an anticapitalist, antiracist world without cops, cages, and capitalism, TBL mythology works to materialize a capitalist, racist world without abolitionists, anarchists, and communists.[22] It is for exactly this reason that a consideration of TBL mythology is a compelling site to take seriously the insidious ways police—understood as a particular type of political power for fabricating racialized exploitation and expropriation—become synonymous with a violently narrow conception of humanity.[23]

A POLITICAL BESTIARY

The entire civilizational drama of TBL—that is, of police power writ large—is a zoological performance, a sort of political bestiary where animal imagery helps to justify an exterminating violence against racialized subjects.[24] Frantz Fanon famously noted how "the colonist always refers constantly to the bestiary,"[25] and from this we can highlight the bestiary as a key technology of police. It is no secret that police are especially fond of likening people to animals

by calling them beasts, savages, animals, mutts, dogs, and so on. There is a pre-
ponderance of evidence of this. TBL is nothing less than a political bestiary as
predators (part human, part beast) lurk in the shadows, readying to attack and
devour humanity at any given moment. It is almost as if Fanon had a critique
of TBL in mind when he wrote of the "colonized world" as a "world divided
in two . . . inhabited by different species," where "the dividing line, the border,
is represented by the barracks and the police stations."[26] This is not merely an
argument about how police dehumanize marginalized populations via racist
language. Rather, the point is to take stock of how the police power is animated by the figure of the beast, or the feral subject; it is to specify that what
is at stake in even the most mundane police practice, according to TBL, is the
securing of humanity from those animalized subjects that still exist within
the violence of nature. TBL imagines police as the central battle line of all
the wars raging within capitalist civilization: property lines, color lines, gender lines, welfare lines, bottom lines, picket lines, and bright yellow "Do Not
Cross" lines. But what TBL reveals in such a powerful way is how bourgeois
ideology comes to valorize police as the dividing line that necessarily splits
humanity into two warring species, with police as the arbiters for deciding
who is human or not, whose lives matter and whose lives don't matter.

The TBL fiction isn't merely that cops police the line dividing civilization
from savagery as if cops are somehow separate from the line. Rather, police
power is imagined as the actual line.[27] Police *are* the front lines, the barri-
cades, the ramparts that hold back an *invasion* of savage hordes threatening
to devour civilization. Chief Parker again provides a classic articulation when
he describes the police as "a thin blue line of defense . . . upon which we must
depend to defend the invasion from within" because, as he stated elsewhere
in 1954, there exists a "lawless criminal army warring against society itself,
and the police comprise that part of society which has been given the task of
being the first line, and sometimes the only line, of defense."[28] As this suggests, police logic can never really decide whether cops are the "first" or the
"last," or even the "only line of defense." This isn't confusion or contradiction
so much as it suggests that from the police perspective everything and anything begins, continues, and ends with the police as power of life and death.
Barry Ryan suggests that TBL "makes apparent that police have something
to do with lines, divisions, connections, and flows" while at once marking

"the capacity of the police to move back and forth with ease across the cartography of norm and exception."[29] But the TBL is always *thin*, perpetually on the brink of being broken or obliterated by bestial hordes, if it were not for the valiant "boys in blue" keeping darkness at bay. TBL marks less the back-and-forth patrolling between norm and exception than it marks the police as always in constant crisis, under threat, inevitably insecure if ultimately triumphant.

The implication is that the "thinness" of the line marks not a temporary crisis, a momentary emergency, or a state of exception. Rather, the normal condition of the line is one of continuous insecurity and instability, and it is this ordinary emergency that provides the alibi for everything police do, have done in the past, and will do in the future.[30] This pushes us toward an articulation of the police project as fundamentally premised on endless emergency where what is said to be at stake in police power is the very existence of civilization itself. The TBL fiction is nothing if not a bourgeois racial fantasy about how police—understood as a specific type of ordinary emergency prerogative that cannot easily be subsumed under law—are first and foremost the most vital of all countermeasures to a crisis of humanity. We can frame this in the form of questions: What sort of emergency does police power imagine itself corresponding to? What sort of emergency is the police emergency? This is an emergency of the very category of the human itself: a crisis of species where the "human" is fabricated as a site of racialized insecurity, always threatened by a regression to a violent, feral nature. It is exactly this crisis of humanity that is signaled by the thinness of the line, as if the very threshold between human and beast is perpetually on the verge of disappearing. Hence, the workaday cop makes possible, so it was written by a police official in 1955, "the very existence of civilization, for without the thin wall of police protecting the people from criminal depredation, the world would soon revert to savagery and bestiality."[31]

TBL is the popular expression of the zoological idea that police are necessarily the power that secures "us" humans from "them" beasts, yet it recognizes this as a never-ending project; hence, police must always be "on the lookout" while "holding the line." Take, for instance, how TBL is often linked to the trope of jungle law.[32] "In every city of the land," writes a commentator in 1925, "stands a thin blue line" fighting an endless war against "the law of the jungle—the law of claw and fang" that threatens to transform

"New York and all our other cities to places of terror by night to our peaceful citizens." With the state of nature framed as the scaffolding on which human drama as police drama unfolds, this unnamed journalist narrates the police project as a war against beasts, "a war that never ends" because "the enemy still thunders at the gate. ... The war must go on."[33] This means, of course, that for the cops "there can be no final triumph." Or consider how Ronald Reagan expressed the idea in similar terms in 1981 in a speech to the International Association of Chiefs of Police when he spoke of police not as mere crime fighters or law enforcers, but as "the thin blue line that holds back a jungle which threatens to reclaim this clearing we call civilization."[34] But by framing "civilization" as horrifyingly threatened by the "human predator" that can only be contained via the TBL, Reagan ultimately posited a police conception of humanity: "For all our science and sophistication, for all our justified pride in intellectual accomplishment, we should never forget: the jungle is always there, waiting to take us over."[35] That is, if it were not for the "men and women in blue," bourgeois civilization, or we might say the very creation of a society built on surplus value and capitalist accumulation, would in all likelihood regress back into a violent, unproductive nature. By positioning police in never-ending opposition to the dark jungle, with savages always threatening to take back or reclaim or repopulate the "cleared" land, Reagan asserts the central premise of racial feralization: bourgeois civilization's particular genre of the human is never a *fait accompli.*[36]

TBL as jungle discourse was strikingly encapsulated in image form in 1964 by famed cartoonist Karl Hubenthal in a comic titled "Your Shield and Mine." To conjure the image of TBL without uttering the words themselves, the cartoon depicts a large arm wearing a shield, which is itself an oversized police badge engraved with the words "City and State Police." In the bottom right-hand corner is a robed angelic-looking white woman kneeling down, and on her thigh is etched the words "our free society," while in her right arm she holds a book titled *Laws.* On the opposite side of the shielded arm, and in the top left-hand corner, are a broken bottle, a thrown brick, and streaking bullets. This anarchic side of the shield is titled "Law of the Jungle."

The vertical dynamics of the cartoon are particularly telling, with the Law of the Jungle essentially placed hovering over the kneeling figure of Lady Liberty as if jungle law is in the dominant position, with only police shielding her from savage violence. One of the most telling aspects of this image of cops as masculinist protectors is how it refuses to conflate police with law. Instead, police power is depicted as the condition of possibility, a prerequisite preroga- tive, for the rule of law to even exist in the first place. A free, civilized society, it suggests, must first be a policed society, or else the city will itself become a jungle. Perhaps most telling, though, is how the feminine figure of Lady Liberty is depicted as becoming human through her possession and retention of laws and freedom, which is in turn only made possible by the protective shield of the TBL.

Let's put it this way: TBL insists that the weight of the world rests on the shoulders of the "men and women in uniform" way before Congress makes laws and robed judges render decisions on the individual merits of "justice." The implication is that one becomes human, first and foremost, by willfully submitting to police authority, which also means to refuse this authority is to lethally mark oneself as bestial. In response to the 1991 beating of Black mo- torist Rodney King by a pack of white LAPD officers, Sylvia Wynter pointed to how common it was for cops to use the racist acronym of NHI, or *No Hu- mans Involved*, to refer to Black victims of police violence. Her concern was to account for how "*humanness* and *North Americanness* are always already de- fined, not only in optimally White terms but also in optimally middle-class" terms.[37] By unpacking the social effects of such a violent logic, Wynter argued that NHI revealed a genocidal animus at play, albeit not necessarily "overtly genocidal" but nevertheless producing "genocidal effects . . . by ostensibly nor- mal, and everyday *means*" (i.e., the caging and policing of young Black males).[38] If NHI is shorthand for the murderous enthusiasm underpinning colonial capitalist order, TBL smuggles in this racist patriarchal nationalism by telling the story of "humanity" as a civilizational drama between police and beast.[39]

On the surface, TBL is less obviously an overtly racist construction than NHI, appearing more as a simple statement on the necessity of security and order for any "civil society." Yet because its most elemental structure is that "society must be defended" from what is fantasized as an attack from savage species,[40] TBL sets into motion what Paul Gilroy calls "racism's alchemical power" to cast outside of humanity (history and culture) those marked as in- frahumans (not reducible to phenotype or skin color but routinely articulated as such).[41] This is not to suggest those who wear the TBL T-shirt are consciously or intentionally racist, even though it is quite telling how TBL has become popular among neo-Nazis and white supremacists.[42] TBL certainly licenses anti-Black racism, but its racism resides in its power to split humanity in half, effectively investing the police with the discretionary power to decide on the humanity or animality—and hence who can be hunted, caged, or killed with impunity—of individuals and entire communities. Racism, as Ruth Wilson Gilmore notes, is "a process of abstraction, a death-dealing displacement of difference" that "produces effects at the most intimately 'sovereign' scale" by fabricating a "hierarchy of human and inhuman persons that in sum form the category of 'human being.'"[43] Taking at face value and essentially celebrating the existence of a fundamental division between warring species, TBL refuses, and even laughs at, what James Baldwin articulated as a "plea for a common humanity."[44]

TBL frames the human condition as always threatened by a predatory present and feralized future. In other words, this police fiction both spatializes and temporalizes the perceived bestial threat that NHI calls into being since, from the police perspective, regression back to a violent nature can reveal itself in even the most normal, unsuspecting, and routine of circumstances. What appears to be a clear geographical division between two separate spaces—civilization over here, savagery over there—ultimately breaks down as cops are constantly on the hunt for the specter of atavism or the once-human subject that has regressed backward in time. Of course, those populations historically targeted by police, such as Black and Brown communities, have long been viewed by police as always already feral and atavistic, as existing within what Anne McClintock calls anachronistic space, or the idea that marginalized populations "exist in a permanently anterior time within the geographic space of the modern empire."[45] If the beast resides within everyone, if more forceful in some, then this means that from the police perspective there can never really ever be any clear territorial division between civilization and barbarism. The jungle is mapped onto the city, and everyone and anyone can be determined by police to be the proper objects of policing's civilizing touch. If the line itself is each and every individual cop, as TBL mythology insists, then this embodied line is constantly moving and patrolling across the untamed wilderness, guarding life and property as well as hunting and tracking predators and keeping a watchful eye on would-be beasts. TBL insists, then, that wherever and whenever the cop occupies space, whether standing on the sidewalk, patrolling the streets, or even passing out candy during a parade, this territorializing agent of the state is always haunted by the "state of nature," whether from those who have never left this violent condition or those who might regress back to it.

THE POLICE INVENTION OF HUMANITY

By narrating police as always in opposition to an original scene of predatory violence—the urban jungle as state of nature—TBL authorizes racialized state violence in the name of humanity: police-as-prerequisite for making and preserving the human species. A critique of TBL, then, encourages a critique less of how the ideology of law claims to make the human possible, what Samera Esmeir calls "juridical humanity,"[46] and more of what we might call police humanity: a story about the police project as the invention of humanity. Of course, legal reasoning certainly plays an important role in all things police, but it is the notion of police as a prerogative violence over and above law, but licensed through law, that TBL expresses so clearly. TBL identifies the police power as the most routine and insidious logic of *necessitas*, or what Denise Ferreira da Silva describes as a prerogative violence deemed "*just* because it is deemed *necessary* for the reinscription of the state's authority."[47] This is directly observed when an officer places a "thin blue line" flag sticker on his handgun,[48] and it is also manifest when TBL imagery is decorated with a popular maxim: "People sleep peacefully in their beds at night only because rough men stand ready to do violence on their behalf." Giving popular expression to the idea that security is the supreme concept of bourgeois society,[49] TBL recognizes the truth of Walter Benjamin's critique of state violence: "the 'law' of the police really marks the point at which the state . . . can no longer guarantee through the legal system the empirical ends that it desires at any price to attain."[50]

This was clearly articulated by Michael Stone, a defense attorney for the white LAPD officers charged, and eventually acquitted, in the beating of Rodney King. Talking to journalists, Stone argued that cops "do not get paid to lose a street fight. . . . And if we as members of the community demand they do that, *the thin blue line* that separates the law-abiding and the not law-abiding will disintegrate."[51] According to this logic, cops are not only paid to "win street fights" but are to win by any means necessary or else the entire social order will collapse. By placing the individual cop as the dividing line between law and savagery, Stone naturalizes the idea that for the un-pacified to be pacified, cops must tap into their own predatory nature to re-establish social order. Here, cops are less agents of law and more a law unto themselves who must "get their hands dirty" by street fighting in the name of delivering street justice. We should recall that the "civilizing discipline" meted out against King was justified, as Cedric Robinson once explained, via "dogmatic cultural convictions" of the Hobbesian variety, which he under-stood as "providing the surface idioms" of the ruling elite's assault against the poor and multiracial working class.[52] King himself and by extension Black and Brown populations more generally were constructed as bestial aggressors that can only be pacified via the application of legal violence, with one officer calling the bludgeoned King "bear-like."[53] Directly before officers beat King, some officers referred to a Black couple in a domestic dispute as "gorillas in the mist," to say nothing of the widespread use of NHI discussed earlier. As one lawyer explained, "They truly believe it's a jungle and there's this thin blue line" and that "the jungle is over there and the good people are over here. They're subhumans over there. They're gorillas. They're lizards."[54]

In its most basic narrative structure, the "thin blue line" plagiarizes the mythological origins of the modern state by recasting the story of the "state of nature" in explicitly police terms. Thomas Hobbes famously spoke of this precivil life as a state of war, of perpetual predatory relations where every in-dividual was pitted against each other like brutes akin to wolves.[55] If life in the state of nature was defined by bestial existence that is "nasty, brutish, and short," then for Hobbes the way out of this problem is a consensually formed "civil government" that appropriates and monopolizes violence in the name of public welfare. Just as those in the state of nature are said to have a natural right to "self-defense" and "self-preservation," sovereign power claims for it-self this natural right of defensive violence in the name of peace, security, and order, which Dimitris Vardoulakis refers to as the "universal justifications" of state violence.[56] Those who threaten or violate the peace, such as by com-mitting a crime or being unruly or disorderly, can be subjected to a violence that is not dissimilar to the violence used to kill nonhuman animals. This is perhaps best articulated by John Locke in his *Second Treatise on Government* when he writes of the criminal as waging a war against someone's life, and "for the same reason that I may kill a wolf or a lion," this warring criminal who has "no rule except that of force and violence" can be "treated as beasts of prey, those dangerous and noxious creatures that will be sure to destroy him whenever he falls into their power."[57] Just as wolves have no respect for private property and are said to be merely predatory, the "criminal," who does not live "under the ties of common law reason," poses a similar threat against the life and sanctity of property and must be dealt with in similar terms as beasts. Here, it must be said that the social contract has never been an innocent philosophical exercise but rather a "description of concrete historical events," as K-Sue Park writes on how it was used to justify colonial conquest and chattel slavery in the Americas.[58] Similarly, TBL is nothing if not a mythology of justification that works to naturalize police prerogative via racialized and gendered depictions of oppressed populations as savages.

At the heart of this foundational mythology about the creation of "civil society" is a profound anxiety about the always-uneasy threshold between human and animal, as the modern state becomes fixated on creating and policing the lines dividing civilization and savagery. Despite all of the different variations and nuances, as Christopher La Barbera has shown, a central premise stitching social contract mythologies together is a story about the invention of humanity via a confrontation with nature and animality.[59] This story about the invention of humanity is of course a fundamentally racial project—a racial contract—that refracts race through the lens of species and species through a racialization lens.[60] Kay Anderson points to how the "state of nature" constructs a racial conception of the human as the transcendence of nature—the full human is the human who overcomes the "external nature" of hunting and gathering and the "internal nature" of "human animal," or the beast within.[61] Critical animal studies scholars point to the ways that "the human" gains its meaning through a negation of its own animality, a process that becomes essentially impossible without the production and naturalization of racial differentiation and hierarchal exclusion. Yet scholars focusing on the historical links between humanism and racism have pointed to how the human is an always already racialized, classed, and gendered construction built on liberalism's "exclusion clauses" that cast outside of humanity those subjects rendered nonhuman or inhuman, as animals and savages that exist only in the violence of bestial existence.[62]

What I am suggesting is that the figure of the state of nature, defined by animalistic predation and bestial aggression, is the most naturalized and fundamental story of all police stories. We get glimpses of this when police speak of their task as creating a "polite society" and a "decent society," which is nothing if not an embrace of police as a power to civilize the uncivilized. Police also often speak of themselves as "teaching a lesson" in how to "not act like an animal" to those racialized populations said to be lacking human qualities. Take for instance how the philosopher of sovereign decision Carl Schmitt characterized Hobbes's *Leviathan* as ultimately a police story that narrates state prerogative—understood as the general apparatus of security—as ultimately a police power responsible for, as he puts it, "transforming wolves into citizens": "This is a familiar definition of police. Modern state and modern police came into being simultaneously and the most vital institution of the security state is the police."[63] Schmitt's use of the wolf as symbol of state of nature borrows directly from one of the most famous passages of political theory, which Hobbes himself cited: *homo homini lupus*, or "man is a wolf to man." We have already seen in Locke the figure of the criminal as a wolf that can be exterminated in the name of order. The historical figure of the wolf, as others have shown, was the foundational basis for the "outlaw" that was banished outside the domain of legal protection and therefore could be killed with impunity.[64] If TBL is at heart a story about the police power turning wolves into citizens or at least eradicating the wolf so that the human can live in peace, as I am suggesting, the reverse is also true: TBL etches into the political imagination the racialized logic of feralization or the never-ending possibility that the human might regress back into a wolf. As Mary Nyquist notes, there is a temporal dimension in Hobbes in that a "threatened regression" *back* to the violence of primitive nature is always on the political horizon.[65] It is this threatening "return" to a state of nature—the thinness of the TBL—that provides the ideological scaffolding on which the police power justifies itself as the invention of humanity.

What emerges here is a theriophobic animus, or an intense fear of wild beasts,[66] animating the police power as a strategy of order building, even if the bestial figure can never fully be eradicated. The theriophobia of the TBL brings to the surface how the fear of a degenerative regression back to a violent wolf-life nature provides the justificatory logic of all police power. This is succinctly articulated in a memoir by a Knoxville officer: "For a cop, the moon is *always* full."[67] The same year this memoir was published, "wilding" emerged in the public imagination to describe Black inner-city youth as "wolf packs," and in 1995 John DiIulio would invoke the wolf while predicting "the coming of the superpredators," a cohort of inner-city youth who were godless and ultraviolent.

It is no coincidence that the wolf is a central figure in the contemporary bestiary of TBL. Over the last twenty years, a story about "wolves, sheep, and sheepdogs" has emerged as one of the most popular and visible police mythologies, with criminals being the wolves that are hunted down by sheepdog-police protecting their flock of citizen-sheep. Popular police trainer and self-proclaimed "killogist" Lt. Col. David Grossman is usually credited with popularizing this story in his book *On Combat*, although he first mentions this in his widely celebrated book *On Killing*.[68] As a result, TBL clothing and other products are commonly adorned with phrases that identify police as sheepdogs and "wolf hunters": "I hunt the wolf in the dark of the night"; "The sheep pretend the wolf will never come. The sheepdog lives for that day"; "There are wolves. There are sheep. I am a sheepdog"; and "Because of the sheepdog the wolf is lean and forced to hunt at night . . . and because of the wolf the sheepdog never sleeps that his flock may live in peace." As a historically enduring symbol of evil, violence, and indigeneity, the figure of the wolf further identifies police mythology as frontier mythology, imagining police as the settler state moving through untamed wilderness, hunting dark predators in civilization's shadows. Consider a meme image posted in April 2019 on the public Facebook page of the North American Police Work Dog Association with the heading "The Thin Blue Line . . .": a sheepdog guarding a flock of sheep from a beastly bipedal werewolf. The image was posted with an additional message from the website administrator: "This speaks volumes."[69]

If we continue tracking the wolf and sheepdog across the frontiers of the TBL, what we find is an image of police as superpredator, or the beast in police.[70] Despite TBL positing some clear divide between civilization and savagery, there nevertheless remains an acknowledgment and embrace of policing's own animalistic, carnivorous nature. For human prey to be protected from rapacious predators, so it goes, police must always strive to be the apex predator that rules all other predators prowling in the urban jungle. "It

takes a predator to catch a predator," writes Stephanie Rogish and Lt. Col.
Dave Grossman in a coauthored children's book on police and soldiers called
Sheepdogs: Meet Our Nation's Warriors.[71] Here, they point to the similarities
between the sheepdog and the wolf, explaining to the children that "sometimes the sheep are frightened by the sheepdogs" because "sheepdogs look a
little bit like the wolves with their fur, sharp teeth, and watchful eyes." But
they insist that at the end of the day, inevitably, when "the wolf comes! . . . the
whole flock tries to hide behind the closest sheepdog." To imagine oneself
as a sheepdog who guards sheep from wolves requires not only recognizing
policing's own animality but also inscribing the cynegetic power of police, or
the predator/prey dialectic, into the laws of nature.[72] "In nature, the sheep is
born a sheep. The wolf is born a wolf. And the sheepdog is born a sheepdog.
That is the way they are born and they can never be anything else." After all,
wolves, sheep, and sheepdogs "are just animals who play important roles in
the balance of nature"—feralization as the very milieu of the capitalist world.

    "The thin blue line is not a fictional concept," an anonymous police offi-
cer and military veteran writes in *Law Enforcement Today*. "It's real—and it's
what separates society from anarchy. It's why you can go to work. Why your
children can go to school. Why you can sleep in peace at night." He writes
this under the screen name Sgt. A. Merica. Police aren't protective sheepdogs,
he claims, but rather wolves hunting down the beasts so that the human may
live free of fear and violence. We find the nature of police in the nature of predation. "I am not your Sheepdog," he writes. "I am your wolf . . . While the
Sheepdog protect [*sic*] . . . I destroy. But I am YOUR wolf. I hunt my prey—
and my prey fears me." The carnivorous appetite of police is what secures humanity from its own bestiality and savagery. For the human to survive, Sgt. A.
Merica insists, the "men and women in uniform" must not simply hold the
line between civilization and savagery. They must also become beasts:

> I am the one who stalks them. As they prepare to come for you . . . I
> pounce. I am not kind. I am not merciful. I take the fight out of them.
> Then I take them out of the fight. Their throat is my prize. Their end is
> my glory.

It is only through the inhumanity of policing—his "glory"—that the human
emerges. "I do it for my children. I do it for my God. I do it for my country. I

do it for you. I am the wolf. And tonight, like every night, I will hunt." The point: it might be true that everyone is always potentially a beast—but only cops are *allowed* to be beasts. The cop beast is a noble beast—a good wolf. That is to say, the police invention of humanity that TBL promises is, in the end, a cruel celebration of the inhumanity of police.

CHAPTER TWO

DISRUPTING ORDER: RACE, CLASS, AND THE ROOTS OF POLICING

Philip V. McHarris

Red and blue police lights cycle day and night outside many New York City public housing developments. The emergency lights, absent any emergency, penetrate apartment windows and the city landscape and are an established dimension of everyday urban life. On a summer day, trash fills the sidewalk of a Brooklyn housing development, while a police car sits directly in front of the pile. The trash makes it difficult and hazardous for residents, particularly elderly residents with disabilities, to make it into their homes. An officer rests his arm just outside the window of an NYPD squad car. The highly visible, persistent presence is framed as a way to maintain safety and deter disorder, and the squad car lights are meant to communicate that order is present in a disorderly environment.

Persistent police presence in cities has come to be taken for granted. When people think of cities, police sirens and lights often loom in the imagination. Through the ubiquity of policing, police power has come to seem natural in the landscape of everyday life. Policing, however, is not natural, and the function of the police is far from clear. To understand the nature of police, it is essential to explore the history of policing. In doing so, three approaches to the scope and power of police emerge: police abolition, preservation, and expansion. While the framework of abolition seeks to shrink and dismantle police power, police preservation aims to maintain police power, even when seeking to reform particular aspects of policing. Police expansion is a framework that aims to expand the scope and power of police in everyday life. Importantly, efforts and reforms consistent with police preservation and expansion often dovetail with one another, as expansion can be a strategy of preservation.

Police killings have persisted since 2014—the year the Movement for Black Lives emerged to protest and challenge police violence.[1] Even during the COVID-19 pandemic, when large numbers of people were inside, police killings remained on par with previous years.[2] The criminalization of the COVID-19 pandemic eventually led to police violence in the name of public health.[3] Despite the perception that police killings are random and unpredictable, the data suggest a stable persistence. The reason for persisting police violence is simple: many efforts historically have centered on police preservation and expansion as an approach to reform while failing to recognize the fundamentally violent nature of policing.

CRIMINALIZATION, SAFETY, AND THE NATURES OF POLICING

Central to the premise of policing in the United States is that society is split into people who are good and those who are bad. The dominant framework suggests that those who are bad deserve to be punished and are largely incapable of change, and as a result, there needs to be an entity—namely, the police—that protects the good elements of society from the bad. These conceptions are socially constructed and shaped by race, class, origin, sexuality, and gender. Those invested in police preservation and expansion posit that the dangerous element, or predators of society that prey on individuals in need of protection, will always try to do harm and wreak havoc on others, thus requiring police to control them and use carceral institutions to contain them. At the core of this "thin blue line" premise lies a religious, Manichaean orientation that splits the world into good and evil.[4] In this orientation, there will always be opposing forces, and police are the critical actors that hold the line between good and evil.

The focus on good versus evil, the latter of which is attributed to an inherent culture or ontological disposition, creates limitations to ending violence within communities, including patriarchal violence. Abolitionists present visions of safe, accountable communities that end and transform cycles of patriarchal violence in ways that do not exacerbate existing harm along the way. As a result, abolitionists challenge the views of human nature that underpin police and carceral logics. The current criminal legal system and structure of policing socialize people to refuse accountability for doing harm in order to prove themselves innocent. The carceral system creates a context where if one is accused of something, the first thing they often try to do is figure a way to discredit and disprove what happened in order to avoid severe punitive response from the state. This has created a culture of refusing accountability because of the realities and fears of the carceral system that have been internalized by society more generally.

Police and the criminal legal system rely on the dubious idea of a fixed human nature in order to justify the preservation and expansion of policing and punishment. Dominant society and elites have historically constructed criminals for the purpose of justifying an institution that exploits and controls those deemed threatening. People from marginalized communities have long been criminalized, and in many ways the expansion of criminalization was largely shaped by desires to control and exploit racialized communities, poor people, and workers.

Marginalized communities—whether the marginalization is a result of race, class, sexuality, gender, or citizenship—disproportionately end up navigating survival economies that are themselves criminalized creating controlling images that the criminal legal system puts forth. A "drug dealer" or "sex worker" is seen as a fixed label—rather than what one does for economic survival. In truth, these same individuals are almost always integrated into broader communities of care and financial networks, which are made invisible through criminalizing labels and carceral contact. The criminal legal system attempts to label individuals based on what it defines as "criminal activity," which does not provide context for particular survival-related strategies or grant people their full complexity and humanity. Once a community becomes labeled as deviant and criminal, it becomes easier for the state to target them with policing, surveillance, and punishment. Abolition requires shifting away from this labeling and how it has long been used in criminological and social science literature.

Data and statistics are also used to legitimize and normalize policing as an inherent public good. Police often make loose correlative arguments to justify particular strategies—and to help legitimize and naturalize their presence in general. Academics and data scientists have assisted with these efforts, multiplying the tools and resources that police have at their disposal.

In creating "hot-spots" and identifying "target" people, the criminal legal system tries to refine who it exacts policing and carceral harm on and creates spaces and people that are inherently criminal.[5] More than people, racialized spaces—such as public housing developments—are also criminalized and targeted by police and criminal-legal attention.

Reformers invested in preservation and expansion have presented police and prisons as approaches to stop gender and sexual violence. An archetype of this approach is the Violence Against Women Act of the 1994 Violent Crime Control and Law Enforcement Bill.[6] But as organizers and advocates such as INCITE! and Critical Resistance have claimed,[7] this act does not effectively address gender violence. Critics further noted that most people—especially those that are racially and class marginalized—don't report their experiences to the criminal legal system. When people do report, police and prisons can exacerbate harm experienced by survivors in many ways: rates of sexual violence in prisons are incredibly high,[8] and sexual violence is also the second most reported police misconduct, followed by domestic violence.[9]

A society in which people can freely enter into processes of accountability and are taught that doing harm does not make someone a deviant, terrible person—or monster—is much more likely to lead to communities that are able to receive what they need to heal from hurtful experiences and facilitate an end to cycles of harmful behavior. In the process, violence and harm can be navigated in ways that would sustainably reduce them—in addition to individuals being able to transform themselves through the process. But the state positions policing as the only well-resourced option for safety, so despite not seeing the police as legitimate, many people regard them as the only option. But decades of research show that communities, when given the resources and tools, are able to manage community conflict, violence, and harm.[10]

The criminal legal system draws on ontological conceptions of nature to justify the very existence of policing and punishment.[11] At the onset of policing, enslaved people and exploited laborers were criminalized and constructed as dangerous elements. The criminalization of race and class has contributed to increasing numbers of people that are considered in need—and deserving—of punishment, violence, containment, and control. The punitive, controlling focus on "good" and "bad" has permeated every aspect of society and has prevented society from creating models of safety that are not steeped in isolation, vengeance, and retribution. Harm and violence are far more complicated aspects of social life than the framework constructed by the criminal legal system suggests, but the orientation has persisted largely by tapping into broader conceptions of human nature that resonate culturally.

Safety is much broader than the criminal-legal definition of it. Crime rates, for example, only tell what is reported to and by the police, and data suggests that a large percentage of people who experience harm such as sexual assault, robberies, and aggravated assault do not report it.[12] Moreover, safety and security also involve economic and material dimensions that are not captured by a criminal-legal conception of safety. Political leaders, police, and the criminal legal system have developed a monopoly over the definition and maintenance of public safety even when it is shown to be counter to the interest of public safety. Scholars such as Stuart Hall have theorized that the identity management work that police and criminal legal systems engage in serves the purpose of maintaining hegemony and racial-class orders.[13] As Hall argues, the state engages in public-facing and strategic identity management in order to reify hegemony; in doing so, societies can be ruled by "consent" rather than coercive violence.

Police and the criminal legal system are not separate, external entities; they are institutions that socialize through routine, persistent contact and teach people what justice is, what adequate responses to harm look like, and the ways safety can be guaranteed. Prevailing societal institutions in the United States socialize people with narratives and worldviews that position police as the stewards of public safety, and, in turn, people seeking safety often ask for more police—especially given that for Black and poor communities, despite what people ask for, police and carceral responses are often the only things that the government provides.

Organizers—many of whom have been embedded in the broader Movement for Black Lives—injected abolitionist frameworks and demands, such as defunding the police, into national discourse surrounding policing in 2020 following the murders of George Floyd and Breonna Taylor. At the same time, many invested in police preservation and expansion have engaged in efforts that have reified the legitimacy of policing and undercut abolitionist organizing. Still, organizers have intervened in decades-old narratives and frames that have centered on a paradigm of safety, punishment, policing, and control that has challenged the naturalized framework of police. As advocates and scholars have noted, harm is dynamic, and most people in their lives will be harmed and engage in harmful behavior. To be sure, not all harm and violence are experienced in the same way, but the obsession with punishing the alleged monsters of society has served as cover for racial and class domination and has gotten in the way of developing a just society where people have safety interventions, reliable mechanisms of accountability, and their basic needs met.

Today, the idea that more police officers will make communities safer—including from violence—remains, despite the fact that police respond to 911 calls involving violence just approximately 4 percent of the time, make arrests for violent criminalized offenses less than 5 percent of the time, and spend a vast majority of their time on noncriminal activities.[14] Moreover, many harmful experiences go unreported, and when they are reported, clearance rates are notoriously low.[15] The durability of this idea that police will make communities safer stems from a long history of the US government legitimizing and empowering police as a means of combating crime. Police departments and police unions have enormous political power. At the local level, they often organize and campaign for additional city-budget funds and seek to repress efforts aimed at holding police accountable and creating change in the criminal justice system. Moreover, the influence often extends to election cycles, where political candidates advocate for "tough-on-crime" stances and commit to pushing for increased funds for policing because they see tough-on-crime policies as politically necessary.[16]

Instead of providing communities with resources and ensuring people's basic needs are met, the state continues to respond with policing and carceral solutions. The only way forward is divesting and working to abolish policing. As is seen today, policing can be carried out by local, state, and federal law enforcement agencies and civilian entities, such as child-welfare and child support systems, schools, and private security, and abolition requires divesting and abolishing policing and prisons—as well as the logic that undergirds them as central animators of institutions responsible for safety—altogether.

EARLY HISTORIES OF POLICING: RACE, CLASS, AND LABOR CONTROL

Dominant power structures have institutionalized the idea that police are the only legitimate providers of public safety—which subsequently justifies their attempts to monopolize the use of violence. For most of history, however, police were not seen in that way. Rather, police were often considered as violent tools serving the interest of those in power, something that has remained true for many communities disproportionately targeted by police violence. Police are said to be the stewards of public safety, but across the country policing emerged as a tool of racial and class domination and control. Over time, we have seen that policing has been centered on maintaining the status quo, which has been shaped by white supremacy, patriarchy, and capitalism. The police violence we see throughout the country in the present is not a fluke or aberration. The criminal legal system today is not broken—it is operating exactly as it was designed: a violent tool of race and class control.

Policing, in various forms, has existed since colonialism and slavery in the United States. The formality, organization, and legitimacy of the police force has changed over time, but the institution of police, both when it was invented and as it exists today, is an apparatus to enforce the agenda of the state and coercively control the nation's citizens. As Alex Vitale articulates in *The End of Policing*, "While the specific forms that policing takes have changed as the nature of inequality and the forms of resistance to it have shifted over time, the basic function of managing the poor, foreign, and nonwhite on behalf of a system of economic and political inequality remains."[17]

The first organized policing entities began as slave patrols in the South. Slaveholders and local civilian officials paid full-time officers to prevent slave revolts. Slave patrollers would surveil private property and public space to ensure that enslaved people were not carrying any weapons or fugitives, conducting any meetings, or gaining literacy. Officers also patrolled the roads to catch any enslaved people who attempted to escape to the North. Although a majority of these slave patrols dominated rural areas and were loosely organized, urban patrols such as the Charleston City Guard and Watch that began in 1783 became increasingly professionalized. With the rise of industrialization, enslaved African Americans had to work in places far outside their enslavers' property, so there were large numbers of unaccompanied enslaved people around the city. Officers were viewed as even more necessary to supervise, monitor, and inspect slaves who worked in these urban areas.[18]

After the abolition of slavery, slave patrols no longer existed, but racialized policing continued. Systems of formal policing became expanded in small towns and rural areas and were used to suppress, intimidate, and control the newly freed Black population and force them into convict leasing and sharecropping. No longer prioritizing the prevention of rebellions, the police enforced laws that outlawed vagrancy in order to criminalize and force Black people into convict leasing through the sharecropping system—which maintained exploitative labor conditions consistent with those under slavery. Officers also routinely enforced poll taxes and checked proof of employment for any Black person on the road. During the Jim Crow era, police often enabled and worked with white supremacist vigilantes such as the Ku Klux Klan to maintain social, political, and economic racial hierarchies. Meanwhile, northern political leaders also feared the northern migration of newly freed rural Black populations, who were viewed as inferior in every aspect. As a result, northern cities established segregated areas and utilized police officers to contain Black people in these spaces. In both the North and the South, the police employed brute means to impose geographical, social, and political limitations on Black communities.[19]

Just as the state utilized the police force to maintain the inferior position of enslaved people and later freed African Americans, policing in the North began as informal, privately funded night watch patrols to control working-class immigrants and growing unrest among the industrial working class. Northern cities experienced an influx of immigrants and rapid industrialization, which instilled a sense of fear and resentment among white elites. They viewed Irish and other working-class immigrants as uneducated, disorderly, and politically militant. Labor strikes and riots broke out, inducing fear and anxiety and demands for the preservation of law and order. Although the informal night watch system was intended to block looting and labor organizing, it failed at preventing them, which resulted in the emergence and expansion of formalized public policing to protect the interests of property and business owners. The creation of the police enabled enforcement of morality laws, such as restrictions on drinking. However, the early urban police were openly corrupt, as they were often chosen based on political connections and bribery. Qualifications to become a police officer did not include formal training or passing civil service exams. Political parties also utilized police to suppress opposition voting and to spy on and suppress workers' organizations, meetings, and strikes.[20]

Because of the high degree of police corruption, business leaders, journalists, and religious leaders united and exposed the corruption of the police beginning in the early 1900s. In response to the pressure, policing became increasingly professionalized through civil service exams and centralized hiring processes, training, and new technology. Management sciences were also introduced.[21] Reformers such as August Vollmer, who drew his ideas from his experiences in the US occupation forces in the Philippines, also implemented police science courses, which introduced new transportation and communication technologies, as well as fingerprinting and police labs. Police reformers of the twentieth century paved the way for the increasingly intertwined relationship between standardized technology, policing, and surveillance. Police militarization—where police adopt military strategies, tactics, and tools in routine policing—began to increase in intensity in the early twentieth century as a result of imperial feedback, where police expanded their infrastructural power using militarization models, borrowing tactics, techniques, and organizational templates from America's imperial-military regime developed to conquer and rule foreign nations.[22] Imperial feedback paved the way for police to adopt strategies and tactics used by the imperial military to control colonial subjects abroad to control racial and class minorities in the United States, such as African Americans and Indigenous communities.

The United States also employed colonial policing through the Texas Rangers, which were formally established in 1835. Texas Rangers were hired to protect the interests of newly arriving white colonists under the Mexican government and later under the independent Republic of Texas. The Texas Rangers hunted down native populations who were accused of attacking white settlers. Rangers also facilitated white colonial expansion by pushing out Indigenous Mexicans through violence, intimidation, and political interference. Mexicans and Native Americans who resisted were subject to beatings, killings, intimidation, and arrests. Throughout the 1960s and '70s, local and state elites also relied on Rangers for political suppression of Mexican Americans' suffrage rights and worked to subvert farmworker movements through similar tactics. Utilizing intimidation, they prevented voter rallies and threatened opposing candidates and their supporters. After organized resistance, communities pushed back against the Texas Rangers, which ultimately helped to pave the path for civil rights for Mexican Americans.[23]

The early forms of policing across the nation served to maintain the interests of the dominant class of white elites. By characterizing newly freed Black Americans, the working class, and incoming immigrants as deviant, morally inferior, and uneducated, both state and local police forces used brute force to ensure that they remained in their perceived inferior positions.

At the turn of the twentieth century, political leaders of the United States radically changed the organization and responsibilities of the police department. For much of history, the general public perceived the police as illegitimate and riddled with corruption.[24] Reformers in the 1920s and '30s attempted to rid departments of organizational corruption and to decouple their close ties with political elites. Instead, they emphasized that the role of police departments was in crime control and arrest. Changing expectations of police led to organizational changes, in which police departments took on a more centralized, bureaucratic, paramilitary organizational structure.[25] Inevitably, the reform era led to police professionalization that further cemented their power and allowed them to do more unchecked harm. These shifts led to changes in how a police department's success was measured, focusing increasingly on higher arrest rates and "efficiency" determined by rapid response time to emergency calls. By the 1950s these priorities were having devastating impacts on marginalized communities of color, beginning with Black communities.[26] Scholars have long shown that poverty and disadvantage, shaped by centuries of structural racism, are closely related to levels of police violence and harm in neighborhoods across the nation.[27]

During the 1960s, a large number of the urban rebellions that rocked the nation were directly prompted by incidences of police brutality.[28] At the same time, the War on Crime and the Law Enforcement Assistance Act provided police with increasing amounts of resources and also helped to create a climate that legitimized police as viable "crime stoppers," even though the effect police even have on what is referred to as crime is largely inconclusive.

The Civil Rights and Black Power Era saw an incredibly violent, repressive policing and carceral backlash.[29] The period was a time of widespread activism—including the work of Dr. Martin Luther King Jr., the antiwar movement, and the Black Panthers. For groups like the Black Panthers, which began in Oakland, California, that activism looked like both protecting Black communities from police violence and launching a wide variety of initiatives ranging from free breakfast programs for children to health clinics and ambulance services.[30]

On the local, state, and federal levels, police engaged in surveillance, violent repression, and criminalization of nationwide protest and dissent against the US government. The violent repression of Black movements through COINTELPRO epitomizes the development of increasingly violent surveillance tools and police violence. One notable example of COINTELPRO's violent suppression of Black activists was the case of Fred Hampton, who was murdered in his home during a raid conducted by the Chicago Police Department and the FBI. Many other activists during this period were jailed, injured, and killed by local, state, and federal law enforcement.

President Lyndon B. Johnson's War on Crime and creation of the Law Enforcement Assistance Act (LEAA) expanded the push towards empowering local law enforcement by legitimating the police as stewards of public safety. The 1965 LEAA authorized the US attorney general to make grants for the training and expansion of state and local law enforcement personnel.[31] As the president told Congress in 1966, "The front-line soldier in the war on crime is the local law enforcement officer." The LEAA subsequently created the first federal funding stream for local policing efforts.[32] At the height of an era that professionalized policing, Johnson's financial support at the federal level and valorization of local police reinforced a paradigmatic shift toward the perception that local law enforcement served as the only legitimate gatekeepers to public safety.

The coming decades would set the stage for the mass incarceration of today. The emergence of police strategies—coming out of Johnson's War on Crime—specifically aimed to violently police and punish Black people, poor people, and marginalized communities.[33] These criminal-legal efforts included the War on Drugs, War on Gangs, and the criminalization of poverty, homelessness, and survival—such as via sex work. During the 1970s and onward, police developed and expanded tools such as hot-spot and problem-oriented policing, stop-question-frisk, investigatory traffic stops, surveillance devices like wiretaps, and data-driven police tactics as new standards. Moreover, police increasingly became involved in immigration enforcement and detention and deportation proceedings. These five decades filled jails with Black people, as well as poor people and people from other marginalized communities. From 1983 to 2012, the United States spent $3.4 trillion more on the criminal justice system as a result of mass incarceration, criminalization, and policing.[34]

Anti-Black sentiments fundamentally shaped policing and punishment as solutions to issues of homelessness, poverty, drug use, housing insecurity, mental health, and interpersonal and communal violence. Consequently, the expansion of and increased funding for policing tore at the social fabric of Black communities, and in many cases worsened already pertinent social conditions.[35] The growth of punishment and policing accelerated when President Richard Nixon declared a war on drugs.[36] Nixon's administration continued to channel hundreds of millions of dollars to local law enforcement in the name of curbing drug use and distribution. Statistics indicate that drug use is at similar levels across all races and that white populations sell drugs at higher rates than Black populations. Nonetheless, the War on Drugs both reinforced the criminalization of Black people and, in practice, disproportionately targeted Black and other racially marginalized and poor communities, facilitating the mass incarceration of large numbers of Black as well as Latinx people.[37] By the 1980s, the War on Drugs reached its peak under President Ronald Reagan, notably because of the anti-Black hysteria around the use of crack cocaine, fueled by the platforms of both Democrats and Republicans. The hysteria drove even more government funds to local police, who were pressured to expand arrests to demonstrate success and justify these new budgets.[38]

During the 1988 presidential campaign, George H. W. Bush utilized the image of Willie Horton—an escaped Black convict from Massachusetts—to portray his opponent, Massachusetts governor Michael Dukakis, as soft on crime. The widespread popularity of this image drove white voters' anxiety and fear around safety and perpetuated stereotypes about the Black community.[39]

In response to concerns about Democrats' image of being soft on crime, Clinton advocated for a tough-on-crime platform. His adoption of this harsh approach to combating crime is exemplified by his signing of the 1994 Crime Bill—the largest bill to expand the criminal justice system since the LEAA. Clinton touted the number of additional police officers that this legislation put on the streets through the Community Oriented Policing Services (COPS) program. COPS was a seemingly liberal attempt to better police-community relations and reduce crime, but it flooded Black and other racially marginalized communities with police officers, fueling mass incarceration rather than reducing violence and harm within communities.[40]

The policies that Clinton, Johnson, and other Democrats advocated for and implemented set the stage for a federal commitment to fund local police departments. Increased spending on policing was often at the expense of social services like schools and community programs—the very programs implemented by the Panthers decades prior.[41] Since the 1960s, there has been little evidence to suggest that the additional funding has had a large impact on driving down indexes of crime or violence.[42] In fact, studies of communities with aggressive enforcement and the hyperconcentration of police found associations with increases in violence, worse health indicators, and adverse educational performance.[43] Governments at all levels have created new threats to safety by failing to develop institutions that address the underlying causes of violence and harm, often shaped by legacies of racial and class inequality, and instead by increasing criminalization, policing, and incarceration.

As a result of the continued investment in policing and the criminal legal system, police today have an immense amount of power. During the decades following the 1960s, police were given more power to engage in contact with the public through the criminalization of traffic stops and emergence of pretextual stops targeting poverty and survival economies, and legislators passed laws to allow for no-knock and quick-strike warrants—the same ones that led to the murder of Breonna Taylor. This rise in power occurred in tandem with rapid increases in police funding: national spending on police rose from $2 billion in 1960 to $16.7 billion in 1980 to $67 billion in 2000 to $137 billion in 2018.[44] That expansion of policing overtime allowed police to engage in increased amounts of surveillance and state-authorized violence.

Supreme Court rulings have also granted protection for and expanded power to the police, specifically during their interactions with the general public. Qualified immunity first emerged during *Pierson v. Ray* (1967). The Supreme Court used it with the rationale of protecting law enforcement officials from lawsuits and financial liability in cases where they acted in supposed good faith. In 1982 it was expanded to protect police and government officials from criminal and civil repercussions unless the conduct is "clearly established" as unconstitutional and unlawful. In 1986 qualified immunity was reinforced to protect "all but the plainly incompetent or those who knowingly violate the law."[45] In the decades to follow, qualified immunity has continued to enhance and embolden police power. Federal policies that inevitably increased police power—at the local, state, and federal levels—also include the emergence of the 1996 Immigration Act and the USA Patriot Act. The War on Terror also saw the onset of new funding, technologies, and focus on surveilling Muslim populations.[46] Throughout history, whenever police and politicians announce a "war" on a particular thing, it has also meant a war on Black people, poor people, and marginalized communities.

In recent decades the rise of "big data"—the use of large amounts of data to analyze and create algorithms—and increasingly sophisticated systems of surveillance have facilitated mass policing by expanding the capacity of police to engage in the sustained monitoring of residents and the use of algorithm-driven policing to focus on members of especially marginalized communities of color.[47] Data and algorithm-driven strategies such as predictive policing, social network analysis, hot-spot policing, and focused deterrence today are seen as "race-neutral," but they target Black and marginalized communities of color and position punishment and control as answers to social issues created by legacies of white supremacy and capitalism. These advances in criminological research that focus on algorithm-driven police tactics have equipped police with the resources and knowledge necessary to utilize "big data," social network analysis, and geographic systems.[48] Police maintain a large degree of discretionary control over how these technologies are implemented.[49] For example, these tools have been used toward gang suppression efforts in New York City with little oversight.[50] Moreover, the use of social media by police in order to surveil and monitor communities has also become increasingly widespread.[51]

The militarization of local police has facilitated the use of surveillance technologies, such as night vision and Stingray military technology. Sponsored by the Department of Homeland Security, Department of Defense, and Department of Justice, these tools have been transferred and channeled through programs like the 1033 Program—which emerged in 1989 and provides excess Department of Defense equipment to police agencies across the United States—augmenting the capacity of county and state police to surveil and enact violence, particularly on Black, Latinx, and other marginalized communities and protestors and to undermine public safety.[52]

MOVING BEYOND REFORM

Through community-relations initiatives, procedural justice, implicit-bias training, and reforms that focus on rooting out "bad apples," police are taught to engage in ways that make communities feel heard and listened to, while doing nothing to fundamentally reduce police violence and contact. Academics and social scientists often help to develop and legitimize the police and the criminal legal system without shifts that lead to meaningful reductions in police violence. Other reforms, such as review boards that have little or no decision-making power, are symbolic rather than transformative shifts that have little effect on reducing police contact, arrest, and violence.

Academics, politicians, and police leaders posit use-of-force standards, force-report requirements, and licensing as solutions to police brutality and misconduct. The police reform era began over one hundred years ago, and procedure, professionalism, and training were framed as a solution to the problems of policing. Minneapolis implemented all the progressive reforms—body cameras; deescalation, implicit-bias, and mindfulness training; reconciliatory efforts with communities of color; use-of-force standards; requirements that police intervene in misconduct; and community policing.[53] The department was held up as a model for progressive police reforms, but it still murdered George Floyd.

Rather than these progressive reforms, the way to ensure police violence does not occur, and the way to help reduce violence, conflict, and harm within communities, is to reduce contact with police and invest in community resources and institutions. It's also critical to remember that police brutality and killings are not the only form of police violence—sexual violence and domestic violence are among the most commonly reported police misconduct.[54] Moreover, the fear and terror that many communities experience from police presence and interactions are forms of police violence as well.

Proponents of limited police reforms include progressive-leaning mayors, such as Ras Baraka in Newark, who proposed a 5–7 percent cut to the city's police budget following nationwide calls to defund the police and reinvest in communities, but the proposed reduction was not the kind of substantial change organizers are envisioning.[55] Moreover, Baraka's violence interruption initiatives and social service programs are directly linked to partnerships with police and the criminal legal system. Linking the two will expand the scope of policing, increase contact with the public, and discourage many from using the services if they are linked to policing and the criminal legal system. On the subject of defunding policing, Baraka stated, "Most of our residents want police officers. . . . They want police officers in our neighborhoods, they want safety, they want security."[56] Baraka captures the heart of the issue here.

Reforms that do not reduce police power and scope will not lead to reductions in police violence and the reimagining of public safety. For instance, Camden, New Jersey, which is often praised as a case study around police reform, is not an example of reimagining public safety.[57] In 2013, the local government replaced the local department (due to austerity measures) with a better resourced, county-level department that has created an intense surveillance culture in the city. The model still rests on punishment, surveillance, and control, even though there are ways to actually foster safety and accountability that do not center on policing and prisons.

There are many ways to reduce violence and intervene in conflict that do not rely on an incredibly expensive, archaic, and violent model of justice that actively harms and kills Black and other marginalized people. Largely a result of the culture of punishment that animates the criminal legal system, most people do not report things that are defined as crime at all. A major intervention moving forward is removing police from traffic safety, which has been implemented in Berkeley, California, where an unarmed civilian entity manages traffic safety. This is gaining momentum in New York City and Los Angeles, as many instances of police violence start during traffic stops, which often become pretextual stops and spiral out.[58]

Since the wave of unrest following the murders of George Floyd and Breonna Taylor, there has been an increase in defund campaigns that seek to reallocate police funding directly to community investments and alternative systems of safety. There is a growing list of alternatives to policing that center on safety and antiviolence work. For some organizations, there may be a need for companion organizing to build alternatives. The resource hub Transform Harm has developed strategies for transformative justice and alternative approaches to community violence and harm. Oakland POWER Projects has advanced alternatives to policing and emergency preparedness and decoupling health care from policing.[59] The Health Alliance for Violence Intervention (HAVI) supports hospital and community collaborations to advance equitable, trauma-informed care for violence intervention and prevention programs. Violence Interrupters in localities such as Washington, DC, and in New York use personal outreach from community members to mediate and defuse neighborhood conflict.[60] In California, the Bay Area Transformative Justice Collective addresses child sexual abuse without the police.[61]

There are existing violence intervention models that have been shown to be effective and do not center on police and systems of punishment.[62] There is also a substantial body of evidence that suggests how other civic and community-based organizations and initiatives can build safe communities without the costs and violence that come along with police and prisons.[63] These include conflict-resolution teams, summer jobs,[64] engaging youth in after school programs,[65] addiction and mental-health treatment, well-resourced community-based violence interruption teams (including for gender-based violence), creating more green spaces within communities,[66] and making sure all residents have their basic needs met.

In 2020 after the murders of George Floyd and Breonna Taylor, tension emerged between individuals and organizations calling for traditional reforms and those making more transformative demands. In the summer of 2020, Campaign Zero launched #8CantWait, a set of policy recommendations based on faulty data science that failed to reduce police power and scope. Because #8CantWait seemed like it might undercut the transformative demands emerging from the Movement for Black Lives, organizers developed the #8toAbolition campaign, which put forth the following recommendations: defund police; demilitarize communities; remove police from schools; free people from jails and prisons; repeal laws that criminalize survival; invest in community self-governance; provide safe housing for everyone; and invest in care, not cops.[67] After #8toAbolition and criticism emerged, Campaign Zero removed the specific data claims from the #8CantWait platform and added a framework of divest/invest and abolition to the platform.

Across the country, organizers are building political power to refuse the century-long reforms that have been recycled and repackaged time and time again, and they are pushing for a transformative shift away from police and prisons altogether. Instead, alternative safety interventions and designing models of responding to conflict, harm, and violence rooted in frameworks such as transformative and restorative justice are the priority, rather than punishment, vengeance, and control.[68]

In 2018, the Movement for Black Lives outlined a policy platform on divest/invest initiatives, a part of the broader Vision for Black Lives policy platform, arguing for *investment* in safety for Black communities through access to education, health care, jobs, and domestic infrastructure such as housing and transportation and *divestment* from "exploitative forces including prisons, fossil fuels, police, surveillance and exploitative corporations."[69] The platform presented an encompassing vision that addressed police violence in addition to the social, political, and economic realities that emerge from legacies of racial and class inequality.

Building on this 2018 policy platform, the Movement for Black Lives released the BREATHE Act,[70] a sweeping omnibus bill that advances a divest/invest framework and significantly reduces criminalization, institutionalized punishment, and police surveillance. The bill is perhaps the largest bill proposed by Black movements since the Civil Rights Act. The four sections of the bill are titled: "Divesting Federal Resources from Incarceration and Policing & Ending Criminal-Legal System Harms"; "Investing in New Approaches to Community Safety Utilizing Funding Incentives"; "Allocating New Money to Build Healthy, Sustainable & Equitable Communities for All People"; and "Holding Officials Accountable & Enhancing Self-Determination of Black Communities."

The BREATHE Act proposes eliminating surveillance tactics that are disproportionately used to target Black, Brown, and Muslim communities by prohibiting predictive policing, racial recognition technologies, drones, and similar tools; eliminating the use of electronic monitoring, including ankle monitors, smartphone applications, and any other tool used to track location; ending civil asset forfeiture; abolishing mandatory minimum sentencing laws; ending life sentences; abolishing "three strikes" laws; developing a time-bound plan to close all federal prisons and immigration detention centers; repealing federal laws that criminalize human movement and border entry; further repealing and replacing the 1994 Violent Crime Control and Law Enforcement Act with noncarceral, nonpunitive investments in communities; and decriminalizing and retroactively expunging drug offenses.

The BREATHE Act also calls for eliminating federal programs and agencies used to finance and expand the US criminal legal system, such as the Department of Defense 1033 Program, the Edward Byrne-Justice Assistance Grant Program, Community Oriented Policing Services, the Drug Enforcement Administration (DEA), and Immigration and Customs Enforcement (ICE). The bill would ensure that nonpunitive, noncarceral elements of these programs are identified so that they can be transferred to another funding source. The BREATHE Act also makes recommendations to dramatically reduce the Department of Defense budget. The act is the most sweeping bill offered to date that can fundamentally reduce the size and power of police and the broader criminal legal system.

The only guaranteed way of reducing police violence is by reducing and eliminating contact with police altogether. Communities, with the necessary time and resources, can develop alternatives to deal with violence, conflict, and harm, as most people who do harm and violence within the current model do not go to jail. In many ways, aggressive policing and incarceration make communities less safe and cause devastating effects that ripple across their social fabric. The criminalization of poverty and survival economies—such as the drug trade and sex work—further inflames communities and seeks to police through an unpoliceable issue.

Activists and organizers have made compelling arguments for abolishing policing, jails, and prisons that have been injected into popular discourse in a way that has not before existed. Organizers have made clear that their efforts are not centered on abolishing safety and help but making a decision—as was made in Minneapolis by MPD150, Reclaim the Block, and Black Visions Collective—to unearth what currently exists.[71] In that excavation process, organizers are calling to design reimagined models of public safety and craft transformative models of justice that create safer communities that have the resources they need to thrive. The current model of punishment is not making us safer and often leads to cycles of harm and violence that devastate communities.

Police have considerable resources, tools, and discretionary power. Across the country, police often engage in contact that is unnecessary and discriminatory. Particular emergencies could be managed by other entities better equipped to deal with the incident—such as crisis intervention teams for individuals experiencing mental health emergencies and homelessness. There have been efforts over the last decades to reform policing through a focus on initiatives such as community policing and training around procedural justice, but these reforms aim to change perceptions without changing the root causes of systemic police violence.

Policing was not designed for public safety but as a tool to exploit, punish, and control Black and other racially and class marginalized communities. The violence witnessed in recent years is not an aberration or accident. The criminal legal system isn't broken. It is working exactly as designed: a system designed, foundationally, as a tool of race-class control. Policing has been responsible for continued injustices and violence, and it has not brought about sustainable safety and an accountable society. On the contrary, police violence and carceral harm have created safety and security threats far beyond the violence that is sensationalized. Policing is at the forefront of enforcing order in a society fundamentally shaped by structural inequality. As a result, policing disproportionately harms marginalized communities.

The expansion of police overtime pay allowed police to engage in increased amounts of state-sanctioned violence at the expense of social spending that would provide people with the basic necessities they need to live and thrive. When communities do not have these resources, violence and harm within communities are more likely. There is no evidence to suggest that policing can be reformed into a nonviolent, just system. Violence is a constitutive dimension of policing—leading some scholars to describe police as violence workers.[72] At their core, police are indeed violence workers who enforce legal codes and orders that are shaped by white supremacy, capitalism, and patriarchy. People need resources in order to thrive, and there is a need for new models of safety that center on safety and accountability, not punishment and control. Legacies of punishment, containment, and control have been disproportionately waged against Black, poor, and marginalized communities. In order to end police violence, policing needs to be dismantled and abolished with new systems that center on safety and accountability, not vengeance and retribution, in its place.

Since the colonial beginnings of the United States, prisons and policing were used as tools of exploitation and racial-class control. The only way to end cycles of police violence and the devastation of incarceration is to

dramatically shrink and abolish what currently exists and reimagine public
safety in its entirety. New systems can focus on alternative ways to prevent,
intervene, and respond to conflict, violence, and harm within communities.
Divesting from policing, prisons, surveillance, and systems of control and re-
investing in communities is a step in that direction.

In recent years, there has been a large focus on integrating W. E. B. Du
Bois into mainstream social theory. Du Bois was a staunch critic of the convict
leasing system and broader criminal legal system he saw emerging as a tool of
control and way to force Black people back into exploitative labor conditions
after the abolition of slavery.[73] In *Black Reconstruction* Du Bois criticizes the
abolition of slavery as a purely legal process, one composed of a focus on formally ending slavery, and argues for an abolition democracy that aims to end
oppressive systems and develop just, democratic systems in their place.[74]

In *Abolition Democracy: Beyond Empire, Prisons, and Torture*, Angela
Davis draws on the concept of abolition democracy and applies it to policing and the broader prison industrial complex. She also emphasizes the need
for an abolition democracy that abolishes unjust systems and builds just,
democratic systems that can meet people's basic needs and be modeled on
transformative visions for safety.[75] As scholar and geographer Ruth Wilson
Gilmore has stated, "Abolition means not just the closing of prisons but the
presence, instead, of vital systems of support that many communities lack."[76]
The creation of life-affirming institutions is central to addressing the underlying causes of violence, harm, and conflict and developing alternative safety
interventions and responses to them that do not center on policing, prisons,
and punishment.

Policing and incarceration have become tools in the United States, and
around the globe, to manage the consequences of unjust social, economic,
and political institutions. To truly address concerns surrounding safety,
it is necessary to provide resources, such as food, water, quality school
choices, a universal basic income, guaranteed housing, accessible health
care, dignifying jobs, alternative emergency response systems, drug treatment, and community-based violence interruption support, to deal with
the underlying causes of harm, violence, and conflict. No amount of policing and incarceration can fully make a community reeling from legacies
of structural inequality and poverty safe on its own. Attempts to control,

punish, and use security measures to facilitate a semblance of safety in the face of legacies of racial and economic inequality has exacerbated harmful conditions within communities.

Fundamentally, abolishing policing, prisons, and systems of surveillance and punishment requires abolishing the idea that police are necessary because there are people who are bad and others who are good, thereby requiring police to hold the line of civility from descending into chaos, violence, and destruction. It also requires shifting away from a framework that positions punishment and vengeance as equivalent to safety, accountability, and justice.

As the United States continues to experience a range of political shifts from the local to the national level, participatory budgeting, a strategy that advocates for direct community decision making in budget decisions, may be the key to divest/invest campaigns.[77] Creating the conditions where communities decide how funds are allocated in their localities offers an alternative, sustainable way to cultivate safety and prevent future budget decisions and resource allocation that hurt, rather than help, communities. There are more than enough resources in this country—and around the world—to make sure everyone has their basic needs met, the resources to thrive, and nonpunitive approaches to safety. But capitalism has created a world of unnecessary suffering and inequality that police and prisons help to maintain. Creating a safe, just world is possible. It's fundamentally a question of building systems and institutions that center lives and people instead of property and capital. But throughout history, policing has been at odds with assuring the most basic human needs—safety and security.

PART II
THE VIOLENCE OF POLICE

CHAPTER THREE

THE WHITE DOG AND DARK WATER: POLICE VIOLENCE IN THE CENTRAL VALLEY

Julie Sze

T his chapter examines how crime/caging, coplands/croplands, and deathscapes are linked in the Southern San Joaquin Valley. It draws on scholarship in racial capitalism, environmental racism, and animal studies. The alienation and dispossession of Indigenous peoples from the land is linked to the alienation of African Americans in an economic and cultural system that political theorist Cedric Robinson calls "racial capitalism."[1] Marxist geographer Ruth Wilson Gilmore's book *Golden Gulag: Prisons, Surplus, Crisis, and Opposition in Globalizing California* examines prisons and space, specifically in understanding the massive explosions of prisons in the Central Valley region of California in the 1980s and '90s. She defines racism as the state-sanctioned or extralegal production and exploitation of group-differentiated vulnerability to premature death. The prisons house overwhelmingly African American and Latinx urban populations from Los Angeles and the Bay Area. Prisons reorder race/space and economics/politics, as a development and jobs program, while simultaneously absorbing and responding to urban and racial "crises" and surplus populations under capitalism. This chapter applies her arguments, specifically her chapter on crime, croplands, and capitalism, from prisons to policing.

Specifically, this chapter examines policing in Kern County, which had the highest per capita kill rate in the United States in 2015. Using a case study methodology (including investigative reports and media accounts), this chapter examines how the police (whether on the city or county scale) maintain the social and economic order based on racial domination in Kern County. Specifically, the police deploy K9 dogs as the proverbial "white dog." Scholars recount the racist use of police dogs by law enforcement against African Americans and others, and the ongoing legacies of these histories.[2] Racialized imprisonment, animalization, and dehumanization have been examined by legal scholar Colin Dayan, who notes that "no country kills more dogs or imprisons more people than the US—inmates and dogs find themselves together in situations that are matters of life and death."[3] Literary scholar Bénédicte Boisseron examines animalization and racism, citing Frank Wilderson's Afropessimist argument that "we are meant to be warehoused and to die."[4] The K9 Kern County case is unsurprising given the scholarship on policing, or what radical police scholar Tyler Wall calls the "horrifying power of the state" through the police dog.

While the racist use of police dogs is not unique, this *particular* landscape of the Central Valley of prisons and industrial agricultural fields is an important site through which to counterpose normalized (slow) and spectacular (fast) violence by the police against Black and Brown bodies. Tracing the contours of this history of racial terror within the historical and political specificity of Kern County and the Central Valley is a necessary task. Pervasive and historical patterns of pollution exposure, toxic contamination, and environmental destruction are not accidental but instead endemic and embedded in systems of exploitation of land and labor. They must also be understood within the contexts of environmental justice activism in the Central Valley.

The chapter asks, What is the nature of police violence in defining and maintaining the racial and spatial order under conditions of petro-capitalism? Petro-capitalism names the specific terrain of racial capitalism as based on energy extraction and labor violence, broadly defined. On what literal and ideological terrain do racism, policing, and animals meet? K9 violence in Kern represents the "normalized" workings of state power. "Problems" come into view only as "matters of life and death" when they somehow exceed the "normal" (i.e., acceptable) state of violence endemic in the Central Valley. K9 policing creates and maintains the order, based on particular extractive landscapes, in Kern County and in the Southern San Joaquin Valley more generally (Kern, Tulare, and Kings). These counties constitute just 2 percent of the US farmland, but use 25 percent of the nation's pesticides (polluting both air and water). Of these, Kern is unique for its oil industries, the histories of the relations between Black and white people in the county, and what anthropologist Michael Eissinger calls the "Deep South" character of the county.[5] Kern County produces four hundred thousand barrels of oil a day and is the largest oil-producing county in California.[6]

Prisons, pesticides, policing, oil, and water are part and parcel of the political deathscape of the region, which is defined by extraction of natural resources and the manipulation of life, death, and value by state and capital. Oil and water are linked through hydraulic fracking, particularly along the Monterey Shale, a geologic formation running the length of the Central Valley. The process of hydraulic fracking requires the injection of water, sand, and chemicals into existing wells at high pressure in order to unlock natural gas and oil. The technique essentially fractures the rock to get at the otherwise unreachable deposits. The fracking in California is primarily for crude oil rather than natural gas and occurs on a smaller scale.[7] Oil and water are layered with each other, in a landscape further defined by poor air quality from pesticides and carbon emissions.[8] Although usually thought of as separate from one another, oil and water are intimately linked, as fossil fuels are combustibles of ancient biological origin, preserved in rock, originating from decaying marine organisms. Beyond mere outrage, I argue that Kern County's K9 problem reveals the structural logic of normalized and spectacular violence in the Central Valley, the primary function of which is to enable the conditions of racial petro-capitalism to unfold in the first place and to create the context whereby (in sociologist Daniel Faber's words) the "polluter-industrial complex" flourishes unabated. African Americans were often the primary targets of the southern-inflected racism in Kern. As in other parts of California, Native peoples in Kern were displaced by multiple colonizers—including the Spanish, Mexican, and Anglo populations. These traces of settler colonialism in the Central Valley continue to haunt how people live and who is made to die under the particular forms of petro-racial capitalism. In contemporary life, Latinx populations are hardest hit by these conditions, in an interrelated matrix of pesticides and chemicals, air pollution, oil spills, police deaths, and water scarcity.

This chapter is organized as follows: The first section outlines how racial and state violence in Kern and the Central Valley are both typical *and* exceptional. I then discuss how the police hunt humans (particularly Latinx and Black people) and the specificity of Kern County as a southern (in both senses: Deep South/Southern San Joaquin) space of resource extraction. Next, I discuss how settler colonialism in the Central Valley continues to haunt how people live and who is made to die under racial capitalism. At the same time, ordinary people respond and fight back. They challenge the police and their dogs, big agriculture, and oil industries. These battles are no small order in a spatial, economic, and political world historically shaped by authoritarianism and state control in the interest of extraction of nature and disposability of Black, Brown, and Indigenous bodies in both historical and contemporary contexts of the Kern County, the Central Valley, and California writ large.

HAUNTING AND SETTLER COLONIALISM IN KERN

Kern County is haunted by its history of racism and state-sanctioned natural resource extraction and violence. Kern County was home to many Native populations.[9] On the valley floor were the Yokut, or the Tulamni.[10] Despite ideologies that foreground the savagery of Black, Brown, and Native populations, Tulamni artifacts showed how petroleum was used to glue together soap root fibers, to make acorn-meal brushes, to waterproof baskets, and for a myriad of other uses.[11]

The past seeps through the present in landscapes of racial violence and resource extraction. As Colin Dayan writes, "The dead do not die. They haunt the living. Both free and unfree, the undead still speak in the present landscape of terror and ruin."[12] The dead body of a human and the living body of a dog haunt one another. This deathly presence is part and parcel of the valley: its prisons, its fields, and the city streets and county roads are constructed as a hunting ground for the police, specifically in Kern County. The thick tule fog that covers the valley in the winter is said to be "a curse visited by the spirits of the Yokut Indians who made their home around Tulare Lake until white men stole their land and drained the lake to plant the bottom in cotton."[13] The lake was, until the mid-nineteenth century, the largest freshwater lake west of the Mississippi.[14] Drained and diverted for agricultural uses, the lake transformed from a fertile site to a dry zone, a story typical in the valley (as recounted by environmental historian Linda Nash).

Oil was discovered in the county in 1864. One year prior, in 1863, the US military killed thirty-five Native Americans in what became known as the Keyesville Massacre. Anglo settlers and a detachment of the Second California Volunteer Cavalry under Captain Moses A. McLaughlin killed Tubatulabal Indians.[15] McLaughlin captured nearly one thousand Indians from the Kern and Owens valleys and "escorted them on a merciless six-month march of more than two-hundred miles to Ft. Tejon and the San Sebastian Indian Reservation,"[16] which some liken to the more well-known Oklahoma Trail of Tears. McLaughlin was no anomaly. California undertook an extensive campaign for Native genocide, which scholars conservatively estimate at sixteen thousand deaths by vigilantes, state militiamen, and federal soldiers.[17] Driven by the gold rush, and manifest destiny more broadly, the Native presence was targeted for annihilation so that mining and other forms of extractive petro-capitalism could flourish. In "A Glossary of Haunting," Eve Tuck and C. Ree explore Native feminist histories, cultures, and the hauntings of settler colonialism. They discuss the Japanese horror film *Dark Water* alongside Ree's artistic installation with dripping water on a ceiling. Both represent "the horror and irrational of the everyday, which glances sideways at specters and the sociological traumas that they haunt." The misrecognition of the site is "a ruin and a remake, is haunted and haunting, is horrific and very plain."[18] The haunting of Kern is also *horrific and very plain*.

The settler, racial, and gendered politics of control reflect the histories of terror and authoritarianism that structure institutions, including the police, prisons, oil fields, and industrial agriculture. As theorists Raj Patel and Jason Moore explain, capitalism *begins* with nature. They write, "Nature is not a thing but a way of organizing—and cheapening—life. It is only through real abstractions—cultural, political, and economic all at once—that nature's activity becomes a set of things."[19] Cheap nature, money, work, care, food, energy, and lives are all connected. The big industrial agriculture story about pesticides and prisons (Gilmore and Harrison) is also related to water, and crucially, in the case of Kern County, to oil and air.

FAST AND SLOW, TYPICAL AND EXCEPTIONAL

Bakersfield, the largest city in Kern County, was identified in 2016 as the city with the worst air in the United States by the American Lung Association.[20]

Kern County was also identified in 2015 as having the deadliest police in the United States by the *Guardian* in a report that showed that Kern County killed more people per capita than any American county that year.[21] These designations (worst in air and police violence) are strategically and symbolically important and crucially interlinked. The thirteen deaths in a county of 875,000 was higher than the nine people killed by police in New York City, which has ten times more people than Kern County and twenty-three times the police officers. The death rate was 1.5 per 100,000 residents, more than triple the rate in Los Angeles County. Since 2005, police—primarily the Bakersfield Police Department (BPD) and the Kern County Sheriff's Office (KCSO)—killed seventy-nine people. The state attorney general opened an investigation against both BPD and KCSO in 2016 that is still ongoing as of 2021.[22]

Although somewhat exceptional, Kern County is also typical of the problems of racialized police violence. And Kern County is in line with the Southern San Joaquin Valley in terms of racial, spatial, and environmental politics. No law enforcement officers in Kern have been reprimanded, and legal limitations of the public's access records suggest vast underreporting of these problems.[23] Kern County is a highly stratified society with a strong law-and-order culture. It is the fourth poorest county in California, and Bakersfield's congressional representative is Kevin McCarthy, the Trump ally who is the leader of Republican House members. He, along with the political delegation from the Central Valley,[24] are overwhelmingly conservative by any measure, but they are particularly conservative in terms of criminal justice and environmental regulation. As one environmental justice activist in Bakersfield describes it, "Locally our pollution control district is an ultraconservative, proindustry air district that says yes to everything from industry and no to the community."[25] The same can be said in law enforcement, with its political culture broadly supportive of both BPD and KCSO.

The police abuse problems of Kern County, and in Bakersfield, have been well documented in the 2004 US Department of Justice technical report and the 2017 ACLU report titled *Patterns and Practices of Excessive Force in Kern County.*[26] The ACLU report found that "both KCSO and BPD use canines in ways that are life-threatening, hazardous for public safety, and at odds with national standards and practices as well as constitutional law."[27] Canines were used against the mentally ill, at traffic stops, and after suspects were already under control. Every person killed by the KCSO since 2009 was unarmed. The "horrifying power of the state" receives attention insofar as it *exceeds* and makes visible what is more usually rendered normal and buried.[28] Thus, the police "problems," including K9 bites, in Kern County are considered spectacles of excess. In other words, these "problems" require "investigation" when thought of as "excessive" rather than endemic.

This excess of violence characterizes the region, defined by the social and environmental conditions of the Central Valley. These include the highest rates of air pollution in the country, high risks from water contamination, carceral landscapes, high poverty and residential foreclosure rates, and low educational attainment.[29] In *Pesticide Drift and the Pursuit of Environmental Justice*, sociologist Jill Harrison examines pesticide drift activism, policy, and science in California, and particularly, the Southern San Joaquin Valley. Pesticide drift is when aerial pesticides drift off their intended target onto homes, schools, and other sites, leading to mass pesticide poisoning incidents. She explores how pesticide poisoning was constructed simultaneously as both "pervasive" and "invisible." The pesticide industry and the environmental regulatory state narrated a particular "story" about mass pesticide poisoning as accidental and exceptional.

The pervasive and invisible normalization of environmental abuse on the most vulnerable populations functions through what literary scholar Rob Nixon calls slow violence. Slow violence is "a violence that is neither spectacular nor instantaneous, but rather incremental and accretive, its calamitous repercussions playing out across a range of temporal scale."[30] It contrasts with explosive and spectacular violence, such as the militarized standoff at Standing Rock, or repressive responses by the state to uprisings and protests of violent deaths by police of African Americans and others. As Wall writes, the "animalization" of state violence, primarily through the police dog, is not "exceptional" but rather acts as a "ritualized, normalized and concealed practice of authorized bloodletting." Rather than an exceptional act of exposure, police violence is the "normal working" of state power. In short, the "animality of police power is *normalized and insidious*."[31]

The question of exceptionalism with regard to K9 violence in Kern is nonetheless *symbolically* important given the weight that a designation of "most" carries (*most* dirty air, *most* police killings, *most* pesticide use). Thus (with Harrison and Wall in mind), 2015 represented a watershed year for K9 violence in Kern within a context of systemic and normalized violence. The rhetorical weight of extremes can be useful from an activist or organizing perspective. It most certainly reflects long-standing ideologies that normalize violence and abuse of particular peoples and landscapes as polluted and pollutable. This issue of expected or normalized pollution is taken up in *What Is Critical Environmental Justice*. Sociologist David Pellow traces how abuse of humans, ecosystems, and nonhuman animal species are connected, as is the notion of expendability. Pellow joins others in discussing how animals/dogs and African Americans in particular are symbolically linked through dehumanization in policing practices and in the context of Black Lives Matter movements.

Racialized and class-inflected animalization has a long history in the United States, of which immigrants and criminals are just the most recent targets. Historical examples include the likening of enslaved people to apes, youth gangs to "wolfpacks," and undocumented people to "animals" (not to mention Donald Trump likening African American women to dogs). It is also a phenomenon throughout the Americas, particularly in the use of dogs to control enslaved peoples and to chase runaways.[32] In California's agricultural fields, concerns about the threat of "invasive" Japanese beetles in the early twentieth century was explicitly anti-Asian as Japanese farmers were conflated with pests.[33] Political scientist Claire Jean Kim examines race and its entanglement with species and nature in the United States. She historicizes the animalization of Black people, Native Americans, and Chinese immigrants through which hierarchical orders of the "races of man" were constructed. She examines the category of the human as a taxonomy of power.[34] Her question parallels that of Sylvia Wynter. Wynter is a key figure in discussions of the human who has questioned how the modern world system conceptualized "Man" and the "specific genre" of the human person in the wake of colonialism."[35] The "idea of the human" is grounded in Western modernity—the question of "how" these notions are naturalized through the discourse of the human is Wynter's and Kim's central concern.

HUNTING AND THE POLICE DOG IN DEEP SOUTH KERN

The contemporary police dog and the violence unleashed on Black and Brown bodies are linked to older historical debates about race and animals and forms of racism in its different eras and moments. Racial terror from the police dog, most spectacularly from the policing of civil rights demonstrators, has a long arc, "from the plantation, the chain gang, and convict leasing... the upstart ghetto, to the neoliberal present."[36]

This neoliberal present and the racial terror of the past are explicitly linked by K9 dogs in Kern County, where the state uses dogs to hunt humans and to maintain "law and order." The Kern County sheriff, Donnie Youngblood, admires the notoriously racist Joe Arpaio and fashions himself similarly on a horse with a cowboy hat.[37] Youngblood sought to have the county designated as a "law and order" county.[38] Kern is defined by a particular regional and economic culture drawn specifically from the southern United States, which shaped the racial and spatial politics of the region's economic development based on extraction—that is, the development of cotton farming and industrial agriculture writ large.

The "fact" of the transplantation of cotton farming from Georgia to Central California materialized a deeply racist white-Black hierarchy, land development, and resource extraction, as documented by Gilmore in *Golden Gulag*. The journalists Mark Arax and Rick Wartzman have shown how the biggest farmer in the United States (first in cotton, then other crops), J. G. Boswell, came from Georgia and then amassed massive amounts of land in Tulare County. With over two hundred thousand acres, Boswell owned over $1 billion of water rights and real estate in California. Eissinger argues:

> No place in California is more Southern than Kern County. By Southern, in this context, I mean not only does Kern County reflect southern cultural food and music, but also the long-standing traditions of Jim Crow and other racist manifestations of Southern culture. Although other parts of Central California have experienced incidents of racism, segregation, and racial violence, since the nineteenth century not another county has so consistently exhibited these attitudes and actions to the degree evident in Kern County.[39]

These "Southern" attitudes were directed squarely at African Americans and deviant women (i.e., prostitutes). KKK leaders held political office in the 1920s and '30s. The high school had a Confederate mascot until the 1960s. The only thirteen Black people in Taft (athletes recruited to the local college) were run out of it in 1975 by a lynch mob. Cross burnings in the 1980s and white attacks of Black motorists in Kern indicate that this racist culture is not an artifact of the distant past. Well into the present, the county has active white supremacist groups, and hate crimes flare up with regularity.

Police dogs are a crucial part of Kern County state violence. The 2017 ACLU report found that four of the ten KCSO deaths involved K9 dogs that were set upon suspects. Dogs were used to attack people for nonserious offenses, they were used against people already under physical control, and their deployment used almost entirely against Black and Latinx populations. K9 dogs have been "specifically trained to attack people."[40] KCSO deputies rewarded "colleagues for aggressive use of batons with a 'baby seal' prize for the best clubbing."[41] The ACLU report indicates that canine units have decals on their cars that say, "We'll bite your ass."[42]

The catalog of police dog attacks and deaths is long. During a regular traffic stop, the BPD set a K9 dog on the driver; the dog bit flesh off the man's leg. David Sal Silva, one of the men killed, had a German shepherd set on him. The dog bit him multiple times, after which six deputies beat him and hog-tied him. After the death of James De La Rosa, Officer Aaron Stringer tickled his toes, jerked his stiff body, and said, "I love playing with dead bodies."[43] When asked about De La Rosa's death, the chief of the Bakersfield Police Department was confused (and unapologetic) when he asked: "Which one was he?"[44] In the chief's words, the deaths were the same, with no distinction between those killed by the police, because they were not seen by him as individuals.

All but one of the people killed according to the ACLU report were Latinx or African American. The Bakersfield police force is overwhelmingly white (74 percent in a city that is 38 percent white, 46 percent Hispanic, and 8 percent Black)[45]; it's also defined by a particular white masculinized braggadocio, and it is corrupt and insular. Youngblood won his election over Mack Wimbish, the father of Rick Wimbish, a Bakersfield police officer who was involved in four fatal shootings.[46] Youngblood himself has been embroiled in various controversies (after which he was reelected, most recently in 2018). His estranged wife was mauled *in her home* by BPD K9 police.[47] Youngblood was caught on tape saying that it costs less to kill suspects than to wound them.[48] His comments about the relative cost of death vs. mere harm bring to light the fundamental workings of state-sponsored violence, necessary for the normal workings of industrial agriculture and necessary for petro-racial capitalism to continue.

Demographically Latinx communities are now hit hardest by a group of interrelated conditions—specifically, the matrix of pesticides and chemicals, air pollution, oil spills, police deaths, and water scarcity. Five years ago, gas pipeline leaks in Arvin in Kern County sickened hundreds. Flames began shooting out of home outlets, and explosive levels of gas were documented. In response, groups formed such as Committee for a Better Arvin / Comite Para un Arvin Mejor. The committee, with other groups and legal partners, sued Kern County for passing a new ordinance that would allow the county to fast-track permits for oil and gas without environmental review of public notice for twenty years, leading to up to seventy-two thousand new wells.[49] In 2018, a Kern County judge ruled in favor of the oil industry.[50] In Tulare County, Latinx communities are disproportionately impacted by water pollution (oftentimes by nitrates and pesticide pollution in groundwater), which groups like Community Water Center seek to address through organizing and policy.[51] The list goes on.

FROM WHITE DOG TO DARK WATER

The white dog remains a powerful symbol: of the racist police as well as the ongoing haunting of death and violence under conditions of settler colonialism and racial capitalism. Thus, the snuffing out of Black and Brown life by the police is merely an extension of the settler and racial landscape of capitalism in the Central Valley. Kern County continues that legacy of state-settler violence: in pesticides, air pollution, water scarcity, police violence, and oil. Domination and extraction are suffused in the social-economic and political order of the valley, maintained through institutions such as the police and prisons. The spectral nature of violence on stolen land haunts the present. Legal scholar Colin Dayan writes, "The ghosts of the ancestors always return. What is abused and damaged rises up to haunt . . . So out of the grit and press of death comes the white dog."[52]

The white dog makes visible the way that violence maintains capitalist order: the extraction of nature and the disposability of lives, land, and labor. Dayan ends her book with a poem and a warning:

The law was angry
The law was rabid
It came upon you in the night
The patrollers
Seeking you out

They always came with a white dog
They were white dogs
With their white cone hoods
And their white capes
Ghosts in the night.[53]

The slave patrollers and dogs merge into an "old history of intimacy and threat" (in the white racists and their dogs). At the same time, "the ghosts of the ancestors always return" because, "what is abused and damaged rises up to haunt."

The haunting is alive in the environmental justice movement and in other activists who challenge the status quo. The poisoned chalice of oil wells, on the one hand, and drought, wildfires, and climate change, on the other, is shaped by the white dog of state violence. Here, I want to return to Tuck and Ree's discussion of *Dark Water* inflected with W. E. B. Du Bois's *Darkwater*. In this book, Du Bois ruminated on the relationship between whiteness and ownership and asked: "But what on earth is whiteness that one should so desire it? Then always, somehow, some way, silently but clearly, I am given to understand that whiteness is the ownership of the earth forever and ever."[54] Writer Pankaj Misra notes now, however, that "many descendants of the landlords of the earth find themselves besieged both at home and abroad, their authority as *overlords, policemen* and *interpreters* of the globe increasingly challenged."[55]

Du Bois challenged authorities of whiteness, ownership, and racism throughout his work. In *Darkwater*, the dog and nonwhite people remain a central part of the problems against which he writes:

> It is curious to see America, the United States, looking on herself, first, as a sort of natural peacemaker, then as a moral protagonist in this terrible time. No nation is less fitted for this role. For two or more centuries America has marched proudly in the van of human hatred—making bonfires of human flesh and laughing at them hideously, and making the insulting of millions more than a matter of dislike—rather a great religion, a world war-cry: Up white, down black; to your tents, O white folk, and world war with *black and parti-colored mongrel beasts!* . . . But what of this? America, Land of Democracy, wanted to believe in the failure of democracy so far as darker peoples were concerned. . . . She aspires to sit among the great nations who arbitrate the fate of "*lesser breeds without the law.*"[56]

More recently, race and animal studies scholars have shifted these historical terrains of race and animalization that Du Bois relies upon. Lindgren Johnson calls "Fugitive Humanism" efforts for African American subjectivity, freedom, and citizenship entangled with discourses of animality and animals. In arguing for such intimacies, Johnson argues that African Americans also fled some of liberal humanism's most "cherished" assumptions,[57] processes of "property making and property taking."[58] Liberalism relies on the "moral primacy of individual freedoms, especially the freedom to own property."[59] In arguing *against* human exceptionalism and whiteness, Johnson and other scholars and activists ask, "Why play along with the game of defining human?"[60]

CONCLUSION

Kern County is a violent place, and that violence is suffused through its institutions, including prisons, farms, and the police. It is "horrific and plain" for all to see. That violence and hierarchy nevertheless do not go unchallenged. While all people are impacted by these environmental and social conditions, Black and Latinx populations are hardest hit. Kern's K9 violence "problem" is not a fixable policy issue of excessive force. Rather, the problems are suffused in the extractive landscapes of petro-racial capitalism itself. Kern's dark waters are thus the oilfields of viscous and vicious politics, suffused in Du Bois's and Tuck and Ree's variegated thoughts on dark water.

The ongoing legacies of settler colonialism and racial capitalism are written into the landscape and in its political institutions. Thus, the struggles by peoples and communities to push against big agriculture, dirty air, corrupt police, and unregulated oil wells can only be seen as important. Communities and tribes fight corporations that seek to extract natural resources like oil.[61] They fight for interventions like "buffer zones," which parallel campaigns for pesticide buffer zones.[62] Victims and families of victims of police K9 violence seek restitution in the courts for their injuries and deaths to make the lives of those rendered invisible and indistinguishable matter.

Historically, the adage "man bites dog" has been used within the newspaper industry to indicate how an unusual story attracts greater attention than the typical. But the typical and accepted conditions of life and death are the actual story, buried under violent histories mostly (but not totally) forgotten. These histories never disappeared from historical memory or across spatial boundaries. Central Valley tribal nations, like the Tejon, have fought for, and won, federal recognition, despite generations of forced displacement from their lands across hundreds of miles within California.[63] Sometimes, the fight back is more microscale or literal, as when a Bakersfield man bit a K9 dog.[64] These stories, and the various "challenges" to property, ownership, hierarchy, and whiteness, show both the perils and powers of the white dog and the dark water in a hyper polluted deathscape.

CHAPTER FOUR

POISONED AND POLICED TO DEATH: KORRYN GAINES, FREDDIE GRAY, AND THE NATURE OF POLICE

David Correia

Before Baltimore County SWAT killed Korryn Gaines in a hail of police bullets, she was born into "a sea of lead."[1] This metaphor—the "sea of lead"—leaps from the first page of an otherwise dry and technical environmental study of lead-paint contamination in the two houses that Gaines lived in as a child. The first, a row house she lived in from birth until she was fifteen months old, sits in the shadow of Baltimore's Pimlico Racetrack. It is today an abandoned home on a street of abandoned homes on Belvedere Avenue. In a deposition that Rhanda Dormeus, Gaines's mother, gave as part of a lawsuit the family filed against their slumlord owner, she described the house as completely "full of lead," every room. One room was so bad it had to be sealed off from the children. Nails stuck out of the floors. Windows wouldn't close. Gaines's father, Ryan Gaines, explained in his deposition how hard it was to safely raise children on Belvedere. Flaking paint chips rained down from windowsills. If the children didn't eat the chipping lead paint, the rats did. Korryn and her two siblings played among the paint chips and lead-laced dust suspended always in the air around them. The building was one of a number of homes owned by the slumlord Lee Barnstein, who, according to one neighbor, maintained them "as if they were condemned."[2]

When Korryn was a toddler, her mother received a letter from her pediatrician. Korryn's brother Ryan had tested positive for lead. There is no safe blood lead level (BLL) in children. Any amount, whether by ingesting paint chips or breathing lead-laced dust, can cause permanent neuropsychological damage and neurodevelopmental disabilities in children. According to the US Centers for Disease Control and Prevention, a BLL in children greater than 5 micrograms per deciliter (mcg/dL) causes irreversible developmental damage to the brain. The news of Ryan's poisoning alarmed Rhanda. She quickly tested all of her children, including Korryn, her youngest, in March 1993. The test revealed that nine-month-old Korryn had a BLL of 7 mcg/dL. They fled the poison of the Belvedere house for a West Baltimore row house on Lorman Avenue, which they found through a City of Baltimore lead abatement program. By the time they made it out, Korryn was fifteen months old, and her BLL had tripled to 22 mcg/dL.[3]

The Lorman Avenue house was around the corner—just more than a block—from where four Baltimore police officers would arrest Freddie Gray on April 12, 2015. Police claimed Gray held an "illegal knife," but prosecutors would later conclude that officers had no probable cause to stop and search Gray; and there was never any doubt that the knife they discovered in their search was legal for Gray to possess. When police arrested Gray after a short chase, he told them he couldn't breathe. He asked for his inhaler, but police refused. While the arresting officers waited for a police van, Gray grew alarmed and began screaming for help and flailing his arms against police. The police forced him to the ground, face down, and used a restraint cops call a "leg lace" on him. As Gray hollered in pain, an officer used his entire bodyweight to twist and force Gray's feet onto his own back. When the van arrived, they bound Gray's legs in irons and loaded him into the back. The van had belt restraints, but they didn't use them. What they intended, and what followed, is known in Baltimore as a "rough ride."[4] Police drove Gray around Baltimore for nearly an hour, erratically and at high speed, swerving, slamming the brakes, and frequently stopping short. When the van arrived at the Western District station, Gray was unresponsive. The rough ride severed his spine and crushed his larynx. Medics arrived and transported Gray to Shock Trauma, where he died a week later from his injuries.

The location of Gray's arrest, around the corner from Korryn's childhood home, is a coincidence, but it is not insignificant. Gray, like Gaines, suffered from, and sued over, his exposure to lead-based paint as a child. In

2008, Freddie Gray's family filed a lawsuit against Stanley Rochkind, another among the notorious Baltimore slumlords who profit from misery, and in whose rented apartment Gray lived as a toddler.[5] Freddie Gray was deposed in the lawsuit and described eating the peeling paint in the windows of his family home. Doctors measured his BLL at 37 mcg/dL when he was twenty-two months old.

The similarities don't end there. Less than sixteen months after Baltimore police killed Freddie Gray, a Baltimore County SWAT unit killed Korryn Gaines in her home while serving a bench warrant related to an unresolved traffic ticket. Two of Baltimore's "lead kids," as the tens of thousands of children poisoned by lead-based paint in Baltimore's slumlord-owned row houses are known, also killed by Baltimore police. This is life in West Baltimore for African American residents, where the routine, everyday nature of lead poisoning is matched only by the routine, everyday nature of police violence, two patterns linked by the poisoned and policed bodies of its victims. This chapter examines these linked patterns. One, the history and pattern of the lead-based paint poisoning of tens of thousands of West Baltimore children, nearly all from Black, working-class families. The other, a history and pattern of police violence in West Baltimore. Poisoned by a slumlord as a child and killed by a cop as an adult.

CHILDHOOD LEAD POISONING IN BALTIMORE

In the wake of Gray's 2014 killing at the hands of police, the routine practice of the "rough ride" came frighteningly into focus. It is a common tactic of "street justice" carried out by cops largely against young Black men and women in West Baltimore. And if the cases of Korryn Gaines and Freddie Gray are any indication, many of the adult targets of police violence in West Baltimore, including those given a "rough ride" like Gray, were also poisoned by a slumlord's sea of lead as children.

Lead is a neurotoxicant that impairs neurological development in children. Half a million children "younger than 6 years have BLLs above the Centers for Disease Control and Prevention recommendations."[6] Environmental toxins such as lead overwhelmingly impact poor communities of color in the United States. The US Environmental Protection Agency phased out the use of leaded gasoline in the 1970s and banned its use by 1996. The City of Baltimore banned the use of lead-based paint on interior surfaces in 1966, twelve years before the EPA banned its use nationwide. But there's no escape from lead in Baltimore. Studies reveal "widespread contamination across" the city. Urban soils, particularly in west and southwest Baltimore, exceed national standards in lead accumulation "at levels that can produce negative human health outcomes."[7] Most chronic childhood lead poisoning in Baltimore, however, happens in the home, where the rate of childhood lead poisoning is "nearly three times the national rate."[8] Korryn Gaines and Freddie Gray were poisoned by lead-based paint beginning in the early 1990s. They weren't alone. In 1993, more than a third of all children from Baltimore— nearly thirteen thousand children—who were tested for lead registered levels greater than 10 mcg/dL.[9] According to one expert, if testing had been more widely available "we would have found 30,000 poisoned kids."[10]

Rhanda Dormeus and her children escaped the sea of lead on Belvedere Avenue with the help of their pediatrician, who referred the Dormeus-Gaines family to a lead-free, affordable housing program. As Korryn's mother later explained, "[The pediatrician] told me generally how it could affect them and all that stuff, and she gave me a pamphlet that identified City Homes as a lead paint-free program, and so I got in touch with them and put an application in, and then it was processed, and I was approved for the property."[11] The now-defunct City Homes was then a private real estate management company registered with a Baltimore lead-abatement program that rented homes throughout West Baltimore. Korryn Gaines and her family moved into a City Homes–owned row house on Lorman Avenue in West Baltimore in December 1993.[12] The row house had been recently remodeled. There were "no paint chips," Rhanda Gaines recalled, "but lots of dust." Korryn, who shared an upstairs bedroom with her sister Sheena, lived in the Lorman house from 1993 to 2007, until she was fourteen years old. "I remember them assuring us that it was 100 percent lead-free," recalled Korryn's father. "Because of the issues that we had at Belvedere, we didn't want to move into another location that had paint problems, but the thing that I did notice about … 1708 Lorman was the fact that it looked like fresh paint, but the fixtures for the bathtub was exposed, and it had green and black mold, and I remember being kind of worried about that because I thought that if you could see mold, then it could be in the air. I'm no expert on it, but that's what I was thinking because of my kids,

and the pipes were exposed so that if the kids went into the bathroom unsu-
pervised, that they could actually touch and play with moldy pipes."[13] Shortly
after the move to Lorman, the painted windows and floors began to chip and
flake. Rhanda complained, and a City Homes representative gave her a solvent
called TSP, or trisodium phosphate, and instructed her to scrub the entire
house with the solvent. TSP is toxic when a person ingests or is exposed to it
at high doses. It also does little to resolve the problem of chipping and flaking
lead paint. Despite the overwhelming evidence of flaking lead-based paint in
their new home, City Homes told Gaines that the home was free of lead-based
paint. A 2013 test for lead at Lorman, however, conducted after the family
filed a lawsuit, found "evidence of lead based paint on 12 interior components
most [of] them friction and impact surfaces."[14] Even the "lead-free" homes
in West Baltimore are plagued by lead paint. While Korryn's BBL declined
while at the Lorman house, it never dropped below 7 mcg/dL during all the
years that doctors monitored her levels.

Chronic exposure to lead sources such as lead-laced dust or lead-paint
chips produces neurological damage in children. The injuries are irreversible,
but not immediate, usually manifesting only after the damage is done. This
was true for Korryn, who escaped one toxic house only to be poisoned by
another. In the first years after the initial test, from the time she was twelve
months old until she was five years old, Korryn passed annual screening
tests for developmental problems. But there was no escape. Every time she
breathed the air in her home or played with the toys in her bedroom, her
body absorbed lead paint. Subsequent school-aged testing diagnosed her with
a neurodevelopmental disability, or brain injury, which identified both causal
and "likely" causal associations related to lead poisoning. Neuropsychological tests concluded lead poisoning caused impairment to executive function,
created an attention deficit, and caused a learning disability in math. She was
also diagnosed with "disruptive behavior disorder," which was considered
"likely" associated to lead poisoning.[15]

THE EXPOSURE PATHWAYS OF POISON AND POLICE

The language of public health relies on words and phrases such as *exposure*
and *exposure pathways* to describe the risks associated with lead-based paint
poisoning. Baltimore's long history and ongoing pattern of slumlord housing,

for example, constitutes a neurotoxicant "exposure pathway" for children living in West Baltimore's rundown row houses. But there is nothing natural about this pathway. It's a pathway paved by slumlords who profit by poisoning children. It's a pathway that travels along a political economy built up through racialized disinvestment, weak or nonexistent oversight and regulation, the lack of affordable housing options for poor residents, and a refusal to prosecute Baltimore's lead slumlords; a pathway subsidized by a public-private partnership in poison and profits. This is the order of things in Baltimore, in which the accumulation of capital by slumlords such as Rochkind and Barnstein not only produces but also requires the poisoning of Black, working-class children. There's no other way to say it: to be a Black and working-class kid in West Baltimore is to have been born into a slumlord's "sea of lead." Somewhere between sixty-five thousand and ninety-three thousand children in Baltimore suffer, or have suffered from, significant lead poisoning.[16]

And, not unrelatedly, to be Black and working class in West Baltimore is also to be the subject of constant police surveillance, harassment, arrest, and violence—to be shot to death like Korryn Gaines in a hail of police bullets or killed by a severed spine like Freddie Gray during a brutal police rough ride. These are not unrelated patterns. Korryn Gaines and Freddie Gray were *exposed* to police violence as much as they were *exposed* to lead-based paint. The political economy of slumlord profitability in West Baltimore requires not only laissez-faire regulation of housing but also the intense policing of a population made surplus by the poisoning and disinvestment that underwrite slumlord profitability. Poisoned and policed to death.

This is the link between slumlordism and police, and it is most visible in the logic of the rough ride. It is a common police practice that serves the police goal of "good order" via a mode of street justice, and it travels the same pathway as lead-based paint exposure. Police violence isn't an occasional, unintended, or aberrant consequence of policing, just as the inadequate lead abatement of housing stock in West Baltimore is no accident. The latter establishes the conditions for capital accumulation by slumlords. The former is the primary mode through which police fabricate order, an order that includes widespread disinvestment in affordable housing, and lax regulatory oversight of slumlord housing.[17] The slumlords who have poisoned generations of West Baltimore children have never been the subjects of police violence. The stop-and-frisks, the traffic stops, the street corner interrogations, the SWAT assaults, the K9 attacks, the intense routine surveillance, the Tasers and handcuffs and leg laces and rough rides are all of a piece—they are the everyday modes of policing reserved for the victims of lead poisoning, not their wealthy tormentors. And the rough ride is a violent journey through this poison pathway.

This is the order that policing fabricates in West Baltimore. The intersection of poisoning and policing constitutes a unique and specific threat to young, Black, working-class residents of West Baltimore; a one-way exposure pathway that leads *directly* to what Ruth Wilson Gilmore calls "the state-sanctioned or extralegal production and exploitation of group-differentiated vulnerability to premature death."[18] The slumlords paved it and the police patrol it. Lead poisoning robs them of their future, police rob them of their life.

THE NEUROTOXICITY HYPOTHESIS, OR HOW TO THINK LIKE A COP

But this is not how many scholars or journalists explain the link between lead poisoning and police violence. There is a large body of public health research based on what scholars call the "neurotoxicity hypothesis" that finds a "significant relationship" between elevated lead levels and aggressive behavior. According to Stretsky and Lynch, lead poisoning manifests in very specific behaviors: hyperactivity and antisocial and aggressive behavior in children and adults poisoned by lead. The academic scholarship, particularly among some criminologists writing in public health journals, is a literature laced by claims that childhood lead poisoning leads directly to criminal behavior. For all its measured outrage at lead poisoning, it is a body of scholarship that shifts attention away from the slumlords who poison West Baltimore's children to focus instead on their victims. A shift from where we should be looking (the poisoning and the policing) to where police prefer that we look (the poisoned as a criminal). This is an ideological body of research in that it seeks no truth. It exists only to defend and justify the aggressive policing of poor, Black residents in Baltimore. The first line from Stretsky and Lynch's 2004 article "The Relationship between Lead and Crime" reads: "Contemporary research suggests that lead exposure is a potential source of crime and delinquency."[19] A 2016 article by Leech et al. argues that research on lead-based paint exposure should be understood alongside the "emerging empiric evidence of elevated criminal activity among those who were lead poisoned as children."[20] Freddie Gray might not have committed a crime before he was arrested and killed by police—he broke no law—but according to medico-legal claims that link lead exposure to crime, it is Gray, not his slumlord, who is the proper object of police violence. After all Gray, like so many other Black residents of West Baltimore, had been poisoned by lead paint and thus constituted a potential criminal threat against whom society must be defended.

It's not just criminologists in obscure scholarly journals making these claims. Many journalists relied on the neurotoxicity hypothesis to explain the violent killings by police of Gaines and Gray. Their deaths, they claimed, were a direct result of—*were caused by*—the permanent neurodevelopmental injuries that they suffered as children from childhood lead poisoning. Consider a *Washington Post* investigation of Freddie Gray's death that examined the "toxic legacy" of Baltimore's history of lead-based paint poisoning. The article, drawing on the work of medical experts in lead poisoning, explained Gray's death as a result of lead-based paint poisoning. Gray, according to the *Washington Post*, was damaged so permanently and irreparably from lead poisoning that he lost "his ability to think and to self-regulate."[21] A *Vox* article about Korryn Gaines went further: "Exposure to lead can produce learning disabilities, lower IQs, and impulsivity, on top of erratic and aggressive behavior. The effects are so bad that some researchers believe the drop in blood lead levels in the past few decades may at least partly explain the United States' massive drop in crime since the 1990s."[22] "Gaines," the article concluded, "may have been another victim of an environmental hazard that most hurts black Americans. But in her case, the effects may have cost her her life." These were sympathetic news stories about Gaines and Gray that sought to highlight the brutal patterns and frightening impacts of childhood lead poisoning, but the logic they rely on is one that places the imagined pathology of Gaines and Gray at center stage, with no concern for the ways this slumlord poison economy has been made possible by police.[23]

The neurotoxicity hypothesis requires an inductive leap to get past the uncomfortable fact of police violence. This is most often accomplished by presenting the consequences of lead poisoning as an inexorable progression: poisoning leads to pathology, which leads to crime, which requires cops, who use violence, which restores order. This sequence—lead, which produces a changed nature, transforms a person into a (potential) criminal, which requires police violence to confront—structures nearly every story on Gaines and Gray and nearly every consideration of police in Baltimore. Read the 2016 report on the investigation of the Baltimore Police Department by the Civil Rights Division of the US Department of Justice, released after police killed Gray and Gaines. In it we find a paragraph on lead poisoning: "The City has nearly three times the national rate of lead poisoning among children. This burden weighs heaviest on poor, African-American communities" and causes "learning and behavioral problems, including decreased cognitive performance."[24] But then, immediately following this, the authors leap immediately to crime: "While the crime rate in urban America has declined significantly since the 1990s, Baltimore has experienced violent crime rates relatively higher than many other large cities." After this evidence-free leap of logic from lead to crime, the authors move directly into an expansive section on the Baltimore Police Department. First lead, then crime, now police. The authors of the investigation present this as an inexorable fact of life in West Baltimore. In other words, it is *in the nature* of those poisoned by lead to be violent and criminal, and it is *in the nature* of police to manage this.

The argument that both Korryn Gaines and Freddie Gray were poisoned by lead as children is beyond any doubt. Evidence presented in the lead-poisoning civil lawsuits filed on their behalf describe permanent neurological damage. Korryn Gaines's lawyer ordered an environmental and health assessment of exposure and disease in 2014 that concluded Gaines's exposure to lead resulted in "a neurodevelopmental disability or brain injury."[25] Gaines described difficulty concentrating in school, and records described "a history of problems with anger and impulsive behavior."[26] Freddie Gray was deposed in the lawsuit his family filed against Rochkind and described eating the peeling paint chips that fell from the walls and windowsills in his bedroom. Rochkind's slums poisoned not only Gray but also Gray's sister Fredericka. Doctors found dramatically high BLLs in both, and both were diagnosed with ADHD and eventually suspended from school for aggressive behavior problems.

But while Korryn Gaines suffered permanent injuries from lead exposure, she did not die from a slumlord's "sea of lead"; she died from a hail of police bullets. News reports described her behavior as erratic and unpredictable, but these behaviors did not bring her into contact with police. Police killed Gaines after she refused to comply with them, refused to leave her own home, and then armed herself against a SWAT assault of her home. Likewise, Freddie Gray did not die from ingesting lead paint chips; he died because four police officers severed his spine. And like Gaines, while his lead poisoning may explain why he struggled in school, those behaviors were not present when police arrested him. The only aggressive behavior displayed during Gray's arrest was by police, not Freddie Gray.

THE POISON-POLICE HYPOTHESIS: AN ALTERNATIVE TO THE NEUROTOXICITY HYPOTHESIS

Police killed Korryn Gaines and Freddie Gray. So why have the individualized stories of lead exposure in West Baltimore, rather than the intersection of poisoning and policing, come to exclusively explain their deaths? The biological explanation has been persuasive for the way it has created a seemingly *natural* link between lead and crime. It was lead poisoning that changed *their nature* in profound and permanent ways, and it is this, not police, that must therefore explain their violent deaths.

The leap from lead to crime requires a claim to a human nature as having been irreparably damaged and changed. There is a long colonial history at work in this leap, one that has imagined a pathology located deep *in the nature* of the victims of police violence. This is a racist history in which "the Black body is constructed as an inherently diseased body."[27] When Los Angeles police officers choked to death more than a dozen Black men in the 1970s and '80s, Los Angeles Police Department chief Darryl Gates suggested that it had nothing to do with policing and was instead a function of Black anatomy. "We may be finding," Gates told the *Los Angeles Times*, "that in some blacks when [the choke hold] is applied the veins and arteries do not open as fast as they do in normal people."[28] Cops kill Black people, but it's because of some inherent pathology found in the nature of the Black body, not because a cop choked the life out of them. In the case of the police killings of Gaines and Gray, some have pointed to a record of aggressive behavior in school as *the* cause of their deaths. But like all logical leaps, it's an argument built on quicksand. As an alternative, we might start by pointing to the long history of the use of tropes like "aggressive" and "delinquent" to pathologize the behaviors of Black students. Consider that Black students are more likely to be suspended, expelled by school administrators, and arrested at school by police than white students for the same behaviors.[29] This is true for Black girls, in particular. As Andrea Ritchie notes, schools "represent a site in which Black femininity is deeply regulated and severely punished."[30] As Ritchie explains, Black girls account for 33 percent of all girls arrested or referred to police. And the words used to describe Korryn Gaines—"erratic" and "aggressive" and "delinquent"—are used disproportionately to characterize the behavior of Black girls.

Consider the events that lead to the police killing of Korryn Gaines. She refused to register her vehicle with the state of Maryland. She affixed cardboard signs where license plates would have been. One read "Free Traveler" and the other: "Any Government official who compromises this pursuit to happiness and right to travel will be held criminally responsible and fined, as this is a natural right and freedom." Police pulled her over in March 2016 because of this. After a long confrontation, in which she calmly, though directly, refused to acknowledge their authority over her, police arrested her on disorderly conduct and resisting arrest charges and impounded her vehicle. Consistent with her refusal to recognize their authority over her, she skipped the court hearing. The court issued a bench warrant for her arrest. A heavily armed Baltimore County SWAT unit surrounded her apartment in August. First they knocked. Then they tried to enter with a master key. Then they kicked open her door and found Korryn holding a shotgun. A nearly seven-hour standoff followed. Gaines refused to surrender, and instead remained in her home armed with a shotgun and her five-year old son, Kodi. "I'm not going to murder you, I promise you that," one officer told Gaines, which was captured on lapel camera video. "One of you will," she responded. "I promise you, you will." Hours later, officers opened fire on Gaines after one cop claimed she lifted her weapon. The autopsy found that police shot Gaines in the left chest, back, right arm, left wrist, and left forearm. They shot her son, Kodi, too, who Gaines had been holding at the time, in his face. Kodi survived; Korryn Gaines died at the scene.

The context of her refusal to comply with police was political, not pathological. She missed a court date for a traffic ticket, and they killed her for it. Her refusal to submit to SWAT authority has been depicted in newspaper and media reports as "irrational" and "outrageous"—she was an "irresponsible mother." A *Washington Post* article described her political opposition to police authority as a form of mental illness. One journalist described these behaviors as "the markings of someone not fully in control."[31] Consider these claims. For these writers, any principled refusal to submit to police authority must be evidence of mental illness, and in Korryn's case must be evidence of an inherent criminality caused by lead poisoning. As Barbara Ransby notes, Gaines's antigovernment politics may have been unorthodox, but they were consistent with a libertarian rejection of government authority and an embrace of gun rights that shared much in common with the sovereign citizen movement, an antigovernment ideology often associated with Cliven and Ammon Bundy.[32] It was not a mental illness but an unorthodox political protest. But when displayed by Korryn Gaines, this behavior was interpreted as criminal pathology. She was lead poisoned, and it made her a criminal, and here was the proof.

Korryn filmed the entire police stop that started it all, and you can find the video online. If you watch it, don't read the comments section below the video. It's full of cruel posts by people that Frederick Douglass, if he were alive, would call "the filthy scum of white society." Korryn's child "is better without his mother," reads one. "Well, she was right about one thing," writes another, "eventually they had to kill her. It sure as shit wasn't 'murder' though." And another: "It's such a self-destructive culture. Korryn Gaines expected to die, and should have." The throughline connecting the postings is the popular version of the claim made by scholars and some journalists that Korryn Gaines was lead poisoned and a bad mother and therefore an appropriate subject of police violence.

Gaines was blamed for her own lead poisoning and demonized as a bad mother, which required police violence. As LaShonda Carter and Tiffany Willoughby-Herard argue, the role of police has long been organized around the control of Black female motherhood and reproduction. The SWAT unit, they argue, fulfilled the "state's role as a policing agent of Black motherhood."[33] Gaines's killing at the hands of police came with a police and popular narrative of her death as unfortunate but necessary in sustaining normative claims to motherhood. She was "irresponsible" in that she openly refused to submit to the authority of the state and the police, and in doing so became, according to police, a legitimate threat. "Black motherhood," as Carter and Willoughby-Herard point out, is often depicted as "pathological, broken, damaging, or anti-social," and it therefore comes under, as Gaines did, the prerogative power of police.[34] Gaines, in particular, refused to submit to police authority in ways that Carter and Willoughby-Herard point out are understood by police as "lethal to state sovereignty" if allowed to stand. Lethal for the way they "reveal and rupture the parasitic relationship between the state and Black people."[35] Police eradicate the threat of lead-based paint by killing its victims. This is what lead-based paint abatement looks like in Baltimore.

ON THE NATURE OF POLICE

Medico-legal arguments that link lead poisoning to crime contribute to establishing the conditions necessary for slumlord capital accumulation via the intense policing of communities ravaged by lead poisoning, such as West Baltimore. Scholarship and journalism that treat "crime" and "delinquency" as self-evident categories caused by lead poisoning obscure the central role of slumlordism and policing in the lives and deaths of Korryn Gains and Freddie Gray. The neurotoxicity hypothesis draws together lead, crime, and delinquency in order to obscure the fact that slumlord profitability is based entirely on the poisoning of Black children and the policing of neurotoxicity's victims. There is one mode of abatement to deal with lead poisoning inside the house, and another—policing—for the streets. This also gives cover to police. The police may have killed them, yes, but Gaines and Gray were *by nature* aggressive, unpredictable, impulsive, and prone-by-poison to violence. It was *in their nature* to be a threat because lead poisoning had arrested their development as fully human beings. These stories of delinquency and crime place police violence at the center of efforts to establish order. Gaines and Gray, according to police, constituted threats, even if we or they didn't know it, and even if we might feel badly about it. They didn't have to engage in any criminal act, in other words, to *be criminals*. Their lead poisoning established their nature as criminal.

Police use violence to fabricate order. The "lethality that infuses American law enforcement" is not marshaled in the service of safety and security for all, but rather as a means to establish the conditions and relations of racialized capital accumulation.[36] The indifference of the state to lead poisoning (even the homes registered with Baltimore's lead abatement program are poisoned by lead paint) is matched by the intensity of police in confronting its victims. Rochkind, the slumlord whose apartments have poisoned a generation of Black children, has profited not despite, but because of, that misery. Gaines and Gray were poisoned by slumlords as children and killed by police as adults. And arguments about nature and pathology obscure the role of police in fabricating and reproducing the order that makes all of this possible. Cops and slumlords have much in common. The lethal practices that bind the work of the slumlord to the work of the cop produce a shared exposure pathway: Korryn Gaines and Freddie Gray were poisoned and policed to death.

PART III
THE NATURE OF POLICE

CHAPTER FIVE

POLICING, PIPELINES, AND THE CAPILLARIES OF CAPITAL IN A WARMING WORLD

Axel González

"**C**apitalism as we know it is over," some have proclaimed. "Due to our increasingly unsustainable exploitation of the planet's environmental resources," the argument goes, "we're transitioning rapidly to a radically different global economy." The "oil and gas majors are in deep trouble," moreover, due to rising production costs, the growing popularity of renewable energy, and supposedly dwindling oil reserves.[1] In 2015, Paul Mason famously argued that "the end of capitalism has begun" and the left should take advantage of this transition to "postcapitalism" by ensuring that we build an egalitarian and sustainable economy in the ashes of capitalism. Like the agricultural and environmental crises that feudalism faced in the transition to capitalism, climate change is, Mason notes, "altering the dynamics of capitalism and making it unworkable in the long term."[2] Climate change, according to this logic, places capital on life support as it forces capital to confront the ecological and social crises and contradictions of its own making.[3]

But, as David Correia has argued, the wealthy see climate change as a "business opportunity." This is why Bill Gates and other CEOs flocked to the 2015 United Nations Climate Change Conference in Paris to push for cap-and-trade and carbon trading schemes.[4] Some conservative and liberal analysts have even suggested that, at a time when climate scientists warn that we have a decade to radically revolutionize our energy infrastructure if we are to avert climate catastrophe, "to a greater extent than ever before, the best interest of many businesses and those of the planet are aligned."[5] Rather than bring about the inevitable death of capital accumulation, climate change will, Geoff Mann and Joel Wainwright have argued, simply push global elites to what they call "Climate Leviathan"—that is, a kind of planetary governance in which capitalist elites push for mitigation strategies that allow them to "stabilize their position amidst planetary crisis." Far from the end of capitalism, the climate crisis might very well bring about an *intensification* of capitalist social relations in which elites mobilize an unprecedented level of global military control "in the name of preserving life on Earth," an intensification that, as I will show, is secured through police.[6]

Does climate change threaten the very system of capital accumulation, then? Or is it a business opportunity? Decades ago, ecological Marxist James O'Connor outlined the "second contradiction of capital," the contradiction between capitalist production and its inability to maintain the conditions of production. In short, he argued that capitalist productive forces "self-destruct" by "destroying rather than reproducing their own conditions."[7] O'Connor was careful to argue for a Marxist, non-Malthusian understanding of scarcity in which we can acknowledge that the "warming of the atmosphere will inevitably *destroy* people, places, and *profits*, not to speak of other species life."[8] However, influential ecological Marxists John Bellamy Foster and Paul Burkett have criticized O'Connor for overestimating the extent to which ecological crisis could threaten the system of capital accumulation. "Capitalism," in their words, "could advance and even prosper indefinitely while promoting what amounted to . . . the irreversible degradation of the earth."[9] Like Mann and Wainright, Foster and Burkett see nothing contradictory about capital accumulation thriving under conditions of ecological breakdown.

O'Connor's argument about the second contradiction of capitalism, however, exceeded a description of the natural limits of capital accumulation. O'Connor also suggested that the ecological devastation wrought by capitalism provided an opening for radical social movements. Ceaseless capital accumulation, for O'Connor, would lead to nothing short of a "rebellion of nature" and "powerful social movements demanding an end to ecological exploitation."[10] For O'Connor, it is not that climate change poses any sort of "natural" limit to capital accumulation; rather, it is that the destruction of nature inherent to the process of accumulation also has the unintended consequence of, to echo Marx, producing capitalism's gravediggers. While we might caution the impulse to see climate change as the final nail in capitalism's climate coffin, O'Connor's analysis helps us see that the climate crisis does indeed plunge capital into crisis by opening up the possibility for radical ecological and social revolt.

Rather than theorize the collapse of capitalism in a rapidly warming world, Mann and Wainright insist that we develop a political theory of climate change that considers what might happen if capitalism is *not* transcended by so-called ecological limits. How will capitalism adapt, they ask, to a world beyond two degrees Celsius of warming above preindustrial levels—a now seeming inevitability—and to a world marked by a growing revolt against fossil fuels and the social relations that drive their consumption? In the wake of the election of Donald Trump in the United States, many on the left have focused on state-supported climate denial as a key culprit in capital's ability to thrive in the midst of planetary crisis. Capitalism, here, adapts to the climate crisis by simply denying climate change and doubling down on ruthless extraction and accumulation.[11] Others take a more nuanced view, noting that even when liberal states acknowledge the climate crisis, the solutions proposed are conducive to capital accumulation and ultimately incompatible with ecological sustainability.[12] Geoengineering and carbon trading are thus exalted as solutions so that capitalists can continue to set fossil fuels on fire.[13]

What is missing from these critical accounts of how capital might adapt to a rapidly warming world is a consideration of *police power* as the most basic yet enduring power securing capitalist social relations in a world going up in flames. Police are not merely an institution, as Mark Neocleous argues, but rather a "broad range of powers through which social order is fabricated."[14] In the midst of planetary crisis, I argue, police fabricate and defend an order of nature that is always conducive to capital accumulation. In a warming world, capitalism is and will continue adapting to the climate crisis with nightsticks, handcuffs, Tasers, and rubber and metal bullets. Although ideological battles in the form of climate denial and of false solutions like geoengineering are important ways in which capital thrives under conditions of ecological devastation, none of these solutions to capital's crisis work without police. In a warming world, police will wage war against those who threaten the order

of nature that capitalism requires, whether climate deniers or liberal proponents of Climate Leviathan are in power. While ecological Marxists have
offered invaluable insights into the ecological contradictions of capitalism,
the relationship between capital accumulation and environmental crises, and
the need to build "ecosocialism," very few have considered in detail the role
that police play in defending an order of nature that is conducive to capital
accumulation. If fossil fuels are capitalism's very "lifeblood," as geographer
Matthew Huber has argued, then we should not forget that it is police who
ultimately secure capital's access to its lifeblood.

And, as the world burns, the revolt that O'Connor hinted at is everywhere, as activists take aim at the fossil fuel infrastructure made possible by
the social relations of capital, plunging it into crisis. From the "valve turners" with the group Climate Direct Action who halted the flow of about 15
percent of the United States oil supply in what has been called "the biggest
coordinated move on US energy infrastructure ever undertaken by environmental protestors" to antipipeline water protectors in Standing Rock and in
Louisiana's Atchafalaya Basin, activists are working to sever what Shiri Pasternak calls the capillaries of capital: pipelines.[15] Water protectors in Louisiana with the group No Bayou Bridge (NBB) are resisting the construction of
pipelines that would circulate capital's lifeblood from the Bakken oil fields in
the northern United States to the petroleum refineries along the Gulf Coast.
Fossil fuels are capitalism's lifeblood and pipelines are the capillaries that feed
the endless, extractive project of capital accumulation. Moreover, if capitalism
is fundamentally "a way of organizing nature," as Jason Moore has argued,
then it is a mode of organizing nature in which capital sustains unrestricted
access to its lifeblood.[16] While the climate crisis certainly poses a fundamental
challenge to a mode of capital accumulation based on fossil fuels, it is not because of the "ecological limits" of capitalism; rather, it is because of the growing movement seeking to abolish the order of nature that capital and police
fabricate and defend by suffocating and starving capital of its lifeblood.

In the wake of this growing antipipeline movement, capital is rush-
ing to defend its lifeblood. In the bayous of Louisiana's Atchafalaya Basin,
where NBB activists have set up a "floating resistance camp" on what many
have called the "end of the line" of the Dakota Access Pipeline, police and
the private security force hired by Bayou Bridge Inc. to defend the pipeline's

construction have been especially brutal.[17] Police have dragged activists from construction sites, placed them in choke holds, Tasered them, and attempted to starve them by cutting off the supply line they set up to their "skypod" along the treeline.[18] Moreover, as the *Intercept* reported, police and private security have used counterterrorism tactics on water protectors to, in their words, "defeat pipeline insurgencies."[19] NBB water protectors have also been arrested and charged under a new Louisiana state law, similar to those sweeping across other states with prominent antipipeline movements. The law "creates a felony for anyone who 'recruits, trains, aids, advises, hires, counsels, or conspires with' an individual who causes significant damage to 'critical infrastructure' such as pipelines."[20] Placing this law in the context of other laws designed to suppress environmental and social rebellion—such as the 2006 Animal Enterprise Terrorism Act—the violent and intense repression of antipipeline activists is a continuation of what many call the "war on eco-terror," or what environmental justice scholar David Pellow calls the "Green Scare."[21]

Capital is waging war on antipipeline activists. Police and the law are its soldiers. This chapter seeks to track that war. Drawing on the insights of ecological Marxism, I argue that capitalism creates a "rift in the metabolism between human beings and nature" and it is police that sustain that rift. If, as Foster and Burkett argue, the climate crisis demands that we "engage in a ruthless critique of capital's rift in 'nature's metabolism,'" then, I would add, we need to engage in a just-as-ruthless critique of police. Police, to be clear, do not simply *help* secure an order of nature in which capital sustains access to its lifeblood. Rather, I insist, we must extend the ecological Marxist analysis of fossil fuels as the lifeblood of capitalism to consider police itself as the lifeblood of capitalism. Demonstrating this dual nature of the lifeblood of capital—fossil fuels and police—NBB posted a photograph on its website of two water protectors handcuffed in front of one of the many machines being used to build the pipeline. Here, the handcuffs and the machines are juxtaposed, police and fossil fuels igniting the flames of fossil capital. Alongside the photo, we see a quote by civil rights activist Bayard Rustin that reads, "The only weapon we have is our bodies, and we need to tuck them in places so wheels don't turn."[22] NBB water protectors are using their bodies to stop the incinerating wheels of fossil capital, wheels fueled by fossil fuel combustion and the nightsticks, handcuffs, and weapons of police.

"THE AIR IS HEAVY WITH TIME": NO BAYOU
BRIDGE IN THE AGE OF FOSSIL CAPITAL

In late 2017, Cherri Foytlin and several other antipipeline water protectors set up a "floating pipeline resistance camp" in the Louisiana bayous to resist the construction of the Bayou Bridge Pipeline, a 162-mile pipeline that travels through Louisiana's wetlands and connects to a much larger system of pipelines carrying oil from the Bakken oil fields in the northern United States (Montana and North Dakota especially) to the refineries on the Gulf Coast. The "L'eau Est La Vie" ("Water Is Life") camp, they note, is "a continuation of our fight in Standing Rock, and furthermore a continuation of the centuries old fight to protect sacred stolen territory."[23] As many have pointed out, Bayou Bridge is the "end of the line" of the Dakota Access Pipeline. Like Dakota Access, Bayou Bridge Inc. is owned by Energy Transfer Partners (ETP), a large crude oil and gas transport company that owns or operates more than eighty-three thousand miles of pipelines across the country. Connecting their struggle to the effort to stop the Dakota Access Pipeline, water protectors in Louisiana demonstrate a growing antipipeline movement rebelling against the fossil fuel infrastructure that sustains capital accumulation and colonialism.

Revolt is happening all across ETP's vast pipeline infrastructure circulating capital's lifeblood, and ETP has responded forcefully. At the Dakota Access and Bayou Bridge sites, the company hired the mercenary security companies Tigerswan and HUB Enterprise to harass, surveil, and attack pipeline opponents. ETP attacked activists in court and claimed that environmental groups like Greenpeace and Earth First! "cynically planted radical, violent eco-terrorists on the ground amongst the protesters, and directly funded their operations and publicly urged their supporters to do the same."[24] In addition to ETP accusing activists of "ecoterrorism," the *Intercept* reported that local police and the private security companies hired to defend the pipelines deployed counterterrorism tactics against activists, comparing activists to "jihadist fighters" and targeting Palestinian and Earth First! activists.[25] As I noted earlier, policing at both ends of this pipeline infrastructure has been brutal; water protectors have been Tasered, thrown to the ground, placed in choke holds, and attacked by dogs throughout the years-long campaigns to stop oil from running through North Dakota and the bayous of Louisiana.[26]

This is of course not the first time we have seen a large-scale rebellion against fossil fuel infrastructure. In fact, workers have been engaging in mass revolt against the machines and fuel of what Andreas Malm calls "fossil capital"—that is, "an economy of self-sustaining growth predicated on the growing consumption of fossil fuels"—since British capitalists first began setting coal on fire in the early- to mid-nineteenth century.[27] The great general strike of 1842, Malm reminds us, was actually known at the time by another name, "the Plug Plot" or the "Plug Riots," because of the practice of "plug drawing" in which about half a million workers marched through the country's industrial zones pulling the plugs on steam engine boilers, "sending the water onto the floor and the steam into the air and bringing the revolutions of the engines to an instant stop."[28] Rather than merely incidental to the strike, as some historians have accepted, the act of "plug drawing," Malm argues, was "*constitutive* of the general strike"; workers were engaging in "collective bargaining by *rioting against the fossil economy*," and the "*working class could impose its will on capital by closing the spigots of the fossil economy.*"[29]

As ETP works tirelessly to circulate oil across the country so that other capitalists can set it on fire for greater accumulation, we must recognize that we are confronting a "historicized climate," that every molecule of carbon dioxide entering the atmosphere is "heavy with time."[30] The process of extracting fossil fuels from the ground and setting them ablaze began in nineteenth-century Britain, as British capitalists looked to confront labor shortages, work stoppages, and worker revolts. In contrast to popular arguments about the transition from water power to coal, Andreas Malm demonstrates that capitalists transitioned to coal *not* because of its superior efficiency. Coal was, in fact, *less efficient, less abundant,* and *more expensive* than water. In short, what drove British capitalists away from water was the "spatio-temporal profile" of coal. That is, coal allowed capitalists' never-ending quest to liberate themselves from labor and nature to be perfected. Water mills had to be stationed in particular places—along rivers—and capitalists often had to bring workers to the mills (which meant constructing homes, social services, and entire towns to reproduce their workforce). Coal, however, could be transported wherever, especially to cities, where a large industrial reserve army awaited. Thus, "a labourer downing his spade would ... have been less of an injury in a steam than in a water mill." Coal, moreover, "promised both temporal and spatial protection from extreme weather events," as steam engines and factories could be placed *anywhere* rather than constrained to a riverbank.[31]

The transition to fossil fuels was not a mistake, then, as many have accepted, a mistake that can now be simply corrected with climate science and our better understanding of the dangers of greenhouse gas emissions. Rather, burning fossil fuels has always been a class project, a project of perfecting capitalism's impossible goal to completely liberate itself from nature and labor. Fossil fuels, again, are the lifeblood of capital, and they only make sense as an energy source under the particular social relations that govern capital accumulation. The transition to fossil fuels in nineteenth-century Britain was not an inevitable shift on the path toward progress; rather, it was won through a class struggle by British capitalists. Workers rebelled against the class project of steam and, indeed, another pathway away from fossil fuels was possible. Of course, British capitalists won this war, setting the course of history on a path of insatiable fossil fuel combustion.

What happened, then, to the Plug Riots, to the rebellion against coal, to the "history of alternatives to spiraling combustion" that "were discarded along the way"?[32] The answer is simple: "At the end of the day, the insurrection could not stand up to the one supreme strength of its adversary: military power."[33] British capitalists and the government called on troops in the form of "watch-and-ward-men, yeomanry cavalry, and hastily assembled volunteer patrols . . . on horseback" to protect mill owners from the striking workers, allowing them to reignite the fires. Thus, on September 4, 2018, as St. Martin Parish police officers in Louisiana wrestled antipipeline activists to the ground, dousing them with pepper spray and attacking them with batons in one of several violent attacks of water protectors by police, the air was "heavy with time."[34] Like the carbon molecules seeping into the air as ETP oil is set afire today, the local, private, and public police force wielding batons, Tasers, and tear gas, and defending the critical infrastructure of fossil capital in the bayous of Louisiana, are "heavy with time."

To be clear, I do not mean to make a careless comparison between the British proletariat strike of 1842 and the Indigenous, environmental justice, and climate activists working to stop pipelines across the United States today. These struggles today are also struggles against settler colonialism and racial capitalism.[35] The Bayou Bridge Pipeline travels through the sacred lands of several Indigenous nations along the Gulf Coast and also through the city of St. James, a predominantly Black community that is part of Louisiana's "Cancer Alley" and already marked by several environmental injustices. Antipipeline struggles are also struggles for Indigenous sovereignty and racial justice, as much as—and sometimes even more than—they are struggles against the lifeblood of capital that is ushering catastrophic "global burning," as Daniel Wildcat prefers to name the climate crisis.[36] My point here, rather, is that the cops brutalizing water protectors in Louisiana, in Standing Rock, and in antipipeline movements across the country and the cavalry of nineteenth-century Britain called on to squash the plug drawers operate under the same logics, waging war against the enemies of fossil capital. Rather than separate institutions that function to fabricate and serve the natural order of capital accumulation, war and police are "*always already together*," marshaled to defend the lifeblood of capital against those seeking to extinguish the flames of fossil capital.[37]

There is nothing exceptional about police violence against antipipeline activists; local and state police in Louisiana are simply continuing to function as police always have in the age of fossil capital: they are continuing a long tradition of soldiers and cops waging war against those who threaten the lifeblood of capital. Police and fossil fuels are inseparable, helping capital secure an order of nature that is always conducive to ceaseless capital accumulation. In fact, as British capitalists in the early nineteenth century debated the merits of water-powered mills against steam-powered ones, Robert Peel—the father of Sir Robert Peel, who is considered by many to be the "father of modern policing"—"took the occasion to praise the inestimable value of steam in drawing factories to centres of population." Peel and other mill owners were gathered in Freemason's Hall to demand a monument for James Watt, an inventor who laid the foundation for the proliferation of coal-powered steam engines. It was in Freemason's Hall that steam power was, in Malm's words, "consecrated as a *class project*," as Peel and others celebrated the transition to steam and its promise to liberate capitalists from workers.[38] Sir Robert Peel, the "father of modern policing," would grow up with a father who understood just how well steam could facilitate the process of accumulation. Perhaps it is inappropriate, then, to simply consider police as that which defends the lifeblood of capital; instead, we might better understand police itself, along with fossil fuels, as the lifeblood of capital, as both serve capital as it confronts the crisis of revolt, a revolt working to abolish the stranglehold fossil fuels and police hold over labor and nature. Modern policing and the fossil economy were, indeed, born together.

MILITARIZATION, PRIVATIZATION, OR POLICE WAR

Anticipating the growing movement in Louisiana to resist the construction of the Bayou Bridge Pipeline, Louisiana sheriff Greg Champagne visited Standing Rock in 2016 to learn from the policing and counterterrorism tactics deployed by North Dakota police and Tigerswan, the private corporation hired by ETP and tasked with surveilling NoDAPL water protectors.[39] Tigerswan—run by ex-military special forces operatives, former FBI officials, navy intelligence veterans, and more—infiltrated water protector camps and protests in Standing Rock and often shared their information with police.[40] Unfortunately for ETP, Tigerswan was barred from operating in Louisiana because of lawsuits still pending in other states, though Tigerswan employees have recently attempted to operate in the state under a different company name.[41] Instead, ETP hired HUB Enterprises to defend the Bayou Bridge Pipeline, another private security contractor that specializes in surveillance, in providing protection for extractive industries, and in working closely with local law enforcement to ensure smooth, uninterrupted operation of its clients' business operations.

Like Tigerswan, HUB Enterprises boasts that "100% of our SRT [Special Response Team] members" are "law enforcement and/or military combat MOS veterans," providing them with the means to be "able to effectively liaison with law enforcement and emergency response organizations."[42] Clearly, the ex-military personnel tasked with surveilling water protectors all along ETP's vast pipeline infrastructure are using and marketing their expertise in dealing with insurgencies in the US-led global war on terror to defend "anti-pipeline insurgencies."[43] The use of private security companies operated by ex-military personnel to suppress antipipeline protest illustrates a growing war waged by police and private corporations against those who threaten the critical infrastructure of fossil capital.

On the left, the entanglement between military, police, and private corporations has often been explained through critiques of the "militarization" and "privatization" of police. These arguments—often implicitly—are often concerned with ensuring that police and security remain "public goods" and that police do not overstep their "bounds" by deploying military tactics and weaponry on US citizens. In contrast to "'the-war-is-becoming-police' approach," to the attempt to describe how an "institution called 'the military'... connects to an institution called 'the police,'" Neocleous argues that "we need to think of war and police as *processes* working in conjunction as state power."[44] Rather than attend to the "blurring" between police and war, he insists that we understand war power and police power in conjunction. Police power and war power are about the "formation of capitalist order" and the "fabrication of bourgeois order is war."[45] Police are not learning war from the military; police are waging war as they always have. In a rapidly warming world governed by capital accumulation, police are waging war to secure an order of nature in which capital can continue to extract and circulate its lifeblood and, of course, light the fires of accumulation.

When Bayou Bridge Pipeline opponent Ramon Mejia was arrested and charged under Louisiana's antiprotest law—the Critical Infrastructure Protection Act—he described how public and private police and security worked together to ensure the construction of the pipeline. "We were on private property," he said, "we were welcomed there, we showed them the [landowner's] letter and here you have uniformed officers who are supposed to be enforcing the rule of law . . . they're presenting themselves as uniformed officers . . . but actually they're just paid off by the oil company."[46] Mejia was unsure whether he was arrested by a parish officer or by HUB Enterprise, as the off-duty police officers working for HUB Enterprise still wear the same uniforms and use the same gear and weapons. Was the cop who arrested Mejia on company payroll?

Critiques of the "privatization" of police often see the use of private police forces as a "function of an increasingly 'hollowed-out' state."[47] These arguments that lament the supposed private takeover of a "public good" obscure the ways that public and private police forces work together and complement each other and that, in fact, "for police, there is no distinction between public and private."[48] Mejia's confusion about whether the cop who arrested him was on company payroll or on the local parish's illustrates how public and private police work together—in fact, sometimes they are the same people—to accomplish the same goal: protect capital against threats to good order.

In a warming world, public and private police wage war against those that threaten the ecological and social relations necessary for capital accumulation, relations that ultimately rely on burning fossil fuels.

Mejia's comments also illustrate how police violated the wishes of landowners along the pipeline construction site who opposed the construction of the pipeline through their backyards. No Bayou Bridge made alliances with several landowners, requesting permission to set up tree camps and other blockades along the construction site. Landowners, NBB, and several other local organizations attempted to stop the project in court, efforts that ultimately failed. The competing claims to property, however, were ultimately settled with the hands and weapons of police. Antipipeline movements like NBB and NoDAPL, as Shiri Pasternak and others have argued, pose a threat because they offer and demand different ways of understanding land, property, nature, and value that conflict with the capitalist mode of production. "Resistance," as they put it, "takes the form of both intervening in capitalist valuations and challenging the capitalist value regime, bringing colonial capitalism to its knees."[49] Antipipeline movements for climate justice, Indigenous sovereignty, and racial justice plunge capital into crisis, a crisis solved with police.

This crisis is, thus, also a crisis of value as antipipeline activists challenge the "capitalist value regime." The competing visions of nature, land, and value we see in pipeline projects and in opposition to those projects illustrate that while "value is simple," "valuation is complex."[50] Geographers Patrick Bigger and Morgan Robertson have insisted on a "process-oriented understanding" of value—the process of valuation—that understands that "value is found, affirmed, realized, or destroyed through ongoing social performances of comparison and measure."[51] The capitalist value form is surely dominant, evidenced by the continuing flames of the fossil economy in a burning world. However, Bigger and Robertson remind us, capitalist value "is situated alongside other types of values" and recognizing these others forms the "basis for political intervention."[52] Antipipeline movements have cost Energy Transfer Partners and other pipeline companies billions of dollars, as they have exposed the violence of the capitalist value form.[53] It is police, though, that ultimately have resisted efforts to surmount the capitalist value form. In a warming Louisiana with increasingly powerful storms and increasing rates of cancer, private and public police wage war against those that threaten capitalist value, ensuring the continuing fumes of the fossil economy. In a warming world marked by the crisis of ecological and social revolt, value is produced, affirmed, and maintained through the violence of police.

THE CRITICAL INFRASTRUCTURE PROTECTION ACT AND THE WAR ON ECO-TERROR

If police war is how capitalism responds to ecological revolt, then we must map the war police and capital are fighting today, a war we might call the war on eco-terror. Placing the policing of antipipeline movements in the context of the US-led global war on terror, we can begin to understand and chart how police wage war to secure a natural order conducive to the endless accumulation of capital. As activists today attempt to pull the plugs of the "critical infrastructure" of fossil capital, we need to understand how police wage war in a warming world. We can begin mapping this war by attending to the production of "ecoterrorism" and the legal infrastructure of the war on eco-terror, a legal infrastructure that, as Walter Benjamin would put it, must be stamped through the violence of police.[54]

In response to the growing, threatening movement against the construction of the Bayou Bridge Pipeline, on May 30, 2018, the Louisiana state legislature passed a law that would issue harsher penalties to activists obstructing the construction or operation of "critical infrastructure." Bill 797 was modeled after the Critical Infrastructure Protection Act (CIPA) written by the American Legislative Exchange Council (ALEC), a right-wing think tank. This act "codifies criminal penalties for a person convicted of willfully trespassing or entering property containing a critical infrastructure facility without permission by the owner of the property, and holds a person liable for any damages."[55] This effort to protect "critical infrastructure" is not brand new; rather, it has its roots in a 2015 bill passed by the Committee on Homeland Security of the same name, although that bill was more focused on protecting against cyberattacks and other threats to technological infrastructure. But the 2015 DHS bill does provide the framework and foundation for ALEC's and the versions being passed at the state level.[56] What is new about the ALEC-backed effort sweeping across states with prominent antipipeline demonstrations—including Minnesota, Iowa, Wyoming, Ohio, and Pennsylvania—is the attempt to redefine what counts as "critical infrastructure."[57]

For example, the Louisiana bill defines critical infrastructure as follows:

<u>Any and all structures, equipment, or other immovable or movable property located within or upon</u> chemical manufacturing facilities, refineries, electrical power generating facilities, electrical transmission substations and distribution substations, water intake structures and water treatment facilities, natural gas transmission compressor stations, liquified natural gas (LNG) terminals and storage facilities, natural gas and hydrocarbon storage facilities, and transportation facilities, such as ports, railroad switching yards, *pipelines*, and trucking terminals, or any site where the construction or improvement of any facility or structure referenced in this Section is occurring.[58]

Thus, the law defines critical infrastructure primarily as energy infrastructure and makes the critical addition of "pipelines." CIPA establishes trespassing, obstructing, or "conspiring" to obstruct the operations (we might read, profit) of energy infrastructure (and specifically pipeline) companies as a felony. Of course, the fact that this is a Department of Homeland Security law—the agency tasked with antiterrorism, border security, cyber security, etc.—is no insignificant detail. We might place CIPA in the context of other ecoterrorism laws, such as the 2006 Animal Enterprise Terrorism Act (another ALEC-backed law), which, among other things, criminalizes any act that "intentionally damages or causes the loss of any real or personal property used by an animal enterprise, or any real or personal property of a person or entity having a connection to, relationship with, or transactions with an animal enterprise."[59]

As the Louisiana Bucket Brigade, a group heavily involved in the effort to stop the Bayou Bridge Pipeline, notes, "Many of these bills seek to frame protests as 'riots' and activists as 'terrorists' or 'jihadists,' in attempts to criminalize protected free speech activity."[60] These ecoterrorism laws, thus, work to protect the profits of various extractive industries—energy companies, animal agriculture, etc.—by criminalizing and issuing harsh penalties for those that attempt to halt the violence of extractive capitalism. As David Pellow reminds us, these are not "trespassing," "vandalism," or "arson" charges; in charging activists with terrorism, AETA (and I would add CIPA here) reveals "the criminalization of political thought."[61] In other words, AETA and CIPA extend the penalty associated with a particular act—property destruction, obstruction of an enterprise, etc.—to include the politics behind the act.

Other examples of the labeling and targeting of environmental and climate activists as terrorists abound. The FBI, for instance, defines ecoterrorism as "the use or threatened use of violence of a criminal nature against innocent victims or property by an environmentally-oriented, subnational group for environmental-political reasons, or aimed at an audience beyond the target, often of a symbolic nature."[62] What is common among the language of CIPA and AETA and the FBI's definition of ecoterrorism is the emphasis on damage to the property and corporate profits of enterprises related to animal exploitation, fossil fuels, energy development, logging, etc. In fact, in FBI domestic terrorism chief James Jarboe's 2002 testimony on the "threat of ecoterrorism" virtually all of his examples of ecoterrorism are of arsons and property destructions carried out by groups like Earth First! and the Earth Liberation Front (ELF).

Aside from government agencies like the FBI and federal and state legislatures, there are also a number of nongovernment, not-for-profit, and for-profit organizations and corporations involved in the effort to repress radical environmental and climate activists through the production of ecoterrorism. SITE Intelligence Group, for example, a small not-for-profit organization based out of Bethesda, Maryland, provides frequent updates of "terrorist" actions and communiques across the world to a list of government, corporate, and individual subscribers. Most of their warnings are either about "jihadi terrorism" or radical environmental and Indigenous activists who plan to halt pipelines, logging machinery, and other extractive industries.[63] This conflation of "jihadi terrorism" with "ecoterrorism" is not something new, though, nor is it limited to SITE. As the *Intercept* illustrated in its exposé of counterterrorism tactics used against Standing Rock water protectors, the private security company Tigerswan often "compared the anti-pipeline water protectors to jihadist fighters." As Tigerswan infiltrated protector camps and attempted to exploit tensions in the camp among, for instance, Native and non-Native activists, they paid special attention to activists of Arab—and especially Palestinian—descent. Furthermore, highlighting the conflation of far-right jihadi movements and radical environmental and Indigenous activists, Tigerswan operatives noted in an intelligence report that "of most concern were the 'Earth First' magazines found on the camp. These magazines promote and provide TTP's [tactics, techniques, and procedures] for violent activity."[64] This growing counterterrorism industry—made up of police, private security companies, government agencies, and nonprofit organizations—illustrates, as Neocleous puts it, the "collusion between capital and security" to protect extractive capital from rebellion.[65]

Highlighting the chilling effects of the passage of the Critical Infrastructure Protection Act, one NBB activist noted, "I can say that the change has been that we now have nine people who are facing felonies. It makes us rethink the way we do things so we're super, super careful. That's for sure."[66] Laws like CIPA and AETA, along with the larger counterterrorism industry that fabricates the threat of "ecoterrorism" are part of the larger war on eco-terror helmed by police, a war intended to suppress threats to capitalist value and order in a warming world. In order to confront the fossil economy, we need to understand how capital will adapt to the climate crisis. This section has begun to map how police wage war in a warming world, and the network of laws, think tanks, and government and nongovernmental agencies that supports that war. Police, the law, and war are entangled technologies of power in the formation of capitalist order, in the fabrication of an order of nature in which fossil fuels can be extracted, circulated, and set on fire.

ANOTHER ORDER: THE *POTENZA* STRIKES BACK

In October 2018, Foytlin and others traveled to Dallas to disrupt an Energy Transfer Partners shareholders meeting. They each stood up during the meeting, decrying the violence of the pipeline, the potential health and environmental impacts, the dangers and unequal distribution of risks, and the pipeline's contribution to the climate crisis. "Just because you're rich doesn't mean you can make others suffer," one activist declared. The activists were quickly pushed and dragged out of the meeting and handcuffed. As they filmed and livestreamed the action with cell phones, the video goes dark as Foytlin proclaims forcefully, "Not today, colonizers! Not today! Not today colonizers!" When the officer arresting her told her she was "out of order," Foytlin responded, "I'm out of order? You're out of order! You're all out of order! All of you are out of order! ETP kills!"[67]

Police, again, are waging a war against antipipeline activists to secure an order of nature for capital accumulation. Police, as Neocleous puts it, are always at war against the "enemies of order" as they work to establish "new grounds of accumulation" in the midst of planetary crisis. However brutal the war waged against antipipeline movements has been, there is nothing exceptional or special about it. Police are simply continuing the long tradition of securing the grounds for capital accumulation, a tradition that began at least in the nineteenth century, as British capitalists called on the cavalry to squash the worker rebellion against fossil capital. On May 13, 1985, Philadelphia police dropped a bomb on the homes and headquarters of MOVE, a Black liberation organization committed to animal liberation and ecological sustainability. MOVE argued that capitalism, war, and police must be abolished for a world with "clean air, clear water and pure food" and a world where "human beings, dogs, birds, fish, trees, ants, weeds, rivers, wind or rain" could flourish.[68] When police ignited buildings where MOVE revolutionaries worked tirelessly to embody and live out a relationship with the more-than-human world untied from the logics of accumulation, police waged war on the enemies of the natural order of capitalism. As the great journalist and Black liberation activist Mumia Abu-Jamal put it, "On that day, the city, armed and assisted by the US government, dropped a bomb on a house and called it law. The fire department watched buildings ignite like matches in the desert and cut off water. The courts of the land turned a blind eye, daubed mud in their socket, and prosecuted Ramona Africa for having the nerve to survive an urban holocaust, jailing her for the crime of not burning to death."[69] As fossil capitalists ignite the world for endless accumulation, police set fire to any order of nature that challenges the logic of capital accumulation, white supremacy, and colonialism. If fossil fuels must be set ablaze, so, too, must the enemies of order.

What the war against antipipeline movements and the bombing of MOVE reveal, then, is not the exceptional violence of police. Rather, they reveal that what *is* exceptional, here, is the threat of antipipeline movements themselves, the threat of establishing an altogether different order of nature incompatible with the logic of capital accumulation. As Foytlin notes as she reflects on how the Critical Infrastructure Protection Act and counterterrorism tactics by police have hurt the movement and forced activists to change their strategies, "But it doesn't change anyone's resolve. I haven't seen anyone pack up and go home."[70] Similarly, Abu-Jamal argued that the MOVE bombing demonstrated the "death knell of a system committing suicide. It proved that a man called John Africa spoke powerful truths when he spoke about the nature of the system as corrupt, as flawed, as poisoned." Elaborating a theory of "ecological autonomism," Andreas Malm reminds us that "sooner or later, the *potenza* strikes back," that regardless of how much control capitalism has over labor and nature, the latter always remains autonomous, capable of striking back.[71] As capitalists work to defend what the ecosocialist network System Change, Not Climate Change (SCNCC) calls "militarized accumulation"—a mode of accumulation that relies on war, terror, and policing that we can see very clearly at play in the efforts to destroy the movements at Bayou Bridge and Standing Rock—we should remember that the *potenza* is striking back, that the crisis capital faces now is powerful and threatening ecological and social revolt.[72] We know that pipelines often suffer from "tiny cracks, often invisible to the eye," as No Bayou Bridge shared in one of many communiques on its website, that "appear as infrastructure ages. Detecting them before they cause spills is a multi-billion dollar global business."[73] The water protectors at Bayou Bridge, though, also want us to remember that tiny cracks form in the fossil economy itself and that in these tiny cracks the *potenza* strikes back.

CHAPTER SIX

SECURING NATURE'S RETURN: ECOSYSTEM ECOLOGY AND ENVIRONMENTAL POLICING AT THE SAVANNAH RIVER SITE

Andrea Miller

Look for the wisteria. So few traces remain of Ellenton, South Carolina, that it is only the heavy purple clusters of wisteria in bloom that allow one to imagine where homes once stood. So explained my guide from the Savannah River Ecology Laboratory as we sat in a University of Georgia truck overlooking Field 3-412, famed for ecological studies Eugene Pleasants (E. P.) Odum, the oft-described "father of modern ecology," conducted there.[1] Run by the University of Georgia, the ecology lab comprises 90 percent of the Department of Energy's (DOE) 310-square-mile Savannah River Site (SRS) nuclear reservation, where ecological studies began in 1951 and predated the site's construction. Originally operated by E. I. du Pont de Nemours and Company and devoted to the production of tritium and plutonium-239 for US nuclear weapons, SRS is now home to the Savannah River National Laboratory (SRNL) and serves as a major site of nuclear waste management and storage, including the recently terminated Mixed-Oxide Fuel (MOX) Fabrication Facility, which converted weapons-grade plutonium and uranium into fuel rods for commercial use in nuclear power plants.

By way of eminent domain, the US government annexed and then cleared the predominantly rural area chosen for the construction of the site, which spanned three South Carolina counties—Aiken, Allendale, and Barnwell. The largest of six towns displaced, Ellenton was a small but bustling community of 739. Once absent its previous residents, the town's former farmlands became the site of Odum's Field 3-412. Here, E. P. Odum and his students began their first ecological studies at the nuclear reservation, using Ellenton's "old fields" to examine the ecological principle of *secondary succession*, where ecological development "proceed[s] in an area from which a community was removed (such as a plowed field or cutover forest)."[2] Within secondary succession, human land uses are subsumed and replaced by nature's inevitable return, an "orderly process of community change,"[3] which is described as analogous to human-driven processes of development and civilizational progress.[4] As the principle area of ecological research that aligned the interests of the University of Georgia via Odum with that of the DOE's precursor, the Atomic Energy Commission (AEC), at the site, secondary succession is a useful analytic through which to interrogate the ecology laboratory as security world, a site of production and enclosure maintained through myriad forms of state and economic violence. I argue that, taken together, both the principle and Odum's studies of secondary succession conducted at SREL function as a mode of environmental policing, those practices of enclosure, dispossession, and governance that work on and through the natural and built environment. Through its capacity to render that which was previously manmade "natural" and to generate "order" in nature, Odum's secondary succession simultaneously enacts and obfuscates colonial practices of policing and dispossession.[5]

In order to interrogate secondary succession as a mode of environmental policing within the security world of the ecology lab, I begin this chapter by thinking with residual traces of Ellenton's built environment still perceptible in SREL's Field 3-412 / Ellenton Bay to ask of the relationships between histories of dispossession and the colonial logics of Odum's secondary succession. Here, succession works to naturalize and enact colonial practices of dispossession, and natural laws exceed human governance in the service of generating and maintaining good order. These material and historical transformations wrought upon the land produce the conditions that make possible the very existence of the ecology lab and the scientific inquiries investigated and developed on its campus. Understanding the ecology lab and the development of Odum's ecosystem ecology as inextricably bound up in the US colonial project, I next trace secondary succession in the scholarship of E. P. Odum, where succession is articulated through a developmentalist framework of progress and civilization. I demonstrate that these colonialist economic underpinnings link Odum's ecosystem ecology to conceptual formations of police power and informed Odum's concept of the mesocosm, an in-between world of both laboratory and field site, natural and built environment.[6] As protected areas that preserve land for the use (as well as enjoyment and currency) of the ecologist, mesocosms function as border zones that must be perpetually surveilled and policed. As one example of Odum's mesocosm, the Savannah River Ecology Laboratory emerges as a security world, where it is through rather than in spite of *practices of policing* that the ecology lab and ecologist are produced as such.[7]

THE CURBS ARE NOT WHAT THEY SEEM

Before we reached the pull-off overlooking Field 3-412 / Ellenton Bay where my guide pointed out wisteria vines as subtle markers of previous settlement, we drove through what had once been the center of Ellenton. The only visible evidence remaining of the town were curbs overgrown with vegetation and dirt, perhaps a fire ant mound or two. As I reached for my camera, I remembered that my guide had told me that I was welcome to take pictures, but none of infrastructure. Photographs of infrastructure were thought to pose risks to national security, potentially leaking information about SRS that could be exploited by state or nonstate actors wishing to conduct acts of terrorism against the site and, by extension, the United States. Ellenton's former curbs, then, introduced interesting questions: What counts as infrastructure within the boundaries of the nuclear reservation? Are these curbs infrastructure? When I asked this of my guide, she paused and shrugged, visibly mulling it over before indicating that she estimated it would be alright to take photographs of the curbs. Just a little while before, she had told me that in deciphering the definition of infrastructure she applied the question, Was it built by humans? Now this rather commonsense definition was supplanted by one that incorporated multiple and shifting layers of implied meaning: temporal distance between use and disuse, recognizability, perceived boundaries between nature and the built environment, and ability to reveal sensitive information about the nuclear reservation. These curbs once mediated the relationship between the natural and built environment in Ellenton. They were once infrastructure. If no longer infrastructure, what had they become?

A few weeks after my visit to the ecology lab and SRS, I met with an emeritus ecologist from SREL. When discussing Ellenton and Field 3-412, he described the field site's significance to the discipline of ecosystem ecology, telling me that "3-412 is enshrined in the annals of ecology because it helped define a functional ecosystem." This same ecologist also emphasized that during his career at the ecology lab he took friends who had grown up in Ellenton back to the site whenever possible. The white ecologist told me of one specific occasion when a Black friend found an old bathroom tile hidden in the wisteria where his childhood home had once stood. The retired ecologist described that the man broke into tears at the sight of it. "I almost let him take it," he went on. Ultimately, the ecologist did not allow the visitor to keep this remnant of the home from which he and his family had been forcibly removed. As arbiter between the displaced resident and the US government, the ecologist determined the tile must remain with the wisteria. By the ecologist's estimation, just as the site where the man's home once stood was property of both the US government and nature, so, too, was the bathroom tile.

Taken together, the twisted vines of wisteria, the single bathroom tile, and Ellenton's curbs function as what Javier Arbona has termed "anti-memorials,"[8] here marking traces of past human life and previous events of colonial settlement and dispossession in the context of the US nuclear project. Further, these anti-memorials serve as signposts for the capacity of Odum's secondary succession to function as a form of environmental policing, through its claim to the orderly transformation of objects and life into *properties* of nature and state at the ecology lab, sometimes repeatedly.[9] For example, time and again over the course of many years, Odum employed local farmers to seed Ellenton's old fields with corn, only to let them once again be overcome by nonagrarian plant and animal life. These perpetual transformations hinge on generating, knowing, and desiring an orderly nature and an understanding of land as ever only developed *or* natural. These understandings of land and nature obfuscate colonialist dispossession as an ongoing and multivalent process while repeatedly enacting it. Here, if dispossession is accounted for at all, it is only in the form of discrete events in a human historical context predating and ending with the construction of SRS. According to the ecological calculus of the ecology lab and Odum's early secondary succession studies at Field 3-412, previous human habitation and relations to the land, from those of Mississippian and Creek and Chickasaw Indigenous peoples to Black sharecroppers, are rendered prelapsarian. Old fields are simply described as "abandoned farmlands" left to the whims of nature—and the ecologist. For example, in a 1960 article on the first eight years of old field succession studies at the ecology lab, Odum only briefly mentions that "approximately 6,000 human inhabitants moved out of an area of 315 square miles to make way for the establishment of the SRP" before turning his full attention to the sixty-seven thousand acres of "abandoned" croplands that were of chief ecological interest.[10] Here, Odum translates displacement as "moving out" and dispossession as the land's abandonment by previous human inhabitants.

While it may at first seem unremarkable that Odum does not mention past human habitation save for its brief appearance in the article's first paragraph, particularly given the essay's topic and publication in the journal *Ecology*, the absence of the human is conspicuous here. It is, in fact, unusual for Odum not to address the relationship between natural and human ecology in his writing.[11] In this case, the absence of the displaced human and nonagricultural land-based filiations not only characterizes the early research conducted at the ecology lab in former Ellenton but also sets the stage for current and ongoing research that either obfuscates entirely or struggles to reconcile ecological studies at the lab with the site's histories of dispossession. In her role as outreach coordinator, my ecology lab guide described to me that she has had great political difficulty coming to terms with having unfettered access to the land of SRS when so many people for whom it is dear can never return. This admission was a singular one and notably by an ecologist whose position is unique within the ecology lab as an explicit bridge between SREL and surrounding communities. With the exception of one other staff person whose family had themselves been displaced by the construction of the site, ecologists at the lab seemed to approach the issue of dispossession with a sense of casual resignation when asked, focusing instead on the good environmental work the ecology lab produces. This apparent contradiction was one that ecologists were not eager to broach. Through my interviews and time spent at the ecology lab, interlocutors articulated the dispossession of former Ellenton residents as an event succeeded by liberal environmentalism and protection, to say nothing of previous histories of dispossession that include Native removal and Black enslavement. Once again, dispossession and displacement are things of a pre-SRS human past, while ecology is the framework of an environmental present and future.

That interlocutors rendered these concepts—displacement/dispossession and ecology—temporally and conceptually distinct says much of the anachronizing work of Odum's ecosystem ecology and studies of secondary succession at the ecology lab.[12] If secondary succession is the teleological maturation of ecosystems, where one community replaces another to achieve order and the "climax" stage of the "'adult' community,"[13] it stands to reason that the notion of ecological *replacement* cannot reconcile itself or account for forms of *displacement*. That is to say that within Odum's ecosystem ecology teleological models of environmental development do not, and perhaps cannot, reckon with all manner of violence and power and, even if unwittingly, erase histories of human violence. Further, as I explore in the following section, these histories of violence and dispossession are materially and practically foundational to the development of these ecological models. To reckon with these histories would be to reckon with the genesis of Odum's ecosystem ecology as a field and its attendant worldviews as products of a relationship to the US military project. In this way, it is not so far-fetched when ecologists such as Odum's colleague and collaborator Bernard Patten make claims such as: "Invasive species could be welcomed as a natural manifestation of biotic dispersal. So could human migrants seeking better lives outside the centers of their reproduction." Notably for Patten, "exponential growth" is also "the mark of a species succeeding, not failing," and global warming is a positive trend that will increase species diversity in the earth's cold zones.[14] Here, human movement and environmental change, and we might also include the dispersal, disappearance, and destruction of all manner of environments, is only movement and change—purely apolitical and purely ahistorical. It is the story of natural law, species diversification, and ecological development.

Further, displacement as replacement and/or movement cannot account for the profound experiences of dispossession such as those described by Louise Cassels, where the loss of her family home in Ellenton reconfigured her very ability to know and perceive her world. In her memoir, Cassels writes of the unnerving period preceding her relocation, along with her sister Mamie, to nearby Aiken in advance of SRS's construction in the early 1950s. Throughout, Cassels describes the so-called evacuation in terms of a "death sentence" that radically reoriented her ability to know and perceive reality.[15] She describes being frightened by her own "premonitions" and "uncanny" feelings,[16] physically reeling backward and collapsing from the shock of opening the door of her church to lively tourists who flocked to Ellenton to consume the town's final days,[17] and suddenly losing her ability to speak when confronted by news media in her classroom, a space increasingly saturated by "dread" as students "*sensed* their parents' problems."[18] For Cassels, the town's built environment became a lively and life-filled network of structures that could at once be experienced as traitorous, as with the railroad now aiding the government's efforts,[19] or mourned as they sometimes slowly and at times abruptly retreated into death.[20]

Nor can the sanitized narrative of ecological succession account for accretive forms and histories of displacement and dispossession endemic to US colonialism and racial capitalism in the region. To obfuscate the displacement and dispossession of Ellenton residents and render this history ahistorical is to further render ahistorical the legacies of Black sharecropping in the area, where Black Ellentonians were disproportionately uncompensated for their displacement and losses as primarily nonlandowners. As Kari Frederickson notes in her history of Cold War militarization in the Central Savannah River Area, an estimated three thousand nonlandowning Black residents were impacted by land seizures. Frederickson describes that "the people most intimately connected to the land, not simply aesthetically but practically, the people most likely to hold the soil daily in their hands, were in the weakest position to keep it from slipping through their fingers and the least likely to have any compensation placed into those hands."[21] In this configuration, while those losses incurred by agricultural white landowning families such as the Cassels are erased through the framework of Odum's secondary succession, then the predominantly Black labor that worked that land is rendered doubly displaced from the historical archive. Not to mention anything of legacies of both Black and Native enslavement and the systematic removal of the Creek and Chickasaw peoples.

Erased, then, is Ellenton's long history of racialized colonial violence, where even those stories attempting to address Ellenton's displacement portray the town as one existing in rural harmony, even if segregated and under the rule of Jim Crow.[22] Here, reflections on an idyllic Ellenton cohere as a Cold War rendition of what Raymond Williams described as a "Romantic structure of feeling," a neopastoralism where nature is counterposed to industrialization and notions of the human and community are subsumed "into the idea of culture, against the real social pressures of the time."[23] For example, unaccounted for within a natural historical narrative of secondary succession is the Ellenton Riot of September 1876, where marauding white Democrats killed upwards of one hundred Black Ellenton residents. Under the guise of avenging the attempted robbery of Mrs. Alonzo Harley by two Black men, Peter Williams and Fred Pope, the intent of the riot was to suppress the Black Republican vote in the upcoming gubernatorial election.[24] There is no place for this violence, deeply connected to local histories of property, race, and political unrest, within the narrative of secondary succession at SRS. To apply the formula of secondary succession, Indigenous presence is succeeded first by "pioneer" colonial settlement and plantation economies, which together form an amorphous prehistory to the construction of SRS.[25] These are all but natural progressions in the teleological narrative of civilizational maturation.

In this way, both Odum's principle and studies of secondary succession at SRS operate as environmental policing, where secondary succession is framed as "an orderly process of community development that is reasonably directional and, therefore, predictable."[26] Within Odum's ecosystem ecology, scientific discourses of succession sanitize the violence of displacement and dispossession and work to contain and mitigate the Savannah River Site's unruly legacies.[27] These unruly legacies include embodied human relationships to land and place, violent political and economic histories, the effects of radiation and heavy metals on human and nonhuman life alike, traces of past habitation such as bathroom tiles and curbs, and the transnational effects of US military violence exported from SRS or imported only to be interred in "the burial ground," where nuclear waste of all manner and origin is stored. It is not simply that these processes and objects are naturalized through Odum's secondary succession theory but that they are *made properties of nature and state*. As David Correia and Tyler Wall make clear, to create and enforce the logics of property is by definition to police and to enact all manner of attendant violence.[28] Additionally, as Correia and Wall point out in their explication of private property as a "core value" of police, to police property relations is to engage in world-making practices,[29] here in the service of creating and maintaining the ecology lab as security world.

Further, and perhaps at once appearing counterintuitive, within the framework of ecosystem ecology, nature is not the wild, disorderly environment that must be tamed and harnessed by human industriousness. Rather, *nature is order*, made so through indisputable laws that, while described by science, exist beyond scientific or human governance. Raymond Williams described this as the first principle of nature, as "a principle of order, of which human activity, by regulating principles, may then rearrange and control."[30] It is the law of nature, so the story of ecosystem ecology goes, that works to quell human and nonhuman disorder alike. "The basic 'laws of nature' have not been repealed; only their complexion and quantitative relations have changed, as the world's human population has increased," Odum instructs.[31] Elastic but incontrovertible, the laws of nature adapt to respond to new and different forms of environmental disorder. And, as Mark Neocleous reminds us, the foremost function of policing is the production and maintenance of "good order."[32]

Indeed, the relationship between ecology and policing is not unique to the US military and state. Eyal Weizman, in collaboration with photographer Fazal Sheikh, describes the historical and explicit relationship between ecological science and the Israeli military as one culminating in "ecological paramilitaries." Established in 1977 and expanded by Ariel Sharon during his tenure as minister for agriculture and again in the 2000s as prime minister, Israel's Green Patrol unit was tasked with "the ecological preservation of the desert's threshold." As Weizman describes, policing the aridity line of the Negev desert functions as a scientific veneer for settler-colonial practices of Bedouin genocide and dispossession. The Green Patrol has systematically engaged in tactics of land seizures, forced eviction, and the demolition of Bedouin settlements along the shifting desert threshold, beyond which no settlements are legally allowed.[33] In the case of Israel, the aridity line of the Negev "has become the sharp edge of a legal apparatus of dispossession."[34] Here, ecological science, law, and policing are explicitly bound up in the settler colonial project. This example outlining "ecology as a political tool"[35] is instructive, demonstrating how ecological science and concepts are not simply taken up by the state to justify all manner of violence but developed alongside and through state practices of environmental policing.

Similarly, the historical presence and continued work of the ecology lab at SRS provides crucial insights regarding the coconstitutive relationship between colonial military projects and ecological science, where practices of dispossession and military development created the conditions for the emergence of an Odumian ecosystem ecology. As ecologist Frank Golley, himself director of SREL from 1962 to '67, described in his account of the ecosystem as scientific concept, it was only through the financial, institutional, and land-based support of the AEC that ecosystem ecology began to flourish in the United States following World War II.[36] Materially and intellectually marginalized within conservative biology and zoology university departments,[37] ecosystem studies and the AEC "created an invisible college" where "this community exchanged members, met as a group in national symposia in 1961, 1965, and 1967, and had a joint research agenda."[38] In the section that follows, I echo Scott Kirsch's call to interrogate these "institutional relations" between ecosystem ecology at SREL and the US nuclear and military projects, "important precisely because they become internal to the nature, and the nature of the science, produced."[39] I demonstrate that Odum's ecosystem ecology was not simply haphazardly enrolled in the US nuclear project and its attendant dispossessive and policing logics. Rather, it is explicitly through the dispossession outlined above and subsequent decades of military and private policing at SRS that Odum's ecosystem ecology was conferred both the land and material resources necessary to conduct experimentation and develop its scientific theory.

ECOLOGICAL SUCCESSION AND THE MESOCOSM AS SECURITY WORLD

In 1959, as E. P. Odum's research at the Savannah River Ecology Laboratory was in full swing, Odum published the second edition of his now iconic textbook *Fundamentals of Ecology*. Here, he described that the advance of science "is analogous to the advance of an army; a breakthrough may occur anywhere, and when one does, the thrust will not penetrate far until the whole front moves up."[40] Presumably, part of what Odum gestured toward in this advance was the emergence of the field of radioecology, a burgeoning new subfield of ecology developed through the relationship between ecosystem ecologists and the AEC in the 1950s. In the second edition of his textbook, Odum included a new section on radioecology to reflect these changes in the field. Also in this edition, Odum defined ecological succession as "the orderly process of community change," as "the sequence of communities which replace one another in a given area," and described the principle as "one of the most important in ecology."[41] Crediting studies of ecological succession at the turn of the nineteenth to the twentieth century as inaugurating the genesis of modern ecology as a field, Odum distilled key concepts from what he deemed a glut of ecological succession terminology, including pioneer community, climax, primary succession, and secondary succession.[42] Pioneer communities are those original communities that "colonize" an ecosystem and are then subject to processes of primary succession. As Odum described elsewhere, "In the pioneer society, as in the pioneer ecosystem, high birth rates, rapid growth, high economic profits, and exploitation of accessible and unused resources are advantageous, but, as the saturation level is approached, these drives must be shifted to considerations of symbiosis (that is, 'civil rights,' 'law and order,' 'education,' and 'culture'), birth control, and the recycling of resources."[43] When these communities are removed, secondary succession takes shape, where "previously occupied territory is more receptive to community development than are sterile areas. This is the type we see all around us."[44] Here, the capacity to undergo teleological maturation produces landscapes of the built and natural environment as such, where both are articulated through a colonialist language of occupation and development. For Odum, civilizational progress and ecological homeostasis are homologous.

Later in his career, in 1969, Odum proposed a rearticulation of *succession* as *development*, where, rather than a "singular straightforward idea," succession "entails an interacting complex of processes" and parallels both biological development and the "development of human society."[45] Here and elsewhere, Odum drew from the cybernetic ecosystem ecology he was developing alongside his brother Howard Thomas (H. T.) Odum and ecologists such as Bernard Patten to posit ecosystems as complex bioenergetic feedback systems.[46] As Gregg Mittman and Scott Kirsch note, for some, this approach to ecosystem ecology and a transition to functional or applied ecology mark a shift toward the ecologist as environmental engineer, where "ecologists were to be professional managers who could monitor and fix the environmental problems created by human society."[47] This is, of course, not entirely inaccurate, echoed by nearly all of the ecologists I spoke with at SRS, whose research they described as inevitably shifting during their tenures at the ecology lab toward questions of environmental remediation and military-industrial applications.

However, this straightforward formulation obscures the complex philosophical and scientific worldview put forth by the Odums in their articulation of ecosystem ecology and ecological development. This worldview was dogmatically holistic, which E. P. persistently argued as the only approach that could address the twentieth-century "predicament of humankind."[48] As Golley notes, emphases on holism and systems in ecosystem ecology reflect popular philosophical and conceptual trends in the pre– and post–World War II United States.[49] Further, and crucial to this project, Golley explains that the development of ecosystem studies was "almost entirely descriptive," rooted in philosophical and "analogical thought" rather than scientific questions. Thus, while thermodynamic physical laws were presented as the basis of Odumian ecosystem studies, its previous philosophical and ethical attachments, which range from holism to eighteenth-century vitalism, remain a guiding subtext and at times explicit framework for theorizations of the ecosystem.[50] For example, rather than reimagine the ecologist as professionalized environmental engineer, E. P. posits the ecosystem ecologist as a political actor whose ethical obligation is not only to seek understanding of the "structure and function of nature" but also to translate that understanding into information that can be deployed at multiple levels to enhance the preservation of the biosphere's life-support systems.[51]

Take E. P.'s remarks at the annual meeting of the American Risk and Insurance Association in 1974. Here, Odum outlined his holistic ecosystem ecology as a complex cybernetic feedback system, where "negative feedback promotes balanced inputs and outputs, and guards against excesses that could destroy the system."[52] For the insurance industry, the political imperative at hand was to function as negative feedback to regulate capitalist expansion and unfettered development.

The insurance industry, as already noted, can be of assistance in the evolution of an optimum growth policy by (1) not investing in speculative land development; (2) insuring owners of only solid residential and industrial development that includes adequate provisions for water, waste disposal, open space, and future maintenance; and (3) not underwriting housing and related construction where objective analysis shows that the area is saturated in terms of environment and services.[53]

In the same essay, E. P. described that the insurance industry can be crucial in mitigating increased environmental risks, where "so-called 'natural' disasters are increasingly people-made."[54] Here, as elsewhere in Odum's body of work, ecology and economy are coconstituting, and humans are embedded parts within the organic-inorganic relations of matter and life that comprise ecosystems. Further, all must work together "to make an orderly transition from pioneer, rapid-growth civilizations to mature civilizations."[55] Within the teleological framework of ecological development theory, the ecologist, the actuary, and the farmer are all vital political agents who must act individually and collectively to achieve mature homeostasis for civilization.[56]

That ecological succession or ecological development theory turns on twinned colonial narratives of progress and eschatology is plain within Odum's ecosystem ecology, including neo-Malthusian codas extolling the importance of population control in nearly all of his writings bridging natural and human ecology.[57] Odum's preoccupation with health, balance, and order at the level of the population provides an ecological corollary to what scholars have variously termed "the marketization of everything," "economentality," and "the economization of life."[58] Michelle Murphy defines the "economization of life" as a biopolitical and deeply colonial project composed of "practices that differentially value and govern life in terms of their ability to foster the macroeconomy of the nation-state, such as life's ability to contribute to the gross domestic product (GDP) of the nation."[59] Emerging coevally with the development and popularization of ecosystem ecology, this economization of life has been subtended by an ecologization of life, whereby the total environment is subsumed in a topology of lifeworlds as orderly systems. Odum himself emphasized that "ecological and economic common sense are directly related. The two words come from the same Greek root, 'Oikos' meaning 'house.' Ecology is the study of the house (people's total environment) and economics literally is the 'management of the house,' which must include all of the environment."[60] Here, the interrelated fields of economy and ecology work in tandem toward describing and optimizing the productive capacities of lifeworlds through the framework of population.

This nexus of ecology-economy also helps in elaborating the relationship between Odum's ecosystem ecology and environmental policing, whereby the ecologist figures as the patriarch (paterfamilias) of the household to be managed (economy) and studied (ecology). As Markus Dirk Dubber argues, US conceptions of police power from the plantation to the precinct must be understood as emerging through a European formulation of police science that posits the state as "macro household" to be governed, owing to the same Greek and Roman political traditions from which Odum derives his conceptual genealogy of the ecological.[61] Further, as Dubber notes, continental police science "became the science of administering a 'population' with the aim of maximizing its welfare. . . . There were human resources, and natural resources. The mode of the resource made no difference to the science of police."[62] Following Odum's own logic, the agential capacity of the ecologist, the actuary, and the farmer mentioned above connotes a form of environmental stewardship as patriarchal power, where the resource management attributed to police is outsourced—what might be more plainly thought of as an environmental analog to community policing.[63] Here, I do not seek to flatten the distinction between the institution of the police, policing as concept, and ecosystem ecology, taking seriously Neocleous's admonition of the tendency within critical theory to render policing so abstract that it is simultaneously everywhere, everything, and nothing at all.[64] However, in tracing the shared conceptual language and origins of Odum's ecosystem ecology with economy and police as patriarchal power, it becomes possible to draw out a shared and more diffuse sensibility of police power that works across multiple scales and takes multiple forms.

The patriarchal valence to Odum's ecologist becomes all the more apparent when we examine his notion of the mesocosm. Beginning with the implied relationships between ecology, economy, and human development, Odum advocated for the proliferation of set-aside land areas to avoid overpopulation and predatory development. He termed these "mesocosms," "middle-sized worlds" bridging the laboratory with the field for scientific and aesthetic enjoyment while functioning simultaneously as a form of conservation, warding off human development.[65] As set-asides, these mesocosms constitute what Kirsch, drawing from Kohler, calls "an unsettled field-laboratory frontier."[66] These protected areas are themselves the very border between laboratory and field, the organic and inorganic, and the built and natural environment. As border zones, mesocosms must also, then, be understood as sites that must be secured, preserving their "frontier" status: untouched, save by the ecologist, the ecologist's equipment, and plant and animal subjects. The mesocosm is, then, an example of what Léopold Lambert describes as "weaponized architecture,"[67] a space maintained through various forms of architectural and embodied policing—be it by wall or fence, the ecologist gathering data, No Trespassing signs, or networks of field and surveillance cameras. Drawing together Lambert's articulation of weaponized architecture with descriptions of colonial practices of worlding by Marisol de la Cadena, Kathleen Stewart, and Déborah Danowski and Eduardo Viveiros de Castro,[68] I argue that Odum's mesocosm is not simply a benign medium-sized world but a security world. A world of police power, broadly construed, the security world is a site of production and enclosure maintained through myriad forms of state and economic violence. The very emergence of Odum's mesocosm as concept is indebted to the security and resources conferred through the relationships between ecosystem ecology and the US colonial state, largely through the AEC, DOE, and US military.

In the case of the ecology lab as security world, those mundane and unassuming policing practices of the ecologist mentioned above emerge in relation and relief to the addition of more explicit security measures: military personnel and heavily armed security guards, constant surveillance and guarded patrols of the site, networks of checkpoints and keyed gates, a laborious background-checking process for anyone seeking access to the ecology lab, and disciplinary protocols such as SRS's "remote worker" program. The "Remote Fieldworker Application," developed at the Savannah River National Laboratory, creates a chain of constant communication between workers and security at the ecology lab and SRS more broadly. Workers leaving their designated buildings must contact their dispatcher, a site security employee, notifying them of who they are, where they will be going, and their start and stop times. If a remote worker fails to report back by their proposed stop time, security will dispatch personnel to the worker's location. The ecologists I spoke with had varied relationships to remote worker protocols. For some, remote worker status ranged from a nuisance that made daily tasks more onerous to a liability that produced moments of vulnerability and danger as ecologists were brought into encounters with site security. I was told of more than one occasion when ecologists holding perimeter keys, which allow them access to the site bypassing security checkpoints, forgot to call in ahead of time announcing their entrance to the site as remote workers and found themselves surrounded by guard vehicles and helicopters. However, other ecologists I spoke with felt reassured by the program, citing that it prevented worrying about graduate students and colleagues working in the site's swamps and forests.

It seemed noteworthy that of the ecologists I spoke with those who held the most animus for the remote worker protocols were those who had spent the most time on the site, many with tenures of more than forty years. In their time at the ecology lab, SRS has grown increasingly focused on issues of security, at times framed through discourses of safety (like the remote worker protocols) and at times more explicitly through discourses of national security. All ecologists I spoke with cited the attacks of September 11, 2001, as a turning point for security at SRS. Almost immediately, previously lax policies were replaced with strict and enthusiastically enforced regulations, and security perimeters were enlarged and fortified. For example, prior to 9/11, the ecology lab campus was publicly accessible. However, following 9/11, its campus was incorporated into SRS's secured perimeter zone and cautionary signage appeared noting the presence of "foreign nationals" in its buildings. All visitors must be formally badged and escorted at all times when visiting campus. As my ecology lab guide informed me, even regularly entering and exiting the facility does not exempt workers from suspicion. Cars are frequently searched, actions called into question, and repeat entries and exits are treated as particularly suspect. Nor did my California driver's license go without scrutiny. "What are you doing all the way out here?" I was asked by a guard eyeing both me and my license. When I explained that I was at the site for research, having moved back to the South from California (I am no stranger to the unwanted attention conferred through association with California in the state of South Carolina), he responded, "Well, at least you're moving in the right direction." My guide and I both acknowledged that it was probably for the best that I had left my vehicle with its California tags off-site. At another checkpoint, a guard greeted my guide warmly and made reference to an inside joke they shared. Describing him as her favorite, my guide reflected upon how strange it was to interact with these guards daily. While they know her name and many other details about her, for her, the guards remain entirely anonymous.

Through its cooperative, even if at times vexed, relationship to the US military and DOE, the ecology lab provides a particularly generative site through which to interrogate the mesocosm as security world. Capitalizing on Odum's original vision and the University of Georgia's partnership with the AEC and later DOE, the lab is conferred unparalleled security for its research sites. While ecologists might have been ambivalent about remote worker protocols, those I spoke with indicated unanimous and overwhelmingly positive responses regarding whether the campus's location within SRS helped or hindered their ability to conduct their research as they desired. Each ecologist cited their ability to leave technologies and equipment in the field without worry of theft or tampering as the greatest advantage the ecology lab offered.[69] Further, the expansion of security perimeters to incorporate SREL following 9/11 codified the significance of the ecology lab for DOE and the US military. While more senior ecologists shared many stories with me about their tempestuous relationships to the AEC during SREL's early years,[70] this spatial inclusion clearly demonstrates that the lab is considered vital to SRS.[71]

It is perhaps tempting to romanticize the ecologist in the checkpoint scenario I described as one in which an unbiased scientist and environmentalist is subjected to undue policing at the hands of heavily armed mercenaries in military fatigues. However, the complexity of these daily interactions belies both the strategic and symbolic importance of the ecology lab to the US military's nuclear program and the importance of SRS to the defense and maintenance of the ecology lab. It is not simply that the checkpoint confers access to the highly sensitive spaces of SRS where the ecology lab just so happens to be. Rather, the checkpoint produces and maintains the SREL mesocosm as a security world in its own right, legitimizing both the import of ecological science to the US government and the credentials of expertise that mark and make the belonging ecologist. Put simply, without the Savannah River Site, there is no Savannah River Ecology Laboratory.

As a visitor, whose access was also mediated by my institutional affiliation and researcher status, I, too, was granted temporary status of belonging within

SRS, even if cast into suspicion by my relationship to the state of California. Although an ambivalent actor, the SREL ecologist is, then, necessarily produced explicitly through relationships with and legitimacy conferred by the security guarding and maintaining the borders of the nuclear reservation and ecology lab campus. The ecologist is made as such not only through practices of research and data collection but also, in this case, through explicit practices of surveillance, security, and identification.[72] Additionally, the ecologist's ability to carry on with their research without perturbation hinges on the security offered by policing the multiple layers of the site's borders. For example, we might consider that it is not by accident but by design that the ecology lab has held the Guinness World Record for the longest daily monitored amphibian and reptile study on the planet since 2000 for a study begun in 1978 at the site's Rainbow Bay. The very possibility for this study to continue in perpetuity is generated through the site's security and the perceived and endless futurity imagined to characterize the US government's nuclear program.[73]

Further, not insignificant within this constellation of security, ecology, and legitimacy, security personnel at SRS are employed by the company Centerra. Originally Wackenhut Corporation, famed for its role in the rise of private prisons in the United States and later acquired by the controversial global security firm G4S, Centerra was acquired by Constellis Holdings in 2017. Constellis itself is the product of a merger between Triple Canopy and ACADEMI, the rebranded corporate identity of the infamous Blackwater firm, known for committing atrocities in the Iraq War under the leadership of Erik Prince before changing its name to Xe Services in 2009.[74] At SRS, then, the Centerra security guard figures as an agent of police and military power deputized through the enduring and historical relationship between the US military and private security, linked through circuits of shared practices, personnel, equipment, assets, and ideologies.

Further, the Centerra guard and histories of site policing and surveillance, which often includes US military personnel and soldiers in addition to contract security, underscore the historical link between the production of ecological scientific knowledge at the site and the police logics foundational to the maintenance of the US colonial project. The anonymous Centerra guards, sharing quips and warm familiarities with my guide, cannot be disentangled from their emergence in various forms across landscapes and

temporalities of war, carcerality, and empire, nor can the ecologist (or graduate student) who is folded into and out of these projects, even if ambivalently.
Neither can the ecology lab as mesocosm be abstracted from its position
within SRS as a spatially bounded asset that must be secured and protected.
The embeddedness of ecosystem ecology within nuclear military-industrial
legacies of violence at SRS demonstrates a relationship of reciprocal security.
Rather than buttress notions of a "*post*nuclear" or "*post*military" landscape,[75]
which as Shiloh Krupar argues both temporally and geographically defers
and displaces the violence of the US military project, the ecology lab explicitly supports the mission of a nuclear and military present and future, just as
SRS ensures the presents and futures of ecosystem ecology at SREL.

ECOLOGICAL SUCCESSION AS PRIMITIVE ACCUMULATION

At the ecology lab, ecological succession functions as a form of colonialist
environmental policing, enforcing the relations of state and natural property
at SRS while eliding all manner of violence and dispossession constitutive
of those property relations. Writing of the ecology lab as an experimental
landscape of inclusion and exclusion, Scott Kirsch describes the relationship
between ecological studies at SREL and notions of land absent its past human inhabitants through the framework of alienation. Kirsch notes that "the
production of this experimental landscape, a proprietary space for scientific
ecology and forestry, always depended initially on the alienation of property,
and the uprooting of previous landscapes and livelihoods."[76] While I agree
with Kirsch that the forging of the experimental landscape of SREL hinges
on the alienation of property and previous inhabitants from their labor, it is
necessary to understand the ecology lab and its emphasis on secondary succession research as constituted through more than a singular event of violence
and dispossession in the construction of SRS. Rather, the annexation and
destruction of property and place in order to make the Savannah River Site
and Savannah River Ecology Laboratory must be understood as ongoing and
positioned in relation to multiple histories of violence and dispossession that
emerge through US colonialism and racial capitalism in the region. Further,
these histories must be understood as foundational to the very production of
scientific knowledge within Odum's ecosystem ecology and the legitimacy
conferred to it as a scientific field.

It is perhaps more useful, then, to read the environmental policing engendered by secondary succession at SREL as a form of what Robin Blackburn describes as "extended primitive accumulation," where primitive accumulation is not "an episode" but an "on-going aspect of the metropolitan accumulation process."[77] For Marx, primitive accumulation "plays approximately the same role in political economy as original sin does in theology."[78] It is "the historical process of divorcing the producer from the means of production. It appears as 'primitive' because it forms the pre-history of capital, and of the mode of production corresponding to capital."[79] While Marx acknowledges that primitive accumulation is wrought through the violent practices of colonialism and slavery, for him, primitive accumulation, as in Odum's secondary succession, signals moments of epochal rupture and teleological development. As a corrective, Blackburn has suggested reframing Marx's primitive accumulation as "not a fateful biting of the apple located in an antediluvian past, but a continuing and relentless process whereby capitalist accumulation battens on pre-capitalist modes of exploitation, greatly extending their scope, until it has exhausted or transformed them."[80] While Blackburn analyzes extended primitive accumulation through the plantation economy and slave labor in the US South, it can also be extended to address land as property and developed territorial asset *versus* land as nature and well of resources yet to be extracted. In this way, extended primitive accumulation is analogous to what David Harvey has described as "accumulation by dispossession," capitalism's imperial and ever-expanding quest to generate new markets, often through "spatio-temporal fixes" that range from the straightforwardly colonial to the development of new financial instruments and terrains.[81]

In the case of the ecology lab, secondary succession studies have worked alongside the AEC (*cum* DOE), DuPont, Westinghouse, and now Bechtel as a way of *making natural* human and capital-driven processes of primitive accumulation through dispossession. Secondary succession at the ecology lab is foremost, as Kirsch notes, "the story of *nature coming back* at Savannah River Site and places like it."[82] To return to Ellenton's curbs or the singular bathroom tile hidden in wisteria, it is the story of making natural that which was (and continues to be) man-made, where discourses of agricultural and infrastructural abandonment alongside processes of plant and animal growth are seen as simultaneously inaugurating a new phase of orderly development and a return to an original, purer state of nature. However, the land of the ecology lab and Ellenton, such as Field 3-412, must also be located as a site of extraction and profit, where the data collected by the ecologist translates into both epistemological and financial value in the context of academic knowledge production and through its applications for government and industry.[83] Discourses of nature and natural law buttress processes of extended primitive accumulation while masking the force and character of capital accumulation. As Nikhil Singh describes, "Capitalism may 'come into the world dripping from head to toe in blood,' as Marx writes, but it manages to clean itself up, at least in certain spaces and places."[84] At SRS, ecological studies of secondary succession appear as the force of "sanitizing rhetoric" described by Shiloh Krupar in the suturing of environmentalism and nuclear landscapes and infrastructures, not only working to remediate toxic landscapes and in service of the vast security infrastructures of military and capital but also working to remediate traces of violence and dispossession that mark and make the site.[85]

While this understanding of Odum's ecosystem ecology demonstrates its import for and emergence through colonial projects, it is not simply a novelty that a curb can be transformed through processes of secondary succession from infrastructure into property of nature and state. Rather, this signals the productive capacity of secondary succession to *make the historical ahistorical*.[86] A technique of environmental policing, studies of secondary succession at SREL function to erase past human presence and violence outside the context of agricultural development and ecological experimentation. Land has either been abandoned, as in the case of old fields,[87] or severed of its pre-SRS ties to the human altogether by rendering those ties prelapsarian and natural. Here, environmental policing through secondary succession is also policing as Jacques Rancière conceives it, as those practices that "define the configuration of the perceptible."[88] Drawing from Rancière's partition of the sensible, Marisol de la Cadena describes that "the division between what is seen and heard in the sphere of politics (and what is not heard or seen) corresponds to a division between the historical and the ahistorical that also implies a distinction between what is and what is not, the possible and the impossible."[89] Working at the nexus of nature and the ahistorical, secondary succession delimits the possibility for an Ellenton dispossessed of both inhabitants and place and for alternative sensibilities and perceptions of land, such as those described by Louise Cassels. Further, it delimits the possibility for an Ellenton marked and made through histories of local economic and racial violence, that necessarily include the history of Indigenous dispossession, Black enslavement and sharecropping, and the wielding of eminent domain to clear the way for SRS. By the account of Odum's secondary succession, these Ellentons are not and were not, imperceptible within the ecological account of the ecology lab's prehistory.

PART IV
THE MONSTER OF POLICE

CHAPTER SEVEN

THE ARMED FRIENDLIES OF SETTLER ORDER

Melanie K. Yazzie

On March 27, 2016, in Winslow, Arizona, Austin Shipley shot and killed twenty-seven-year-old mother and citizen of the Navajo Nation Loreal Tsingine. Tsingine had been walking the two blocks back to her residence from a Circle K convenience store when Shipley, a white police officer with the Winslow Police Department (WPD), pulled up next to her in his police cruiser. Twenty-three seconds later, Shipley opened fire on Tsingine at close range, shooting her five times. Tsingine collapsed to the sidewalk and died a few minutes later. According to Shipley's body cam footage, Tsingine was clearly still breathing and moving during these vital minutes between the shooting and the arrival of paramedics, yet neither he nor Steve Cano, his partner and another white officer with the WPD who was on the scene, administered first aid despite having the proper equipment in their cruisers.

News of the shooting quickly spread and Native-led protests organized by grassroots organizations like The Red Nation erupted in Winslow, followed swiftly by demands from the Navajo Nation for an investigation. Winslow, a white-dominated town just outside the reservation boundaries of the Navajo Nation and sitting along Interstate 40, is a notoriously racist bordertown where Navajo and Hopi citizens routinely report acts of discrimination from police, businesses, and townspeople. Tsingine's death at the hands of a white police officer heightened these existing tensions and brought renewed attention to the high rates of violence Native people experience at the hands of police in the United States. With this increased attention also came predictable calls from police reformers for police departments to address cases of "excessive force" (which is how many labeled the shooting) and require officers like Shipley to take "cultural sensitivity" training.

Because the logic of police reform dominated the reports and news stories that were critical of Shipley's conduct, the fact that Shipley's behavior that day fully conformed with normal police procedure remained largely unexamined by critics. According to official testimony, every aspect of Shipley's conduct during his encounter with Tsingine was entirely normal—as normal as the racism experienced by Tsingine and other Native people on a regular basis in bordertowns like Winslow. A 320-page internal evaluation about the shooting issued by the Arizona Department of Public Safety (AZDPS), for example, found that Shipley's actions were not only justified but also in full compliance with the expectations and procedures that police officers are expected to follow in their daily conduct on the job. Contrary to the claims of police reformers, official reports found there was nothing excessive, nor lacking in sensitivity, about the shooting. From the moment Shipley made contact with Tinsgine to her final breath, he was following procedure and acting completely normal.

That Shipley's treatment of Tsingine was considered "normal" by other police is important for understanding the larger ecology of counterinsurgency that informs contemporary policing in the United States. In this essay, I build on the AZDPS claim that Shipley was acting in full compliance with the normative expectations of policing, but I advance a perspective that is likely contrary to the cop logic that drives AZDPS's conclusion. That is, I argue that Shipley's behavior conformed with the standard operating procedure of anti-Indianism that structures the larger dynamics of settler colonialism in bordertowns like Winslow, which have their origins in US imperialism and colonial aggression toward Native nations. From this perspective, Tsingine's only crime was being an Indian in Shipley's eyes—and, moreover, a Native mother of future generations of potential insurgents who needed to be snuffed out in order to protect US sovereignty.

In her 2007 book *New Indians, Old Wars*, Dakota scholar Elizabeth Cook-Lynn places the twenty-first-century US wars in the Middle East within the larger context of US imperialism that started with the nineteenth-century Indian Wars in the so-called American West. Recounting the horror she felt in January 1991 as the US military dropped thousands of bombs on Iraq—which marked the beginning of the first Gulf War—she argues that "the old Indian wars are the backdrop" for America's modern-day wars in the Middle East.[1] The horror of those wars, she reminds us, originated in the "political terrorism against the tribal nations" that birthed the United States.[2] Besides outright war, this political terrorism crystallized in the domestication of Native nations through settler laws. The most belligerent of these legal strategies, the Marshall Trilogy (1823–32), unilaterally changed the status of Native nations from foreign nations—which was their status according to treaties—to colonized subjects of the United States. Between 1823 and 1832 the US Supreme Court's first chief justice, John Marshall, "defined the status and rights of Indigenous nations within the United States as 'tribes,' uncivilized peoples dependent on it" and subject to its complete authority.[3] These decisions not only stripped Indigenous nations of their independence but also became the foundation for all subsequent laws pertaining to Indigenous nations (what is now known as federal Indian law).

The Marshall Trilogy cemented a growing hegemonic consensus that Indigenous sovereigns, as foreign nations with their own laws in relation to the land, posed one of the greatest threats to US economic and political growth. The permanent placement of Indigenous nations under the dominion and jurisdiction of the US government—also known as domestication—was a key method for neutralizing this threat. It helped to establish the conditions for mass land dispossession and granted the US government the absolute right to rule over the supposedly heathen Indigenous nations, treating them as wards/children of the state and denying them sovereignty in perpetuity. Cook-Lynn defines this process of domestication as a form of colonialism that worked in tandem with imperialism to consolidate US sovereignty, what she calls a "a national policy of territorial acquisition through the establishment of economic and political domination of other nations."[4] She notes that the wars of today are driven by the same "colonial aggression and imperialistic nation building" as the wars of old.[5] "If there is one policy behind the scenes that links the Iraq experience of the twentieth century to the Lakota/Dakota Sioux experience of the nineteenth," she writes, "it is the policy of imperialist dominance. Trampling on the sovereignty of other nations for most of its several centuries of nationhood has been the legacy of the American Republic's power."[6]

Often thought to happen in far-off lands, US imperialism is rarely understood as having begun with the domestication of foreign Indigenous nations in what is now considered the contiguous United States. By contextualizing the first Gulf War within the Indian Wars of the nineteenth century, Cook-Lynn helps us see the former as a continuation of the latter, which is an analytical shift that sheds light on how the logic and language of counterterrorism that became so popular during both Gulf Wars actually has its origins in early imperial efforts by the budding United States to subdue Native sovereignty and resistance. Chickasaw scholar Jodi Byrd extends this argument in *Transit of Empire*. According to Byrd, US imperialism is an enduring structure that deploys a "rhizomatic West" in which "Indians without ancestry" or nations serve discursively as the "transit of empire," or the field that "serves all regimes of signs" that constitute the US imaginary.[7] Anticipating the successful eradication of Native nations, America's imperialist imaginary recycles and reproduces the stateless "Indian" "so that empire might cohere and consolidate."[8] Never a done deal, this cohesion and consolidation requires constant vigilance, reinforcement, and investment, which is where the foil of the "Indian" comes into play as the figure against and through which US settler sovereignty makes and remakes itself. Put another way, as the original and most intractable enemy of the fulfillment of American empire, the sign of the "Indian" must be constantly resuscitated in a never-ending Wild West scenario to give legibility and legitimacy to US sovereignty. Given its structural significance, the "Indian combatant" figure is central to the legal regimes that form the substance of sovereignty claims by the United States to territories and peoples. Or as Byrd puts it, the "Indian combatant" is the "*homo sacer* to the United States," the figure that can be killed—and must be killed—in order to shore up the "law and order" that US settler sovereignty depends upon.[9] As agents of the state tasked with upholding "law and order," police carry out an essential—indeed, sacred—duty on behalf of US settler sovereignty: Indian killing. If Indians and Indian nations are "the origin of the stateless terrorist combatants within US enunciations of sovereignty,"[10] as Byrd points out, then all forms of policing and warfare are, at their base, about killing Indians and making anyone who defies US authority into an Indian that must be killed.

With this understanding, we can see how potentially all forms of coun-terterrorism—including those performed "domestically" and "internation-ally" by police and soldiers—are simply a continuum of the original imperial war to destroy "terrorist" Native nations and "Indian combatants." All ene-mies of the United States can be and are fashioned in the image of the orig-inal "Indian" insurgent seeking to undo US law and order. In its usage as military jargon in the United States, the term "off the reservation," for exam-ple, refers to someone disobeying the authority of the United States. A reser-vation, of course, is the diminished territory over which current-day Native nations have limited jurisdiction, a consequence of the enclosure that Indig-enous people experienced following their domestication by the United States during the Indian Wars. To be on the reservation, as logic would dictate, is to be an obedient ward of the state who complies with one's fate, a status akin to a domesticated farm animal. Anyone "off the reservation" is deemed an "Indian"—with the totalizing threat of insurgency attached—and automat-ically dealt with as such. Loreal Tsingine, who was simply walking down the street in Winslow, Arizona, was considered "off the reservation" and sum-marily executed by Austin Shipley to reestablish "normal" law and order in a place where Native proximity vis-à-vis the Navajo Nation is seen as a constant threat to US sovereignty and settler dominance.

THE PUNISHER

Through highlighting the intimate links between counterinsurgency and anti-Indianism in the US imperial imaginary, it is possible to reframe our collective understanding of contemporary policing. Rather than replicating reformist or cop logic in our analysis, I argue it is important to contextualize critiques of police within the larger structures of imperialism and settler colo-nialism that animate US state formation more broadly. Such a shift certainly requires us to center Native critiques of power and domination (as well as Na-tive people's experiences with police, about which very little is written), but it also asks us to think about the multiple ways that the "Indian combatant" is used to justify not only the existence of police but also all forms of state vio-lence. For Native people specifically, counterinsurgency and anti-Indianism work together to eliminate any form of Native agency or action that is seen as a threat to US sovereignty, which by definition encompasses anything that can be deemed disobedient or "off the reservation." But as Byrd reminds us, the banal anti-Indianism of settler "law and order" that led Austin Shipley to shoot, kill, and refuse to administer first aid to Tsingine in those crucial minutes after she collapsed applies to anyone who can be racialized as an "Indian combatant," an insurgent and potential enemy of America who must be policed, murdered, suppressed, and disciplined by cops, soldiers, and settler citizens in the name of upholding US sovereignty. Conversely, Indian killers are not only those credentialed as cops. Soldiers, vigilante militiamen, abusive husbands, and racist business owners can all occupy the subject position "Indian killer" whenever they are executing the standard operating procedures of settler "law and order." They are the white cowboys in Byrd's rhizomatic West that must perpetually vanquish "Indians" as a matter of ensuring the continued existence of the nation. And the proverbial frontier is everywhere and anywhere savagery meets civility, a seemingly endless series of borders and war zones constantly in need of men to defend the sanctity of the US state against a forever "Indian" enemy intent on destroying it.

The forever-enemy sign that animates US imperial logic—and the settler cowboy ontologies and myriad practices of counterinsurgency that extend from it—are no more patently obvious than in the figure of the Punisher, a comic book character fetishized by cops, soldiers, and militias in the United States, including Austin Shipley. Photos from Shipley's police cruiser were included with the AZDPS internal report about the shooting. Sitting on the passenger seat of his cruiser was the range bag he took whenever he was out on patrol. Affixed to the front of the bag was a patch featuring the Punisher skull, with the words "God Will Judge Our Enemies, We'll Arrange the Meeting" encircling it.

Netflix released *The Punisher* as a streaming television series in 2017. The Punisher is a prominent character in the Marvel comic universe, and, following 9/11, became the foremost icon of military and police culture in the United States. A simple Google search shows that the patch on Shipley's range bag is available in dozens of colors from multiple retailers. It is rare to drive down the street in any major city or town without seeing the Punisher skull affixed to private vehicles as a bumper sticker or decal, or to walk through public spaces without seeing someone wearing a T-shirt adorned with the Punisher skull. And with the rise of the "Blue Lives Matter" movement in

2014, the Punisher has become increasingly popular with police as a logo, so much so that police often display both it and the Blue Lives Matter emblem on their uniforms, vehicles, and gear. Similar trends have also occurred in military style and civilian militia aesthetics in the United States.

In the Netflix version, Frank Castle—the Punisher's civilian name—is a former marine who served in the Gulf War. He is also someone who carries deep sorrow and loss. The first scene of the first episode gives us an aerial shot of Frank playing a guitar, alone and shrouded in darkness. Moments later, we are drawn into one of Frank's flashbacks, which shows him lovingly teaching his daughter how to play the guitar in a light-filled room. Fast-forward to the present again and we are brought to rural Alabama, where Frank is chasing a biker gang down a lonely highway, a tattered photo of his wife and two kids affixed to the dashboard of his car. We are then transported to El Paso, Texas, where we see Frank snipe a cartel kingpin in Juárez, Mexico. This section of the episode concludes with Frank cornering a sleazy businessman in a bathroom stall at JFK airport in New York, strangling him as the man looks into the hollow eyes of the famous punisher skull that adorns Frank's T-shirt.

The world Frank inhabits is dark and depressing. Between meals and work, he has constant flashbacks of his family. Though brief, the flashback scenes are in stark contrast to his present tense: they are filled with light, love, and joy. The flashbacks are frequent enough that the viewer gets the sense that Frank's family is no longer alive.

The term *flashback* became associated with modern psychology in the late 1960s around the same time that *post-traumatic stress disorder* was coined to describe the condition of many Vietnam vets. Vets reported suffering from recurrent and abnormally vivid recollections of traumatic episodes they had experienced during the war. These recollections were called flashbacks. Flashbacks became a common feature of PTSD and the discourse surrounding the horrors of the Vietnam War more generally. Unlike Vietnam vets who experienced flashbacks because of the trauma of war, however, Frank's trauma comes from a different source. We are introduced to Frank's flashbacks not through his experience with war but through the loss of his family. Midway through the first episode, we find Frank skulking in the hallway outside a room where a support group for veterans is meeting. We initially expect him to walk in and join, but he doesn't. He listens to participants share stories of trauma—a former marine admits feeling like an outcast in society upon returning home from active duty, and an older overweight man donning an NRA hat talks about liberal persecution of the "Christian American patriot," while other vets, some with missing limbs, sit quietly and listen. Frank waits until the meeting finishes and participants disburse before entering the room. Viewers discover that Frank has come to talk to the meeting leader, who appears to be a friend or confidant, about the loss of his family and the revenge he has exacted on their killers (the Punisher, is, after all, a famous vigilante). At the beginning of the second episode, Frank returns to talk with this friend, believing his participation in a secret CIA-led operation in the Middle East during his military service may have caused his family's death.

Frank first appeared in *The Amazing Spider-Man* #129 in February 1974 while the Vietnam War was still ongoing. Like his Netflix version, that version of Frank served in the US Marines. Unlike his Netflix persona, however, 1970s Frank was a Vietnam veteran. Vietnam-vet Frank might have walked into that room to join the support circle. Gulf War Frank, however, stays outside.

While it is clear that Frank is a profoundly wounded man who moves through the world in pain, the source of his inner turmoil in the 2017 world of Netflix is not his military service but the loss of his family. After all, he has flashbacks of his family, not of war. Rather than being a source of trauma, his active duty as a marine prepares him to avenge his family's death. It is what gives him the skills and the power to enact justice against criminals, which is now his purpose in life. The Frank Castle of today is not traumatized by his experience with war, he is strengthened by it; it's what makes him a badass. It's what makes him lethal. It's what gives him his moral code. This helps to explain his popularity with twenty-first-century soldiers, cops, and militias. In his best-selling autobiography *American Sniper*, former Navy SEAL and famed sniper Chris Kyle described why he loved *The Punisher*:

> We called ourselves the Punishers.
>
> Our comms guy suggested it before the deployment. We all thought what the Punisher did was cool: He righted wrongs. He killed bad guys. He made wrongdoers fear him.
>
> That's what we were all about. So we adapted his symbol—a skull— and made it our own, with some modifications. We spray-painted it on

our Hummers and body armor, and our helmets and all our guns. And we spray-painted it on every building or wall we could. We wanted people to know, *We're here and we want to fuck with you.*

It was our version of psyops.

You see us? We're the people kicking your ass. Fear us. Because we will kill you, motherfucker.

You are bad. We are badder. We are bad-ass.[11]

For Kyle, being a badass meant you found the bad guys, you killed the bad guys, and you didn't let anything as pedestrian as military bureaucracy or someone else's rules get in the way of getting the job done. The Punisher obeys no one. He stops at nothing to get the bad guys. He's the judge, jury, and executioner.

In a 2019 comic called *About Face*, graphic artist Nate Powell documents the progression of fascist aesthetics in the United States through the eyes of his younger self growing up with G.I. Joe in the 1980s.[12] The subtitle of *About Face* states, "This is about surface and style normalizing the language of force," which blurs the distinction between military and civilian life. The story's protagonist notices that following 9/11 a new "forever-war" (a term coined by the *Intercept* writer Jeremy Scahill) dress standard starts to emerge with the adoption of a "paramilitary aesthetic." Most visible in this aesthetic is facial hair, and beards in particular. Trickling down into police and private security culture, the aesthetic of facial hair doubles as "an outward badge of honor for a historically unpopular war" and, in this day and age, serves as a badge of honor for a historically unpopular white supremacist presence in police departments throughout the United States. Combined with the prolific use of the Punisher skull, the black flag, and black trucks with tinted windows and blacked-out license plates, the beard shields those donning it "against shame and trauma," writes Powell.

A few frames later, Powell shows how the return of troops' facial hair, "banned for a century to accommodate airtight gas masks in an age of chemical warfare," mimics the style sported by their predecessors from wars such as the Civil War or, unfolding at the same time on the westward imperial frontier, the Indian Wars. For example, George Armstrong Custer, who was famously killed by Lakota, Northern Cheyenne, and Arapaho warriors in 1876 at the Battle of Greasy Grass, donned a massive, bushy mustache and sometimes a goatee.

Custer would likely feel at home in today's military and cop style and attitude. Which is to say, the iconography of facial hair that Powell documents in *About Face* collapses time and history, making the Battle of Greasy Grass and the Battle of Abu Ghraib but two chapters in a "mythical, centuries-old forever war" in which enemies of the United States never stop trying to destroy America, and therefore settler cowboy heroes can never stop killing these enemies to defend American honor. It is an endless counterinsurgency against Indians (zombie Indians, as Byrd puts it) who simply will not die.

Such circular logic would be laughable if it were not for the fact that this forever-war aesthetic is now the form *and* function (read: politics) of contemporary fascism. Indeed, in a forever war, anyone who does not obey the *form* of counterinsurgency is deemed *functionally* as an insurgent. As Powell notes in his discussion of the increased popularity of black flags within fascist culture, "It's no stretch to see how emphasis on rigidity and lack of depth helps reframe any spectrum as weakness: vibrancy, nuance, interpretation are signs of vulnerability." Conformity, on the other hand, is a sign of strength.

Black flags have historically been used to signify that *no quarter will be given*. When translated into modern language, this means that captured enemy combatants will be killed rather than taken prisoner. Like the Punisher, those who embrace the black flag shoot first and shoot to kill. To them, everyone and anyone who does not obey the style of counterinsurgency is a potential enemy. The cop who waves that most iconographic of the black flags—the "Blue Lives Matter" flag—must prove he's in charge, he's a badass, he's immune to pain. Anyone sporting a beard and driving a bitchin' tinted-out truck with a Punisher decal can proclaim that trauma is for losers; only enemies feel pain at the end of their guns. As Powell notes, fascism is "a declaration of power foremost"—indeed, "power establishing itself as beyond good and evil."

AN EMPIRE OF FORCE

Powell notes that the Punisher's presence initially "helped lend voice to veterans' experiences of their own treatment and public perception after the Vietnam War," which was equally as unpopular as the twenty-first-century wars in the Middle East. However, today, the Punisher is above the law, beyond good and evil. He is force manifest. For him, everyone is an enemy, and everything is war. And the role of police—indeed, all who can be remade in the image of the white settler cowboy—is to prevent evil by killing anyone (or any nation) that is a threat to what America holds most dear: the law and order that give shape to its very existence as a nation. This is perhaps why police identify so strongly with the post-9/11 version of the Punisher: they, like he, are the only things standing in the way between good and evil. Such a vocation is not only uniquely dangerous; it is extraordinarily heroic, a sacred duty performed on behalf of America. It is from this logic that the closely related concepts of the "thin blue line" and "Blue Lives Matter" are derived, which dictate that police are exceptional, that their lives matter more than others and must be protected and celebrated by any means necessary, that they are under siege by an endless stream of suspects and enemies, and that they deserve our undying loyalty, obedience, and compliance. Trained in this "Punisher" version of policing—what I call in the opening section of this essay an ecology of counterinsurgency— Austin Shipley was simply upholding the status quo of US imperialism and settler colonialism when he moved swiftly to eliminate the threat Tsingine posed to the sanctity of settler law and order, including his own life.

The phrase "God Will Judge Our Enemies, We'll Arrange the Meeting" that adorned Shipley's range bag the day he murdered Tsingine is the mantra that police repeat to themselves and to a nation of settlers who perform that most sacred ritual of settler sovereignty: Indian killing. Although the phrase is often attributed to Frank Castle, it has its origins in 1980s US military jargon. Much like the incorporation of the Punisher into "thin blue line" discourse, the combination of this military phrase with the Punisher skull demonstrates the extent to which settler identity is defined by counterinsurgency and anti-Indianism. Within these discursive regimes exist two kinds of soldiers, two kinds of cops, two kinds of men, two kinds of vigilantes: the ones who regret killing Indians (those traumatized by the horrors of war) and the ones who cannot survive without it—those who, like the Punisher, see war as the answer to all their problems. In this sense, every US war is an Indian war, every cop an Indian killer. And the Punisher walks the line daily between soldier, cop, and vigilante; he is the rhizomatic white cowboy defending America against the rhizomatic Indian on the forever frontier of US imperialism. He is the settler manifest, an empire of force collapsed into one figure, one icon, fighting zombie Indians who keep getting resurrected over and over and over again. He is, in essence, the armed friendly of settler order.

IT IS TIME TO END THE INDIAN WARS

Taken to their logical conclusion, the fetishization of the Punisher by white settler men and the idea that police lives are sacred demonstrate how dependent US sovereignty is on authority, discipline, obedience, conformity, and a profound hatred and fear of Native people. For Powell, this combination of authoritarianism, xenophobia, and conformity constitutes modern-day fascism. I would like to go one step further and claim that these aspects of modern-day fascism are actually original and structural elements of US settler sovereignty that have always shaped US legal and ontological institutions like police, citizenship, and popular culture. Given this reality, it seems important to point out that political positions that might be critical of (or stridently opposed to) fascism, imperialism, war, or police ought to take Native politics more seriously than they currently do. Antifascist, anti-imperialist/antiwar, and abolitionist work would be strengthened by a sharper analysis of settler colonialism and deeper knowledge of Native movements for sovereignty and decolonization.

I say this not only because policing in the United States clearly has everything to do with upholding settler colonialism and subjugating Native nations, but also because historically Native people have refused US imperialism, some to the point of refusing to recognize the United States as a legitimate nation-state. For many Native people and nations, the United States has never, and will never, win the Indian Wars because Native people will never relinquish who they are nor their bonds with the lands the United States claims as its own. They ignore the authority of US "law and order" every time they practice and enforce their own forms of governance and political will. This refusal of US settler sovereignty is one of the defining features of Native resistance under colonialism and, given the anticolonial and decolonial resolve exhibited in current #LandBack efforts, will no doubt continue to be at the center of Native politics.

This means we need to get on board with the program for Native liberation if we want to end US wars, stop fascism in its tracks, and abolish the police—all related goals I imagine many authors in this volume share. In addition to centering Native resistance in larger efforts to stop state violence, it may be worth remembering that Native nations were the first victors in wars against the United States. Our memories of these victories run deep, probably as deep as the memories of defeat that gnaw at settlers and manifest as counterrevolutionary violence like what we saw on January 6, 2021, when a group of MAGA supporters stormed Capitol Hill in Washington, DC. Native nations are not just the reminder to America of its failure to conquer Native people. We are its greatest threat, for in Native bodies and nations are the political orders, the economic systems, and the relationships that predate the United States. These same orders, systems, and relationships will be the undoing of the United States, as well as the foundation for the future.

"It is indeed time to bring the Indian Wars to a close."[13]

CHAPTER EIGHT

THE MONSTER AND THE POLICE: *DEXTER* TO HOBBES

Mark Neocleous

On February 25, 2002, Rafael Perez, a former officer of the LAPD's Community Resources Against Street Hoodlums unit (CRASH), appeared in court accused of various crimes: covering up a bank robbery, shooting and framing an innocent citizen, stealing and selling cocaine from evidence lockers, being a member of the Los Angeles gang called the Bloods, and murdering the rapper the Notorious B. I. G. In his statement to the court, he pointed out that above the doors that lead to CRASH offices there are philosophical mottos, such as, "Some rise by sin and some by virtue fall" and "We intimidate those who intimidate others." Perez commented: "To those mottos, I offer this: 'Whoever chases monsters should see to it that in the process he does not become a monster himself.'" The quote from Nietzsche might appear unusual coming from the mouth of a former police officer, but it is far from uncommon—*Whoever Fights Monsters* is the title of one police memoir, in which Nietzsche's aphorism also appears as an epigraph. The appearance of the aphorism is a reflection of the extent to which police discourse is saturated with the idea of the monstrous. We read of "catching monsters," "fighting monsters," and mediating between "monsters and men."[1] What I want to suggest here is that we might want to consider the relationship between the monster and the police.

Take as a starting point the fictional monster that appears in the TV series *Dexter*. The series is essentially about what might be called an ethical serial killer—a killer who kills people who deserve to be killed. The main character, Dexter, had a traumatic moment at an early age when he saw his mother brutally killed with a chainsaw by drug dealers. This bloody murder haunts him to the point where he is obsessed with blood, which becomes a positive, so to speak, by focusing his anger on people who deserve to die: essentially, those murderers or rapists who have somehow escaped the criminal law, often on a minor legal technicality, and who are thus walking free. Not only does Dexter kill these people, but he does so in a brutal and bloody way, chopping them up and disposing of their bodies, and in the process sating his own need for blood. The first thing to note about this is that Dexter is framed by the series as some kind of monster. "I know I'm a monster," he says when about to kill the character Prado (in season 3). The trope of monstrosity appears in various forms: comments by other characters on the various monsters who murder and rape and destroy lives, such as in season 2 when Dexter's romantic partner Rita comments on a serial killer (known as the Bay Harbor Butcher, which is in fact Dexter) and says that it makes her angry "that there's a monster out there," or in season 4 when a police forensics expert comments on a woman who got away with murdering her husband, saying, "If she did it, there's a monster walking free." But it is in Dexter's voice-over narration that his own monstrosity is clarified. He reminds us that "monsters come in all shapes and sizes" (season 4, episode 4) and will often add some finesse to the observations made by others: "I'm not the monster he wants me to be" (season 1, episode 4). The point comes up time and again; when Brother Sam comments that "men can change," Dexter comments in voice-over, "Men, maybe, but what about a monster?" (season 6, episode 2).

Dexter's monstrosity is also articulated through the primal moment of his (second) birth in the shipping container, where he witnessed the bloody murder of his mother. In season 1 (episode 7), when he revisits the shipyard container he comments that "something nameless was born here." The allusion is to Mary Shelley's *Frankenstein*, in which the monster has no name, and this Frankenstein theme continues throughout. His adoptive father, who rescued Dexter from the scene of his mother's murder and who understands Dexter's need for blood and helps him channel it, says that the doctors who treated Dexter "didn't even see the monster inside" (season 2, episode 4), and when the father enters into one of Dexter's killing scenes he recognizes that he has lost the ability to control the monster he helped create and so commits suicide. The same theme emerges in the final season when the psychoanalyst who first treated Dexter makes the same point: "I helped create you." Other characters who know Dexter make a similar point. Lila, his lover in one of the seasons, says to him "You make yourself a monster" (season 2, episode 2).

So, Dexter is framed in the series as a monster. Left at that, there isn't much to concern us; another serial killer, another media construction in which the writers play on the fact that we use "monstrous" to describe those creatures who defy moral codes and kill, another inhuman human, another candidate for the title of this year's "Mr. Monster."[2] However, one of the reasons Dexter can be so successful a serial killer (and thus monster) is because he works in the forensics team of the Miami Metro Police Department, specializing as a blood spatter analyst. In other words, Dexter works within the police. He is not a police officer per se, though often masquerades as one, but like many serial killers he has a place within the general system of police power.[3] Indeed, the fact that he is not a uniformed police officer as such alerts us to the wider concept of police power to which I will be alluding below. Dexter is a monster born into the police power—his adoptive father, who helped "create" him as a serial killer as he matured, was a police officer whose own history was of being restricted and frustrated by the rules under which the police must operate, which in turn feeds into his own willingness to teach Dexter a "code" by which the latter can kill without guilt. And the fact that he is "a very neat monster," as he describes himself in the very first episode of the first season (a point repeated in season 2, episode 10, when he says, "For a very neat monster I'm making an awful mess"), comes in the form of aping police practice: the blood slides, the cataloging, the perfectly organized set of weapons. When he goes about his killings, he enacts key aspects of the police procedural. He investigates a suspect, establishes the suspect's motive, finds clues, establishes guilt, hunts, captures, questions, and punishes.

All of which is to say that what is interesting about Dexter is not that he is somehow stepping in to enforce some kind of natural law of justice or punishment (which is said by cultural analyses of Dexter to be the way he becomes somehow *our* monster).[4] Rather, Dexter's whole modus operandi is a systematization of the police enterprise itself.[5] He fights monsters but has become one, a monster within the police power. The series *Dexter* is a reminder of the intimate and abiding connection between the monster and the police.

It is remarkable how frequently this connection between the monster and the police is overlooked in discussions of the power of the monstrous. What I want to suggest is that we cannot really grasp the idea of the monstrous without simultaneously considering the idea of the police. The common refrains about the monstrous tend to discuss its power in terms of the way communities are ordered, subjectivities are constituted, identities are bounded, and societies are bordered. It is said that monsters define the limits of civilization, are deeply connected to insecurity, indicate a breakdown in hierarchy, and point to the unruliness of matter. What is often overlooked in such claims is that these are the very same issues that underpin the police problematic.[6] I want to therefore suggest that to grasp the power of the monstrous we might need to consider it in terms of the ubiquity of the police idea in bourgeois modernity.

"YOU HAVE ALL THESE SAYINGS TO DESCRIBE WHAT YOU DO"

In a discussion about his actions with Hannah in the final season, Dexter tries to explain himself. He speaks not the language of revenge, justice, punishment, or law but rather uses a particular phrase to which Hannah, a killer herself who understands his drives and would perhaps be said to share his monstrosity, responds: "You have all these sayings to describe what you do." What sayings are these? In their conversation just before, Dexter described his killings as merely "taking out the trash" (season 8, episode 7). The comment harks back to a scene early in season 1 (in episode 3) when Dexter is disposing of the body of someone he has killed and who we are expected to believe really deserved to be killed: he's "taking out the garbage," he says. Later in the same season (in episode 7) he comments that "deep down, people will appreciate my work: Taking out the trash."

Dexter's description of his monstrous behavior is obviously meant to reinforce his monstrosity. He is so monstrous he can regard some other human beings as trash. "Taking out the trash" and "cleaning up" are familiar tropes among serial killers explaining their crimes. "I were just cleaning up streets, our kid. Just cleaning up the streets," commented Peter Sutcliffe, the so-called Yorkshire Ripper (a nickname given to him by the press; the name he gave himself was the Streetcleaner).[7] Yet we should also note that the idea of cleaning the streets and disposing of the garbage resonates throughout modern police discourse. Study after study has reported the extent to which the police regard themselves as having a "mandate to keep the ... streets clean,"[8] and ethnographies of police officers often comment on the extent to which police officers refer to their work with metaphors of garbage collecting or street cleaning (e.g., "refuse collectors, sweeping up the human dross").[9] "The police view their position as marking the boundaries of the social order," notes Peter Manning. They seek to stand "between the higher and lower, the sacred and the profane, the clean and the dirty."[10] Constantly "treading water in human waste,"[11] the police see their task as keeping the streets clean from the filth of humanity. The "clearing up" of crimes is associated with the "cleaning up" of the streets. "The idea that crimes can be *cleared up* reasserts a belief in a world where disorder can be brushed away to restore structural purity and where incongruity can be cleaned up to recreate a perfectly ordered universe."[12] This is why the same ethnographies constantly note that police officers routinely speak of members of what they see as the criminal, dangerous, and miserable classes as "social dirt," "slag," "polluted," and "scum."[13] The dirt in question is connected to the fact that the same persons are regarded as "refuse," "waste," and "garbage." The police regard themselves "as a kind of uniformed garbage-men,"[14] just like the monstrous serial killer but in the garb of the state; both take out the trash. (And if we take Foucault's reference to the figure of the "villain-monster-madman" seriously enough we might add that people considered mad were once dealt with by being placed in "loony-bins.")

The easy interpretation here is that this is about disrespect. A longer historical view suggests something else. When modern police officers speak of cleaning up the moral filth and social dirt, they are unknowingly holding on to and yet also twisting one of the original powers of police—namely, street cleaning and refuse collection. Police once had the responsibility of ensuring that the streets were clean, and virtually all the police theorists of the seventeenth, eighteenth, and early nineteenth centuries, from low-ranking cameralists to the high-ranking philosophers of state power, listed garbage collection as one of the police functions. The reason they did so was because dirt and its associated matter such as rubbish is an *offense against order*. It is not lack of cleanliness itself that is the problem but the fact that the lack of cleanliness undermines good order. "I enjoy my work. It brings order to the chaos," says Dexter, and the comment applies to both his work in the police and his work as a serial killer (season 2, episode 1). The removal of the dirt and the taking out of the trash is the reimposition of order, a replacement of matter into an ordered system.[15]

From Dexter's reference to taking out the trash we have very quickly arrived at the central category of police power: order. From the late fifteenth century, political discourse in Europe centered very much on the concept of police, a term that denoted the legislative and administrative regulation of the internal life of a community to promote general welfare and the condition of good order. The idea behind it was encapsulated in phrases such as "police and good order," "good police and order," or "well-ordered police state." The instructions and activities considered necessary for good order were known as police ordinances and referred to the management and direction of the population by the state. That "order" was the central police concept is evident in the heterogeneous range of affairs and minutia of social life that came under the police power. "Matters of police are things of every instant, which usually amount to but little," notes Montesquieu, adding that "the actions of the police are quick and the police is exerted over things that recur every day." As such, police are "perpetually busy with details."[16] Such details included public security; public health ("medical police"); poor relief; food adulteration; the maintenance of roads, bridges, and town buildings; expenses at christenings, weddings, and funerals; the performance of trades and occupations; the wearing of extravagant clothing; morals and manners; the behavior of servants toward their masters; and, of course, street cleaning and garbage collection. This is why police texts concern themselves with "the general and common good of society." As political administration, "police" was nothing less than the fabrication of social order. As Emer de Vattel wrote, "By a wise police, the sovereign accustoms the people to order."[17] This project shifted as policing developed in conjunction with the shifts in the nature of both state power and the development of capital. We can divide the history of police into three stages, with the first two separated by the Thirty Years' War and the third stage really coming into being with the "new police" forces of the early nineteenth century. Nonetheless, one can still find a consistency in the police function throughout these stages, rooted in the problem of order and as part of the "science of governing men."

I am making this point for reasons that are probably clear to anyone thinking about the power of the monstrous, but to spell it out: all of the key issues that occur in debates about monstrosity—insecurity and community, hierarchy and rule, class and power, subjectivity and identity, borders and boundaries—point to the problem of order posed by the monster. Now, the roots of this disorder might be said to lie in the key original frame of reference of the monster—namely, natural history. "The study of the sixteenth- and seventeenth-century literature on monsters" treats them as "aberrations in the natural order," say Katharine Park and Lorraine Daston, and others follow suit. As Andrew Gibson writes, "The idea of the monstrous involves a disruption of the supposed orders of nature."[18] But the use of "monstrosity" to describe aberrations or disruptions in nature was very easily applied to aberrations or disruptions in the social order (the metaphor of the body politic looms large here, as we shall see), and far greater interest is now expressed in what might be called social or political monsters. Yet one cannot talk about order without talking about the fact that order is the fundamental police problem.

To say that order is the fundamental police problem is to suggest that the key police concept is order rather than crime or law. The stress on the sociopolitical dimensions of monstrosity tends to focus attention on law, often said to be the second frame of reference of the monster due to the fact that aberrations of nature were also thought to breach legal classifications.[19] This is why the criminal has played such a central role in the study of monstrosity, as Foucault has made clear. The penal justice system that was developed and refined with the consolidation of the bourgeois state would find monster after monster within the social body, a figure who had fallen outside the social pact and who was thereby associated with a possible criminality.[20] In *Discipline and Punish*, Foucault comments that "the criminal designated as the enemy of all, whom it is in the interest of all to track down, falls outside the pact, disqualifies himself as a citizen and emerges, bearing within him as it were, a wild fragment of nature." This creature appears as a villain or monster or madman.[21] "Every criminal could well be a monster," Foucault adds in lectures given at the time of writing *Discipline and Punish*, "just as previously it was possible that the monster was a criminal."[22] Pasquale Pasquino has extended this argument by suggesting that criminology emerged around the figure of *homo criminalis* and penal theory constructed a whole knowledge and set of apparatuses concerning *homo criminalis*, but the ancestor of *homo criminalis*

is the monster.[23] The role of the serial killer as our archetypal social monster
plays heavily on this connection, as my opening comments also suggest.

Yet this focus on the way the individual who commits crimes comes to be
regarded as monstrous is somehow not enough. Why? Because it treats monstrosity as a "challenge of law" when in fact the basis of the original juridico-
natural frame of reference was order rather than law.[24] The twinning of "law"
and "order" in the commonplace "law-and-order" masks the fact that from
the police perspective "order" is the key concept; conversely, "police" does *not*
equal "law." Note Montesquieu on the police again, repeating a point that appears in virtually all police theory of the time: "It has regulations rather than
laws," and so one must not confuse "violations of the laws with the simple
violation of the police." Lest Montesquieu's comment appear as out of date,
note the following features of police powers vis-à-vis "the law."

First, police powers are almost always situated either fully in the executive or across executive and judiciary, never solely within the juridical realm.
Second, the police have constantly extended the boundaries of "legal" behavior to the point where the law itself has been transformed—for example, in
Britain by a change in the Judges' Rules by which the police operated, then
through important judicial findings, and finally in new legislation. Hence,
third, rather than police carrying out law as made by Parliament, Parliament
has made laws that have legitimized existing police practice. "Law reform" is
often little more than a product and legitimation of police operational practices, with the law rewritten to suit the exercise of police power. Fourth, the
police operate with a huge amount of discretion, which, far more than legal
codes, shapes the way the police behave. The flexibility in the police concept
we noted earlier offered a vagueness that historically left a great deal to police discretion, and this has never been removed. It runs from stopping and
searching people on spurious grounds (e.g., "moving quickly" and "moving
slowly" are both the basis for a stop) to violent assault and killing; we might
even add acts of police discretion that have only recently come to light and
which have been described by victims as being "raped by the state."[25] The expansive nature of discretion has its foundation in the permissive structure of
law and the powers given to the police to preserve order. In effect, and fifth,
the police power has often simply ignored demands that something called the
rule of law be followed. Indeed, research suggests that most officers believe

that to fully impose the rule of law on police work would render it impossible, and senior police officers are on record saying that there is a "moral justification for getting round the rules."[26] All of this happens through a coordinated effort on the part of the police to legitimate their actions by persuading judges, politicians, and the public that what they are doing is necessary to curb crime and in the name of that most bourgeois of fetishes: security.

Looked at politically, then, the police power needs to be read through the lens of order rather than law. But then this might mean that looked at in terms of "disorder" the power of the monstrous needs to be read through the lens of police. It is the difficulty in categorizing the monster in the "order of things" that makes the monster represent something far more challenging to the bourgeois imagination than mere illegality—namely, disorder.

"HERE I AM, IN THE BELLY OF THE BEAST"

In the series of lectures published as *Abnormal*, Foucault suggests that although every criminal could well be a monster, the most threatening is the political criminal, the one who breaks the social pact and who, by being against society, is seemingly against nature. Foucault points out that although the political monster might in fact be the king or queen or some other "monstrous" sovereign, there is also the monster "that breaks the social pact by revolt."[27] This is the "monster from below" to match the "monster from above," and Foucault places it at the heart of the juridico-medical theme of the monstrosity.[28] Yet if we accept the revolt of the *monster from below* as more significant both politically and historically, as I think we must, then it is also surely the case that the revolt of this monster is at the heart of the police problem.

One might consider this in the light of the thinker who most obviously placed the concept of order at the heart of state power, who did so through an articulation of the problematic of security, and who did both these things by organizing his work around the famous monsters of Leviathan and Behemoth. To title works with the name of two biblical monsters was truly provocative, as Hobbes knew full well; not for nothing did he earn himself the nickname the Monster of Malmesbury. But what do they mean, and why might they help us grasp the monster with the police?

The biblical creature Behemoth appears in the Bible in the book of Job, just prior to the appearance of the beast called the Leviathan, which Hobbes had used to symbolize the stately creation that brings peace, security, and order. Interpretations of Hobbes's use of "Behemoth" for the title vary, but the dominant one is that Hobbes chose "the odd name of *Behemoth*, which signifies in Hebrew language an Elephant, seeming to think that the civil dissensions of such a numerous and powerful people, as the English nation, might be justly compared to the wild and formidable motions of that enormous animal when provoked."[29] Although Hobbes seems to be referring to the "Long Parliament," the Behemoth comes to symbolize more generally the "circular motion of the sovereign power through two usurpers."[30] The two usurpers in question appear to be the disorderly anarchy of revolution and the lawlessness of rebellion. As Franz Neumann puts it, Behemoth "depicts a non-state, a chaos, a situation of lawlessness, disorder, and anarchy."[31]

Set against Behemoth is Leviathan, and whatever the two creatures are meant to signify in the book of Job (an elephant or hippopotamus-like land monster on the one hand compared to a whale-like sea monster on the other) in the Hebrew tradition in general and the Old Testament as a whole, "Leviathan is the epitome of all the monsters of the sea, just as in the same tradition Behemoth is the epitome of all terrestrial monsters, and they are conceived of both as antagonists and as elemental opposites."[32] More to the point, whatever the two creatures are meant to signify in either the Hebrew tradition or the Bible (and although Hobbes refers to the book of Job when mentioning Leviathan he does not do so when mentioning Behemoth), it is clear that Hobbes employed the monstrous Leviathan as a symbol for the state of peace, security, and order and the monstrous Behemoth as a symbol for the state of civil war, rebellion, and disorder and offered the former as the only alternative to the latter. It would appear that one monster, an enormous security system known as the Leviathan state, exists in order to continuously hold down another monster, the revolutionary people understood as the Behemoth.[33] Stephen Holmes puts it succinctly: "It takes one monster to subdue another."[34] And yet this does not quite tell the whole story.

David Williams notes that "Leviathan is the marine representative of a group of monsters whose chief significance is in their devouring activity." The Leviathan swallows its victims whole but does not destroy them. The victims "go through the process of being devoured . . . but without, in fact, being annihilated."[35] This devouring points us to the image used as the frontispiece of

Leviathan—the Sovereign incorporates his subjects by devouring them.[36] We are immediately reminded of the importance of the belly to the body politic: Hobbes's sometime employer Francis Bacon had commented in his essay "On Sedition" that "rebellions of the belly are the worst,"[37] and Hobbes's Leviathan has to deal with "wormes" (too many corporations), "intestine disorder" (errors made when instituting a commonwealth), and bulimia ("enlarging Dominion"). We might also be reminded of Bishop Bramhall's suggestion that Hobbes be allowed to set up a Leviathan state among the American Indians, believing that "if he should put his principles into practice as magisterially as he doth dictate them, his supposed subjects might chance to tear their Mortal God to pieces with their teeth and entomb his Sovereignty in their bowels."[38] And maybe we are also reminded that in the *Philosophical Rudiments Concerning Government and Society*, published the same year as *Leviathan*, Hobbes had suggested that *all kings are to be reckoned amongst ravenous beasts.*"[39] Whatever we are reminded of, the point is that it is not so much that one monster holds down or subdues the other but that one monster *devours* the other and *preserves it inside the belly of the beast.* "Here I am, in the belly of the beast," says Dexter one day in the office of the Miami Metro Police Department (season 2, episode 2).

Yet as well as depicting devoured subjects, the image on the frontispiece of *Leviathan* also presents the individual subjects as forming the protective armor of the body politic. This is a beast whose body "is made of rows of shields, shut up closely as with a seal," notes the Bible; "one is so near to another that no air can come between them" (Job 41:15). The image therefore also presents Leviathan as an airless prison of the very kind that awaits those who are willing to seek the security offered by the sovereign.[40] The double meaning points us to the centrality of the prison system to modern state power: "Here we are, in the belly of the beast" is the comment made time and again by politically astute prisoners, and the Red Army Faction adopted as their prison nicknames the characters from *Moby-Dick* as a sign of their fight against the whale-like Leviathan state that was devouring them.[41] But it also points us to the prison of security more generally.

The first point to therefore be made is that the police power instituted with the modern state might be thought of as a power to devour one and all, everything it encounters, including other monsters, subsuming them within its own force and keeping them within its security frame. (And we might ask in parenthesis: allowing them to emerge only as excrement, as shitty subjects?) The monster from below is also the monster within. Yet this also does not quite tell the whole story.

The reference to the monstrous Leviathan might appear to preempt a reference to Nietzsche's suggestion that the state is the coldest of all monsters. But as Nietzsche adds, the state also lies about this. The lie that creeps from its mouth is "I, the state, am the people."[42] And if there is one thing that "the people" does not wish to imagine itself as, it is monstrous. Indeed, if Job's suffering, fear, and insecurity in the book of Job as a whole are meant by Hobbes to refer more or less to the condition of man in the state of nature, and if the implication is that this condition is overcome only by submission to the new mighty sovereign, then any "monstrous" features of this new order really must be hidden away. The state's emergence alongside civil society and "the people," and the state's administration of civil society and "the people" in the name of order and security, requires that the state appears to be not only above the beastly condition of the state of nature but also somehow *above all forms of monstrosity*. Any hint of the state's own monstrosity must therefore disappear from view.

So far must the state's monstrosity disappear from view that in Hobbes's account the monstrosity in question is barely hinted at in the first place. The Leviathan makes four appearances in Hobbes's text: in the introduction, in which it is understood as a huge artificial man, a huge artificial animal, and a huge machine; in chapter 17, where it is described as a "Mortall God"; in chapter 28, where it is referred to in the discussion of the chapter in Job; and as an image on the frontispiece, which shows a huge person.[43] In none of these appearances is the key feature the Leviathan's monstrosity. Rather, its key feature is its *power*. The passage from the book of Job at the top of the image and repeated in chapter 28 makes this clear: "Upon earth there is nothing to compare with his power." This is a point repeated by Hobbes at the end of the same chapter, where he reiterates the claim that there can be nothing greater than the Leviathan. And of the many points made about the Leviathan in the introduction, the one stressed is that this creation turns out to be "of greater stature and strength" than any other body or creature.[44] Moreover, among the various meanings that lexicographers and commentators had ascribed to "Leviathan,"

Hobbes would have encountered definitions such as "prince," "king," "association," and "society." A commentary on the book of Job by Jacques Bolduc published in Lyon in 1619 and Paris in 1637 writes of "liviath" now meaning "crown," following its roots in "joining together," making the link with the aquatic beast on the grounds that the beast's scales are close together, as a unity, and suggesting that "leviathan" is now also a name for a collectivity of men.[45]

In other words, the point of the Leviathan is to appear not as an omnipotent monster but as the omnipotent technology of an organizing power: as machine, as organic being, as mortal god. It ultimately does not really matter which of these forms the state takes, since what matters is that any hint of monstrosity is replaced by the far more neutral and far less threatening "science of governing men." The use of "Leviathan" as the title of the book may well have been designed as a provocation,[46] and no doubt Hobbes believed that his readers would quickly grasp the allusion to the biblical monster, but the hint at the monstrosity of Leviathan only serves to reveal the emergence of absolute authority as a technology of power for preserving the peace. The abiding concern of Hobbes is, at the end of the day, the problem of order, presented by Leviathan as an omnipotent technology exercised in the name of security, the supreme concept of bourgeois society: *the concept of police*.[47]

In this light we might tweak slightly a comment from Thomas Carlyle, one tweaked in turn by Carl Schmitt when he alludes to it in his commentary on Hobbes: Behemoth versus Leviathan is the world of rebellious anarchy versus the world of police.[48] Hobbes's account of the creation of the Leviathan rests heavily on the perpetual war of the state of nature within which the fear and insecurity, danger and disorder, will push people to seek the protection of the sovereign. But the transition from the state of war to submission to the Leviathan leaves open the possibility that the war continues in the form of internal rebellion—continues, that is, in the form of revolutionary movements within the body politic, inside the belly of the beast. So the fundamental fear and insecurity which permeate the perpetual war of the state of nature are assumed to also exist in the condition of rebellion and revolt, which are "but warre renewed" (as "intestine" rather than "foreign" war, as Hobbes puts it).[49] The sovereign is expected to offer security and protection from all such fears in exchange for obedience, for "the end of Obedience is Protection."[50] What is conjured up is, as Derrida puts it, an "insurance policy" (*police d'assurance*), which basically entrusts to sovereignty the very powers of security and protection that will be called police.[51] If we now read the fear of rebellion and civil war as a fear of the Behemoth, then what is being offered is in fact security from the monster, and the dialectical relationship that Derrida reads between "the beast and the sovereign" might thus be reconsidered as a relationship between "the monster and the police." The security *offered* by the state displaces the monstrosity *of* the state and is turned toward the monstrosity of disorder. The monstrousness of the Leviathan is no longer the issue, for the state becomes instead a police operation against the monstrous Behemoth.

This is why it is more important to keep in sight the monstrosity of the Behemoth rather than the Leviathan. "Behemoth" is the Hebrew plural form of a word meaning "beast" but also signifies an "aggregation of monsters."[52] Behemoth is a plurality of forces and thus, in a sense, the beastly and multifaceted multitude. To keep the Behemoth in sight is thus to hold on to the observation that in being devoured by the Leviathan the Behemoth continues to exist inside the police power, as the permanent enemy within. It is also to keep in sight the fact that as "rebellion," "revolution," "civil war," and "disorder," Behemoth is a monster with many heads.

In *The Many-Headed Hydra*, Peter Linebaugh and Markus Rediker argue that the merchants, manufacturers, planters, and officials of the dominant European states found in the multiheaded monster a key motif for the rebellious disorder of the lower classes. This motif worked alongside the understanding of the figure of Hercules.[53] Hercules was regarded as unifier of the territorial state by the Greeks, signified imperial ambition to the Romans, and was associated in general with a vast labor for the fabrication of order: draining swamps, developing agriculture, securing commerce, and even keeping things clean (specifically, the Augean stables). The ruling class has long regarded its task of constructing a bourgeois order and instilling the discipline of wage labor among the unruly workers as "Herculean."[54] In 1649, for example, Antony Ascham noted in his *Of the Confusions and Revolutions of Governments* that "*Governours of men are like keepers of beasts*; Every man as he is an Animal, participating halfe with the brute. . . . When an irregular passion breaks out in a state, an irrational beast hath broke out of his grate or cave, and puts the Keeper to a great deal of trouble." This beastliness culminates in the monster of revolution, and Ascham's call was for a new Hercules, who was also known as an executioner, "to tame Monsters or usurpers."[55] The specific monster that Hercules was meant to tame or destroy was the many-headed hydra of Lerna. As Hobbes puts it, dealing with subjects is a task "like that of Hercules with the Monster Hydra, which having many heads, for every one that was vanquished, there grew up three."[56]

Linebaugh and Rediker show just how far the many-headed hydra was understood in terms of the rebellious and dangerous classes:

> When the proletariat was rebellious and self-active, it was described as a monster, a many-headed hydra. Its heads included food rioters (Shakespeare); heretics (Thomas Edwards); army agitators (Thomas Fairfax); antinomians and independent women (Cotton Mather); maroons (Governor Mauricius); motley urban mobs (Peter Oliver); general strikers (J. Cunningham); rural barbarians of the commons (Thomas Malthus); aquatic laborers (Patrick Colquhoun); free thinkers (William Reid); and striking textile workers (Andrew Ure). Nameless commentators added peasant rebels, Levellers, pirates, and slave insurrectionists to the long list. Fearful of the energy, mobility, and growth of social forces beyond their control, the writers, heresy hunters, generals, ministers, officials, population theorists, policemen, merchants, manufacturers, and planters offered up their curses, which called down Herculean destruction upon the hydra's heads.[57]

It is in this context that we need to keep in sight the monstrosity of the Behemoth. In Hobbes's *Behemoth*, one part of the dialogue runs as follows:

> B. You have read, that when Hercules fighting with the Hydra, had cut off any one of his many heads, there still arose two other heads in its place; and yet at last he cut them off all.

> A. The story is told false. For Hercules at first did not cut off those heads, but bought them off; and afterwards, when he saw it did him no good, then he cut them off, and got the victory.[58]

The Herculean task of the capitalist ruling class has been to construct the new bourgeois order, and the myth of the many-headed monster simultaneously expressed the fear and justified the violence of the ruling class in carrying out this task.[59] Building such order and exercising violence against any force obstructing that process is the definition of police power. It is to conduct this Herculean task that Leviathan exists: a political machine of/for security and a political body of/for police to defeat the multiheaded enemy.

Yet the problem for the ruling class is that this struggle is never really over—the victory never really "got," as Hobbes puts it—because despite buying off or cutting off the various heads as they appear, the monster lies within the body politic. This is why police discourse from the sixteenth century to the present has never stopped telling us of the permanent wars being fought against the enemy within: the disorderly, unruly, criminal, indecent, disobedient, disloyal, lawless, and mindless, each of which morphs into the other, constantly changing shape in monstrous fashion, lining up with or brushing up alongside the killer, the regicide, and the terrorist, and even performing the filthy trick of appearing to be human.[60] This multiheaded hydra is a creature the ruling class fears will devour it, and so the creature must itself be devoured; an uncontainable creature which must nevertheless somehow be contained. The need for the creature to be contained is why the concept of keeping—in the sense of guarding or holding but also from "the keep," referring to the inner stronghold of a castle—is so important in *Leviathan*. Keeping the subjects in obedience, keeping them from discontent, keeping them quiet, keeping them from rebellion, keeping them in space, keeping them in order, and keeping them in awe, all rolled into the core principle of police theory: *keeping the peace*.[61] Leviathan is the police power of containment, keeping us safe and secure from our monsters, ourselves.

REMEMBER THE MONSTERS? REMEMBER THE POLICE

In the final episode of the final season of *Dexter*, there is a flashback scene to the moment of the birth of Dexter's son. Dexter is worrying about whether he will make a good father, and Deb, his sister, reassures him that he will. "You've always taken care of me," she says, especially when they were young: "You made me feel so fucking safe." In particular, she reminds him of her greatest fear during the night: "Don't you remember the monsters?" she asks, and then reminds him that he made her feel secure by explaining that "the monsters were just the shadows." Deb's suggestion that Dexter protected her from the monsters is immediately undermined by Dexter's voice-over: "You were so wrong, Deb." Wrong because there really are monsters and Dexter *is* one of them? Perhaps. But maybe she was right, in that this monster nonetheless did protect her and keep her safe and secure. This monster had more than a touch of the police power.

Security and protection are two of the most fundamental mechanisms that underpin the police power. But in security there is always insecurity and in protection there is always fear. One of the functions of the power of the monstrous is that it is crucial to the political construction of fear and insecurity. Circulating around and operating through the fears and insecurities of bourgeois modernity, the monster and the police come together. With the continual iteration of issues concerning order and disorder, security and identity, borders and boundaries, containment and excess, the discourses of monstrosity and police share a fundamental conceptual ground: a problem to be contained and a process of containment. It is for this very reason that all of the main themes in the discourse of monstrosity point to the police problematic.

That it does so is connected to the fact that capitalism teems with monsters. Aliens, fiends, vampires, and zombies dominate the cultural scene; reports on scientific developments are frequently presented in terms of their potentially "monstrous" implications; and journalism resorts to describing as "monstrous" a whole host of persons, from the pedophile to the serial killer to the despotic leader. More recently, it has been suggested that capitalism is itself monstrous. Yet like everything else it lets loose in the world, capitalism has to manage its monsters.[62] It has to manage itself, its own monstrosity, and its own monster within. This is the monster that capitalism brings into being *through* the police power and which it must constantly manage *with* the police power. Bourgeois modernity gives us the monster and the police.

CHAPTER NINE

PROOF OF DEATH: POLICE POWER AND THE VISUAL ECONOMIES OF SEIZURE, ACCUMULATION, AND TROPHY

Travis Linnemann

> The spectacle is capital accumulated to the
> point that it becomes images.
> —**Guy Debord**

In late 2013, Melissa Bachman, a would-be television personality, generated a hearty backlash after tweeting a photo of her South African big-game hunt. The photo depicts Bachman proudly grinning, rifle in hand, as she kneels above her prey, a large lion. The tweeted caption reads, "An incredible day hunting in South Africa! Stalked inside 60-yards on this beautiful male lion.... What a hunt!" Outraged Twitter users responded immediately with a torrent of criticism, dismissing the hunt as an act of cowardice and calling Bachman among other things, a "pathetic, sad excuse for a human." Even comedian Ricky Gervais chimed in, noting the "big difference between the natural need for a species to kill and eat prey & just shooting an animal simply as a *ghastly trophy*." Bachman, whose personal website featured a virtual "trophy room" of her other kills, is no stranger to this sort of public response. In 2012 she was dropped from a National Geographic television program after an online petition demanding dismissal of the "contract trophy killer" collected more than thirteen thousand signatures in twenty-four hours. Following the lion photo, displeased viewers began another petition, this time demanding she be not only prohibited from future hunts but also barred from visiting South Africa altogether.[1] While Bachman may be just another of the mounting casualties of a crowd-sourced politics of outrage, her case also neatly maps contemporary visual economies and underlines the irregular force and effect of visual self-representation.[2] Though Bachman's lion photo was in many ways identical to those produced by trophy hunters in the United States, there was clearly something about her photo that engendered the disgust of much of the viewing public. It could be that for her mostly Western audience, the exoticism of the lion deemed it more grievable than animals hunted legally in the United States. It might also be that viewers saw the killing as shameless promotion of Bachman's television program. Viewers may also have sanctioned Bachman for transgressing the masculine boundaries of gun culture and big-game hunting. Whatever it was, viewers did not meet Bachman's photographic message approvingly.

In order to consider the composition of not only what registers photographically, but also pain and suffering rendered as objects of consumption,[3] this chapter engages a pervasive yet somewhat overlooked image, the trophy shot. As understood here, the trophy shot is a visual self-representation of accomplishment or possession or both. This may be as banal as a photo of a new graduate proudly clutching her diploma, or, as Eamonn Carrabine has adeptly shown,[4] it may be as ghoulish as soldiers presiding over the torture at Abu Ghraib. In Bachman's case, we can assume that she meant to represent herself as an accomplished hunter, possessing both the prowess and will to stalk and kill a large animal. The paradox is that the qualities Bachman aimed to represent—her will to kill and dominion over nature—are precisely what incited viewers' anger. Because of the oft-conflicting dynamics found therein, the trophy shot provides particularly fertile ground to engage the politics of visual self-representation and to question why some images escape public scrutiny while others do not. As developed here, the *police* trophy shot is an unvarnished representation of the state's prerogative to search, seize, and accumulate private property. Police trophy shots often accompany official press releases announcing a "major bust" and are also produced by individual officers informally in order to commemorate a particular arrest or event.[5] At a moment when social media has dramatically altered the one-way, top-down model of police-public dialogue, this sort of electronic visual self-representation is increasingly central to the production of the police image. While drugs, guns, and money feature prominently, trophies are not limited to drug war contraband but always represent the state's prerogative of search, seizure, and accumulation.

For instance, in September 2014, police in West Virginia announced the seizure of 190 pounds of illegally harvested ginseng, distributing several photos to local news media of officers posing with their haul. Similarly, when NYPD agents arrested the prolific street artist COST, press releases featured photos of arresting officers posed with COST's seized materials. Understanding the police trophy shot as an artifact of state power, the article "NYPD Gloats About Arresting Graffiti Artist" documents a certain vindictiveness— the desire to revel in or "gloat" over one's accomplishments—permeating the police trophy shot and the police image more generally.[6] Here, the police trophy shot discloses a narcissistic dimension of the police power, which is linked to or derived directly from the ability to exert one's will over another. This becomes more apparent in police trophy shots that position human bodies as trophies. In 2009, several police dispatched ahead of the protests at the G-20 summit in Pittsburgh, Pennsylvania, were observed and filmed featuring an arrested protester in a group trophy shot. Unedited video of the incident shows anywhere from fifteen to twenty riot-gear-clad police posing around a young man, hands cuffed behind his back and forced to kneel, as other officers gleefully document their work visually.[7]

Another image trafficked widely on the internet depicts a police agent lifting a prisoner's shirt in order to expose the words FUCK THE POLICE tattooed across his chest. In relation to the officer who is grinning proudly, the photographic message reads quite literally, *Fuck me? No, fuck you!* Each announcing a victory, these are just a few examples from the immense archive of images that produce and reproduce the police power through the power of the visual.[8] Demonstrating the state's prerogative to search, seize, and accumulate private property, police trophy shots thereby provide a powerful record of how it works to regulate individual market relations and fabricate social order.[9] Yet if we expand our understanding of trophies and trophy shots beyond the parameters of typical drug war contraband—drugs, guns, money—to the corporeal, we might more readily see the police power as the sovereign power over life and death. Here trophy shots that feature a captured subject like those described above and even routine booking photos reaffirm the state's lawful violence,[10] its powers to hunt, capture, and if necessary kill its subjects.[11] Taken together, in the context of precarious late-capitalist economies, the practice of taking trophies and staging and circulating trophy shots reveals how the police power is actively involved in seizing the necessary material of existence and administering if not celebrating everyday domination and death. The aim in confronting the police trophy shot then is to develop an optic that apprehends and contests what we might call *visualities of domination* or the scopic regime of the police power.[12]

NARCISSISM, VISUAL CULTURE, AND THE WILL TO REPRESENTATION

In order to position the police trophy shot within a broader visual economy, it is useful to recall Christopher Lasch's culture of narcissism.[13] Lasch anticipated a social order conditioned by hyperconsumerism, economic specialization, and a sweeping organized kindness, where external validation of individual tastes, desires, and accomplishments are key, if not primary structures of identity. While Lasch, writing first in 1979, did not and probably could not have foreseen developments in visual culture taken up here, his criticisms of social life map neatly onto one of the most inescapable forms of contemporary self-representation—a photograph taken of oneself with a smartphone or webcam and shared via social media—the *selfie*.[14] Jenna Brager describes the selfie as a looped gaze, a self-referential image whereby the photographer and subject occupy the same position.[15] Echoing Lasch, this looped gaze helps to position individual tastes (such as one's dinner or clothing), accomplishments (physique, weight loss), and desires (wealth, celebrity) as fundamental to identity.[16] With an estimated thirty billion selfies produced in 2014 alone, this visual economy now enlists products such as the "selfie stick," which promises to help "take the perfect selfie," and even games where participants compete to produce the most unusual or outrageous selfie, such as in front of a casket at a funeral or next to a homeless person.[17] Of course, all of this has given rise to an ethics of the selfie, leading some to conclude that it marks a significant shift in youth culture and a radically refigured imagined community.[18] Whatever the case, the selfie is now an important currency of contemporary visual economies, representing accomplishment, possession, and hence capital.[19]

While the exponentially multiplying number of selfies archived on social media might be evidence of widespread narcissistic self-indulgence, Brager makes the important point that self-representation also allows subjects to be recognized when they otherwise may not. For prisoners in California's Pelican Bay Secure Housing Unit (SHU), who are denied almost all human contact and may not have even seen their own faces in years, the annual booking photos provide a modicum of "proof of life." She writes, "Under these conditions, a single snapshot against a white backdrop is a kind of proof of continued existence, of time passing in an otherwise completely liminal space. Without the photograph, the body seems to disappear completely, and without the selfie, or rather any control over one's image, the self is evacuated."[20]

Here the visual and self-representation promise to make even the most abject suffering visible.[21] For our purposes here then, it might also be useful to understand the selfie as a political act, a visual record and *proof of the life* we wish others to see. Majid Yar has urged critical scholars of crime and media to consider the ways in which the narcissistic desire for mediated self-representation might also be bound up with the genesis of criminal behavior.[22] He writes, "Today we see the spectacle of (predominately) young people performing acts of crime and deviance in order to record them, share them and upload them to the Internet. This kind of 'will to communicate' or 'will to representation' may be seen in itself as a new kind of casual inducement to law- and rule-breaking behavior."[23] That some criminal acts are conceived and carried out in order to mediate oneself electronically reveals the force and effect of what Yar calls the *will to representation* in contemporary visual culture, derived from Schopenhauer's *The World as Will and Representation*, which saw representation as a mental image of object relations, including one's own body Yar describes how subjects represent themselves visually in order to produce a particular imagined understanding of self. Consider, for instance, the case of six teenage girls in Florida who not only planned and carried out the ruthless beating of a schoolmate but also did so with the express aim of documenting and posting a record of the beating to YouTube.[24] Given the proliferating number of cases such as this, we might say that *image* precedes or overtakes the *act*. Yar's insights complement other important theoretical interventions into expressive criminality and the production of violent and criminal inter/subjectivities. Not unlike Jack Katz's influential *Seductions of Crime*,[25] Willem de Haan and Jaco Vos understand street robbery as an instrument employed not simply for material gain but also to produce and perform a "badass" and "ruthless" self/identity.[26] Simon Cottee and Keith Hayward have also argued that those who commit violent acts of terror do so not only to accomplish geo-strategic goals, but also because of the desire for excitement, glory, and existential meaning.[27] Here "glory" is an exalted but accomplished identity of one who acted violently or died for "the cause." In the social media age, we might say that to produce and perform a *badass/ruthless*—even exalted—identity, it's not enough to simply exert one's will over another human being; the act itself must be documented visually and shared publicly. If the will to representation is implicated in new forms of law- and rule-breaking behaviors, it stands to reason that police officers might also be subject. Lt. Andrew Hawkes of the Collin County, Texas, sheriff's department, a self-described "highway drug interdiction expert," offers a useful window into this question. Not only does he use the term to describe the property he seizes through the course of duty, but, like Bachman, Hawkes also hosted a "virtual trophy room" on his now seemingly closed subscription-only website highwaydruginterdiction. com, and encouraged subscribers to submit their own trophy shots for display: "Trophy Room! Check out the brand new photo album with trophy shots sent to me from officers around the country." If Hawkes is any indication, it is clear that police view the material that they have taken from members of the public as personal trophies and more generally proof of the police power—the power to seize and accumulate private property.

Drug interdiction is part of a broad repertoire that Markus Dubber calls "policing possession," described as the "policing device of choice in the war on crime," Dubber argues what defines the police power in the contemporary moment is not the aim of crime control but rather the intent to police possession of prohibited materials and the threats these objects are thought to represent.[28] In other words, policing is a (precrime) security project aimed at identifying and eradicating threats of crime and disorder. In the context of the police trophy shot, each seized weapon signifies a murder or robbery averted and the familiar mounds of seized drugs, unknowable death and destruction. As such, we should understand the police trophy shot as a dynamic image that produces and reproduces the police power by reminding state subjects of threats eliminated on their behalf and of the police who keep them *safe*.

Yet, to seize property or take from another by force is, by definition, robbery.[29] Therefore, within the celebratory images of its extraordinary work is a secondary representation of the lawful violence of the police power. Of course, the right of the police to take by force is authorized by law and thus not *seen* as criminal. In cases of eminent domain, for instance, where the state seizes the property of a private citizen in order to accomplish something deemed in the best interests of the public, the state is required to provide fair compensation. However, in cases where the state has already ruled that a business, land use, or property is not in the best interests of the public, it may abolish businesses and "take" property without compensation as a lawful exercise of the police power.[30] Under the guise of a drug war purportedly waged in furtherance of safety and security, state and federal, civil and criminal asset forfeiture laws authorize this sort of lawful "taking." In many instances, state subjects need not be convicted or even accused of a crime for police to seize cash, automobiles, homes, and other property if the objects in question can be linked however tenuously to criminal activity. In such cases, it is the object and attendant threat, not necessarily the owner, the state deems suspicious. Legal architecture such as this has produced cases with improbable filing names such as *United States v. One Pearl Necklace* and *United States v. Approximately 64,695 Pounds of Shark Fins*.[31] So widespread are these practices that in 2014 alone Justice Department agencies made a total of $3.9 billion of civil asset seizures, far outpacing the $679 million in assets seized in formal criminal cases actually involving drugs.[32] While individual accounting practices make it difficult to estimate, asset forfeiture at the state level is no doubt just as lucrative and perhaps even more so. In 2011, police in the tiny resort city of Bal Harbour, Florida, seized more than $5 million from a group of suspected money launderers and then used the seized cash on salaries, confidential informants, and a boat and surveillance truck totaling more than a quarter-million dollars.[33] It is also important to note that police do not only target valuable property and "kingpin" traffickers. As the *Washington Post* recently reported, each year the city of Philadelphia seizes millions of dollars, much of it the "pocket change" of its poorest residents with nearly 60 percent of all civil asset forfeitures for amounts under $250.[34] Critics have argued that in an environment of increasing fiscal austerity, civil and criminal asset forfeiture laws permit, if not encourage, local policing agencies to supplement their budgets with the property of private citizens. As one midwestern police chief explained during a public citizen / police review board hearing, the decision to seize private property is "based on something that would be nice to have, that we can't get in the budget for instance. . . . It's kind of like pennies from heaven, you know it gets you a toy or something you need, is the way we usually look at it."[35] Used by all levels of US police for decades, automobiles "seized from local drug dealers" perhaps best characterize incentive-based policing or "policing for profit." Yet these are not simply the vehicles of criminals but the trophies attesting to the impunity of the police power.

As the policeman who appears to be gleefully flashing "gang signs" next to a vehicle "confiscated from your local drug dealer" demonstrates, woven into the representational dynamics of the police trophy shot is the narcissistic desire to gloat over one's accomplishments. For instance, when local news in Saginaw, Michigan, interviewed Sheriff William Federspiel for a story on a Ford Mustang "taken from a local drug dealer," the sheriff posed next to the car sarcastically displaying a matching T-shirt emblazoned with "This t-shirt was taken from a local drug dealer."[36] In this instance we might say that police work is animated by not only some benevolent "duty" but also the joy derived from exercising power over others and representing it visually. Following the lead of geographer Trevor Paglen,[37] who shows how the insignia and iconography of American military units offer a unique and particularly revealing look into the unspoken thoughts and murky politics of state power, we can see how even the insignia of the DEA's Asset Forfeiture Program, complete with a large dollar sign, jewelry, a luxury jet, and automobile married with the line "You make it—We'll take it," discloses the vindictiveness of the police power.[38]

If the will to representation is indeed criminogenic as Yar suggests, it is reasonable to assume that individual officers may cross boundaries of policy and law in order to win acceptance and recognition, if not material benefit. In fact, the many public critiques and legal appeals challenging civil asset forfeiture laws argue precisely this. This is not to suggest that police trophy shots document the proverbial "bad apples"; rather, they suggest a fundamental yet overlooked dynamic of the police power. In *Critique of Violence*, Walter Benjamin offers some insight to the ways in which the police power operates outside the boundaries of sanctioned legality in order to uphold these very same boundaries. Drawing parallels between the state's prerogative of capital punishment and police violence, Benjamin insists that in the exercise of the highest violence—the power over life and death—"the origins of law jut manifestly and fearsomely from it." He writes,

It [police violence] is lawmaking, for its characteristic function is not the promulgation of laws, but the assertion of legal claims for any decree, and law-preserving because it is at the disposal of these ends. The assertion that the ends of police violence are always identical or even connected to those of general law is entirely untrue. Rather, the "law" of the police really marks the point at which the state whether from impotence or because of the immanent connections within any legal system, can no longer guarantee through the legal system the empirical ends that it desires at any price to attain. Therefore, the police intervene "for security reasons" in countless cases where no clear legal situation exists, when they are not merely, without the slightest relation to legal ends, accompanying the citizen as a brutal encumbrance through a life regulated by ordinances, or simply supervising him.[39]

In Benjamin's view then, we might see everyday searches, seizures, and accumulation carried out under the guise of "security" as springing forth from and operating within the contested liminal spaces of capitalist social order. We might also say, then, that in the visual representations of their "takings" police and state power actively reproduce the authority and necessity of a social system dependent upon wage labor and private property. In its visual representations of what the state deems illegal, the symbolic register of the legal emerges. Drawing upon Benjamin's understanding of the police power as that which enforces what is beyond the limits of law, Michael Taussig adds that in order for the police to enforce the law, they must first be "free of it." Taussig's point is that in instances of corruption, police do not sometimes slip from legality to operate as criminals but rather that cops and criminals are always "erotically intertwined and that the thin blue line separating them is more like a veil in a striptease." Police are, as he puts it, "not thieves, but 'cop-thieves.' *Double-men*."[40] A similar point is made by Mark Neocleous's revisiting of Hobbes's two biblical monsters, in which he argues that the security offered by the sovereign *Leviathan* is of course security from the chaos and disorder of the monster/beast from below, *Behemoth*.[41] To find refuge and security from the monster, political subjects must submit to the violent monstrosity from above, the sovereign state and its police. The security offered by the police power negates the sovereign's own monstrosity. There is, in his words, always a monster in the police. Egon Bittner, an early sociologist of the American police, also recognized this duality, which he described as the dragon within the dragon-slayer. He writes,

For in modern folklore, too, he is a character who is ambivalently feared and admired, and no amount of public relations work can entirely abolish the sense that there is something of the *dragon* in the *dragon-slayer*. Because they are posted on the perimeters of order and justice in the hope that their presence will deter the forces of darkness and chaos, because they are meant to spare the rest of the people direct confrontations with the dreadful, perverse, lurid, and dangerous, police officers are perceived to have powers and secrets no one else shares. Their interest in and competence to deal with the untoward surrounds their activities with mystery and distrust. One needs only to consider the thoughts that come to mind at the sight of policemen moving into action: here they go to do something the rest of us have no stomach for![42]

Recognition of the dragon in the dragon-slayer, Bittner suggests, renders the police somehow less trustworthy. Yet following Benjamin, Taussig, Neocleous, and others, we might say that distrust stems not so much from the fact that they do what "we have no stomach for!" but rather from the recognition of police as double-men—cop/criminal, dragon/dragon-slayer. *The monster in the police!* The idea that police mark the boundaries of order and chaos, sheltering the public from the "dreadful, perverse, lurid, and dangerous," is the fundamental myth of the police power and one that trophy shots, as representations of extraordinary police work—threats eliminated, insecurity secured—help to invoke and reproduce. Perhaps more subtly, police trophy shots remind state subjects of the legal brutality and thievery built into the police power, the sovereign power to regulate markets and adjudicate the manner in which state subjects may earn a living. A thoroughgoing critique of the police trophy shot then might begin to counter the political and cultural forces that keep state subjects from *seeing* the entwinements and abiding connections between cop and criminal, monster and police. As Taussig reminds, "What should hold us are the curious properties of the distinction *uniting* the criminal with the policeman, something Nietzsche, for one, made clear when he argued that the police are worse than the criminal because they do the same things, but in the name of Law."[43]

This is a duality that is not lost on the police themselves. Writing on the qualities said to motivate both "cops and criminals" for the policing publication PoliceOne.com, Hawkes elaborates both the will to representation and erotic entwinements of cop and criminal. "After years of working patrol," he asserts, "we can all agree we see five traits are possessed by most people, the good and the bad—the cop and the criminal." His five traits:

1. **Adrenaline:** Whether you are a criminal who wants to escape or fight, adrenaline plays into the decision to do so. Likewise, the adrenaline of a police officer pushes him/her to win the foot chase, subdue the suspect, or catch the burglar.

2. **Revenge:** How many times have we heard, "I'm going to pay you back for what you did." Revenge drives bad people to do bad things like assaulting a spouse or an enemy, stalking someone who has done them harm, or any number of wrongs committed against them. Revenge may not be a character trait we as cops really want to discuss, but to say it isn't a motivating factor to get a conviction in a case of a known criminal that you have dealt with time and time again would be to ignore human nature.

3. **Acceptance:** We all have the desire to be accepted by our peers. If you wear a badge, you want your peers to accept you as a good cop—as someone they can depend on to watch their backs. On the other side of the coin, a meth cook wants the whole meth world to acknowledge that their product is the best on the market. They want acceptance.

4. **Recognition:** The human desire to be recognized for what we feel is a significant accomplishment. Recognition can give an officer confidence, especially when he/she is recognized by citizens for a job well done, or given a service bar from agency administration for rising above expectations. Similarly, criminals often want to be recognized—they want "street cred" among their peers. Bragging about a crime comes from the desire to be recognized.

5. **Victory:** In the end, we all—whether cop or criminal—have the desire to win. We want to succeed at whatever we undertake. The good guys want to catch the bad guys, and the bad guys want to get away. Winning is a big part of what we do, and it's naive to think the criminals don't feel the same way.

For Hawkes, too, cops and criminals are entwined, "driven by the same qualities of human nature." Yet he is clear in his assertion that "possessing the traits of human nature is one thing, using them for right and just ends is an individual choice."[44] Whereas Benjamin, Taussig, and Neocleous would likely argue what defines "cop and criminal" is the authority of law and lawful violence of the state, for Hawkes separating the two is simply each individual's choice of cop *or* criminal. However simplistic and misguided, Hawkes's take on human nature does usefully reveal the ways in which the police trophy shot is animated by the will to representation. For Hawkes, police work is an *adrenaline*-fueled battle in which the "good guys" exact *revenge* upon the "bad guys," claiming *victory* for themselves and the imagined community they represent.[45] From the trophy shots littering his website and the cover of his *Secrets of Successful Highway Interdiction* how-to book, it is clear that for this particular police officer mediated self-representation—proof—is crucial to winning the *acceptance* and *recognition* he desires.[46]

Understanding the ritualistic display of the trophy as method to win acceptance and recognition reveals another binary relation of the police power, being that of *hunter* and *hunted, predator* and *prey*. In *Manhunts: A Philosophical History*, Grégoire Chamayou describes policing as the "most amusing form, the supreme expression, of hunting."[47] Here the lawful violence of the police power is enlisted to track, search, seize, and accumulate the property and bodies of those deemed illegal. Building upon Chamayou's insights, Tyler Wall portends the rise of the police drone as the logical extension of the police hunting power, a "magical" technology providing the state a position of dominance drawn from an unassailable scopic verticality.[48] If, as Wall suggests, part of the police drone's promise lies in its ability through technological efficiency and superiority to minimize the potential of the police to be humiliated by a failed manhunt, we might see the police trophy shot as precisely the inverse, the photographic record of a *successful hunt* and an affirmation or reaffirmation of the state's hunting power.

Expanding our understanding of the trophy shot beyond the inanimate, we can see what also underlies and animates the trophy is the power over life and death.[49] So for instance, the well-known practice of taking trophy scalps long misattributed to Native people of the Americas was actually introduced by English and French colonists as a way to monetize the pacification of unruly natives. Here scalps are not simply ghoulish trophies but the commodified and monetized *proof of the death* of a human being.[50] In

Primate Visions, Donna Haraway describes natural history dioramas and the dead animals that comprise them as a politics of reproduction.[51] Only after killing and representing the animal, Haraway argues, could it be seen once and thus again by Western eyes. What is reproduced is an implied narrative that leans heavily in favor of white man's dominion over nature and "uncivilized" people. Similarly, Thomas Strychacz takes up Ernest Hemingway, the great white hunter figure of all American literature, to describe the distinct and virulent masculinity reproduced through hunter's relationship with his trophy and audience.[52] As we've seen with Bachman, the display of taxidermy and photographic trophy shots of dead animals engender a violent masculinity imbued with the will and power to kill and reaffirm boundaries between human and animal/other.[53] As in the Hegelian master/slave,[54] the hunter's masculine prowess and will to kill are negated if not represented for an audience as trophy.[55] When featuring a body, trophy shots invoke a politics of reproduction exerting command over both material accumulation and the biopolitical.

Of course, corporeal trophy taking as proof of death extends well beyond the realm of sport to landscapes of violence and war. In *The Body in Pain*, Elaine Scarry writes, "To have pain is to have certainty; to hear about pain is to have doubt."[56] Which is to say, while indescribable, physical pain is infinitely knowable to the sufferer. Yet pain is communicated, hence politicized, when attached to a referent external to the human body through a process she calls "analogical verification or substantiation." So while pain is first and foremost the knowable terrain of the body in pain, it can lend "realness" and "factuality" that is communicable and external to the sufferer—amplified and made visible to those outside the person's body.[57] The infliction of pain is also a politics of reproduction, in that the ideas and images that emerge, like those from the prison at Abu Ghraib, invoke a spectacle of brutality, a drama that is played out in order to compensate for the state's waning power. In this way, acts of violence, humiliation, and torture substantiated through analogy or artifact work to make the state seem powerful but at the same time serve, in Scarry's words, as an "announcement to ourselves and the world that we've lost belief in ourselves."[58] Here the trophy is no mere memento and the trophy shot not simply a visual representation; rather, both are productive or reproductive of the powers of violence and domination, rendering the pain and suffering of those positioned as trophy a livable artifact in the world. It is no wonder, as Mark Hamm notes, that copies of the trophy shots of the death and torture at Abu Ghraib are available at "marketplaces from Egypt to the Philippines, evoking the worst suspicions of Muslims everywhere: that Americans are corrupt, heartless, and hell-bent on humiliating Muslims and mocking their values."[59]

Like the hunter with his prey, trophies and trophy shots reveal the relations of violence and domination between state and subject. In May 1944, *Life* magazine published the photo of a young woman gazing longingly at the skull of a dead Japanese soldier, mailed home by her boyfriend fighting in New Guinea. As historian James Weingartner documents,[60] the trophy skull of a "good jap . . . named Tojo" sent home to an adoring girlfriend was the predictable outcome of American soldiers who saw themselves as "Jap Hunters" and had distributed mock hunting licenses declaring "open season on that vile stinking viper known as Jap-Snake" to commemorate the event.[61] Of course this sort of macabre proof of death practice continues. In 2011, American news media began to report on the so-called "Kill Team" discovered by military authorities. This group of army infantry stalked Afghan civilians and after murdering them took thousands of trophy shots with their lifeless corpses. The leader of the group even commemorated his kills with tattoos and took a finger from each victim with designs of a "finger bone necklace."[62] Not unlike serial killers thought to take items from their victims as a form of "invidious consumption" and surplus enjoyment helping them relive their crimes,[63] "Kill Team" members took trophy shots and pieces of flesh from their victims to commemorate their murderous acts and substantiate their *badass/ruthless* identities.[64] Here trophies as vile as a stolen finger or as commonplace as a digital image represent to the world the *adrenaline* thrill of combat, mark a *victory* won in battle, and help revisit *revenge* taken upon one's enemies.

Jihadists have recently taken to social media to circulate grisly trophy shots featuring the severed heads of their executed victims. In a style described by Cottee as "gonzo," this sort of gratuitous visual propaganda or "performance violence" does not intend to achieve any particular strategic goal and is more concerned with the grisly spectacle itself.[65] Cottee suggests that an overtly sadistic element, which glorifies destruction for its own sake, sets "gonzo" productions apart from other forms of political terror. Likewise, in Mexico's so-called cartel wars, bodies or body parts are displayed publicly as a "message" and warning to all those who might interfere with the drug trade. Cartel gunmen are known to pose with the bodies of their victims and even record their executions and post them to the internet. One particularly brazen member of the Knights Templar named Broly maintains an active social media presence posting selfies posing with weapons on the way to "jobs" and with kidnapped victims soon to be murdered.[66] As with the "gonzo" images produced by jihadists, trophy shots and body messages are vital to the identity of cartel gunmen and the collectives they represent. As one Mexican security official reasoned, "I don't think they [because of their presence on social media] are irrational. They are psychopaths for sure, but I believe there is a method in this madness.... They are fighting to defend their *reputation for brutality and the image of control* in the territories they claim."[67] As with taxidermied heads of dead animals prized by trophy hunters, we might say that in the context of war and the contemporary drug/terror war, to take and display the head of a dead enemy is perhaps the most powerful symbolic representation of physical domination. As Philip Smith argues,[68] even the guillotine, which was conceived as a rational, bureaucratic, and sober means of execution, could not escape the "grotesque and Gothic symbolism" and "unknowable horror" of the headless body and twitching spasms and facial contortions of the severed head. The symbolic detritus of the decapitated head represents not just an execution or murder, then, but also a death within death, a symbolic horizon where the possibilities of resurrection and afterlife disappear. Here it is useful to revisit Slavoj Žižek's recuperation of Jacque Lacan's *two deaths*. Whereas the guillotine is a device designed to remove its victims from the realm of the living—the Lacanian *Real*—the decapitated corpse interrupts the figure of a whole human being, thereby producing another *Symbolic* death that transforms the victim from human to *head*—a symbol of violence, death, and erasure.[69]

It is an interesting coincidence that a key strategic principal of the United States' global drug and terror war is so-called kingpin or decapitation strategy exemplified by the maxim "cut off the head and the body will die." In the second invasion of Iraq, decapitation strategy was represented visually by playing cards that set out a hierarchy of enemy leaders and codified the aim of "cutting off the head of the snake" Saddam Hussein, the ace of spades.[70]Although proven marginally effective at best, decapitation strategy unpinned the hunt for Osama bin Laden and more recently the capture of Joaquín Archivaldo Guzmán Loera, commonly known as El Chapo, leader of the Sinaloa Cartel. In a prepared statement, US attorney general Eric Holder announced the "major victory," noting how capture of the "head" of a major drug-trafficking group was recompense for "the death and destruction of millions of lives across the globe through drug addiction, violence, and corruption."[71] The "*hunt* for El Chapo" and the ensuing discursive work accomplished by the deluge of self-congratulatory press releases and "perp-walk" trophy photos reinforce the efficacy of kingpin/decapitation strategy and US police power more broadly.[72] Decades earlier, the US-backed hunt for Pablo Escobar, leader of Colombia's Medellín Cartel, ended similarly. Whereas Guzmán was whisked away to a Mexican prison, Colombian police featured Escobar's corpse in their own commemorative trophy shots. Yet, as touched upon earlier, the triumphant display of human trophies is not limited to the "heads" of major drug cartels and is very much the repertoire of routine police work.

In May 2015, the *Chicago Sun-Times* reported on a photo that was evidence in the dismissal proceedings of a Chicago police officer named Timothy McDermott. Taken sometime between 1999 and 2003, the image shows McDermott and another police officer named Jerome Finnigan posing with rifles, kneeling above an "unidentified African-American drug suspect," tongue dangling from his open mouth, antlers fixed to his head. This particularly grotesque trophy shot was turned over by Justice Department officials to Chicago Police investigators two years after Finnigan received a twelve-year prison sentence for his role in "leading a crew of rogue cops in robberies, home invasions and other crimes." Hoping to save his job, McDermott pleaded, "I am embarrassed by my participation in this photograph. . . . I made a mistake as a young, impressionable police officer who was trying to fit in."[73] As we've seen with Hawkes's take on "acceptance" and "recognition," staging such a ghastly photo in order to "fit in" reveals as much about McDermott's understanding of the police power as it does his own character. What he was trying to "fit in" with then was a permanent institutional and political culture that prizes its ability to capture, display, humiliate, and in fact dominate others. As such, we should not dismiss the officers' decision to affix antlers to the head of "unidentified African-American drug suspect" as a disgusting joke but rather understand it as further evidence of the entwinements of cop/criminal, the police hunting power, and the desire to position state subjects as dehumanized trophies.

POLICE TROPHY SHOTS AS PROOF OF DEATH

The epigraph that introduces this chapter explains that *the spectacle is capital accumulated to the point that it becomes images.*[74] Debord's point, it seems to me, is that even capital cannot escape transformation into a series of somewhat immaterial images that mediate the relationships between individuals. Does this not perfectly describe the police trophy shot and underlying will to representation? After all, the police trophy shot is precisely this: a visual representation of capital accumulated at the point of a gun. Conversely, however, the currency and capital of our social media age is increasingly the image, trafficked in order to gain acceptance, recognition, and admiration.

Without serious engagement and critique, police trophy shots invariably testify to the benevolence of the police power and necessity of the drug war from which they emerge. In order to understand such images as anything other than representations of extraordinary police work, it is first necessary to reject the notion that possession is policed because the items themselves are inherently dangerous (all are legal in some form or other). Instead, we must recognize policing's trophies as the untaxed currency of an illicit and ungoverned economy. To police possession is to adjudicate the ways in which individuals may earn a living. Rather than threats eliminated and insecurities secured, police trophy shots should thus be seen as powerful evidence of how the police power is always at work reinforcing individual and collective market relations and actively fabricating capitalist social order.

As much as the police power desires to be seen as the thin blue line between order and chaos, its own celebratory images betray its utter dependence upon lawful violence. Through a critical engagement and critique of the state's own celebratory images—the proof of the life it wishes us to see—we begin to untangle its entwined and mutually reinforcing powers over material and body. Property seized often with little evidence of wrongdoing troubles the ever-blurring line between cop and criminal, monster and police. At a moment of increasing economic precarity, to seize and narcissistically display the currency of illicit economies—untaxed income, vehicles, drugs, weapons—is to revel in the continued subjugation and domination of society's most abject and dispossessed. Likewise, triumphant images that feature the body of a captured subject—even routine booking photos—expose the monstrous violence of the police power and its prerogative not only to "take" the inanimate but also to hunt the living. Finally, in the future is certain to arrive, when dead bodies and body parts are positioned by police as trophies,[75] we might understand such images as we do the "gonzo" images of jihadists and body messages of drug cartels, as *terror* (as usual).[76] Perhaps then we will see police trophy shots for what they are: *proof of domination and death*, borne not only of the drug war but also of the much older and broader class war waged by police upon the poor.

THE PLAGUE OF POLICE

David Correia and Tyler Wall

"The plague is met by order." This is Michel Foucault's argument in *Discipline and Punish: The Birth of the Prison.*[1] When the plague arrives in town, each of us must submit to—must pass through— "the representatives of power." Foucault calls these "disciplinary institutions." The militia, the police, the agencies of public health, they all confront the order of the plague with a different order. Strict spatial partitioning, quarantine, surveillance, constant inspection, and permanent registration. None of this is voluntary or optional. Submission is required on pain of death. The plague town becomes a "segmented, immobile, frozen space" where all must shelter in place as the disciplinary institutions "sort out every possible confusion: that of the disease, which is transmitted when bodies are mixed together; that of the evil, which is increased when fear and death overcome prohibitions."[2]

Foucault's archeology of the origins of discipline in the modern world rests on two assumptions. First, every plague is the same as every other plague and, second, the disciplinary institutions confront the plague with efficiency and defeat it with authority. The order of the plague upends a previous order, and a different one emerges to fight it. This new order, according to Foucault, survives the plague. Like the virus that it defeats, it quickly spreads. Suddenly "a whole set of techniques and institutions for measuring, supervising and correcting the abnormal brings into play the disciplinary mechanisms to which the fear of the plague gave rise."[3] It is as if the disciplinary institutions mutated in the face of the plague. "Inspection functions ceaselessly. The gaze is alert everywhere."[4] The life-or-death struggle to defeat the plague and the success of disciplinary institutions in doing so offers a lesson that transforms police, schools, factories, hospitals, and prisons. It marks the birth of a new social order. Look at how efficient power now operates since all limits on pure authority have been removed in the presence of the plague. "Rulers," Foucault writes, "dreamt of the state of the plague."[5] In the perfectly segmented, surveilled plague town, Foucault finds the "utopia of the perfectly governed city."

If you are reading this, it is because you lived through the plague of SARS-CoV-2, the virus that causes COVID-19. You require no primer from Foucault on the plague town. You understand it much better than he. You are perfectly aware of the measures taken when the virus came to town. As we write this, sheltering in place and finishing this book, but now also marching and organizing in the streets against police, we are struck by the fact that Foucault's analysis of the "political dream of the plague" includes no consideration of the plague itself, or any notion that the plague may also be police. What use is an analysis of disciplinary institutions in the time of plague, such as police, that ignores the specific and particular nature of the virus that gives rise to it? What happens to this analysis when we take the virus—take nature—seriously?

Consider SARS-CoV-2. It is novel, fugitive, and lethal. We know very little about it. What we think we know remains elusive. It appears to strike some cities and countries worse than others with no simple explanation to account for the difference. It strikes men worse than women, unless it doesn't. Children can be infected but appear largely immune from its effects. There are baffling postinfection immune responses among some children, and these appear to come without respiratory distress. Some people are infected, fall ill, recover, and then appear immune. A few, however, fall ill again. They are not immune. Some survivors suffer few symptoms, while others describe horrors. They can hardly breathe. Their symptoms linger for weeks. Their bones feel as if they are broken. Confusion clouds their thinking. They struggle to breathe as if held in a police leg lace, robbed of air. What use is the word *order* in these circumstances? And yet some things from the old order stubbornly persist. The virus preys on working people and people of color. It spreads like wildfire through a world already scorched by what Ruth Wilson Gilmore has called the "organized abandonment" of structural adjustment.[6]

It spreads silently, often by asymptomatic carriers. Some spread the virus widely, others infect no one. A French schoolboy "attended three schools and a skiing class while showing symptoms of COVID-19 but did not infect a single person."[7] Genetic evidence suggests it has been lying in wait, "hiding out in nature possibly for decades."[8] The drug Ribavirin induces mutation in viruses, but SARS-CoV-2 proofreads its own genetic code, thus resisting mutations that might weaken it. No existing drug or treatment offers a cure. It imposes its own order.

Most coronaviruses either target the upper respiratory tract or infect cells in the lungs. SARS-CoV-2 does both. Once it finds its host, the virus tears open cell membranes and merges its own membrane with those of its new host. It commandeers the cells of its host to produce more virus. All hell breaks loose. Immune systems go haywire. Organ failure follows. It attacks eyes, lungs, hearts, intestines, blood, sperm, livers, kidneys, spleen, and brains. It would be quicker to list the organs it doesn't attack.

For all that is compelling and fascinating in Foucault's analysis of the plague town and its relation to police and the police powers, a glaring absence remains. Foucault seeks to understand the nature of police without concern for the nature of the plague. But we have lived through this plague and we know that the specifics of the virus matter. The various disciplinary institutions Foucault writes about were unprepared for it in our time and failed to confront it. Some used the plague as a pretense to intensify the policing of migrants and communities of color. Foucault argued that the political dream of the plague inaugurated an intensification of power, one that ramified through society and transformed disciplinary institutions in ways that produced a disciplined society—one more productive, more efficient, more orderly. This cannot be said to be true for this plague.

The very institutions that Foucault identified as having been remade by the plague and that, in turn, remade the world—factories, schools, hospitals, militaries, police, penitentiaries—are the very institutions made suddenly helpless by our plague. Foucault argued that the plague taught disciplinary institutions like prisons and hospitals to efficiently—almost effortlessly—order human multiplicities.[9] Our plague undermines this. We find nothing effortless or efficient in our plague town. Students cannot safely return to schools because no manner of social distancing, surveillance, or discipline seems capable of bringing the virus to heel. Schools, prisons, and factories have become key sites of contagion, not nodes of efficient and effortless discipline and productivity. Untold thousands of prisoners in the United States have been infected; at the time of this writing, 80 percent of all inmates caged in Ohio's Marion Correctional Institution have tested positive. Half of all those infected with SARS-CoV-2 in Arkansas are caged in prisons or are living in nursing homes. Nearly 150,000 farmworkers were infected. If you're hunting for the virus, there's no better place to start than a meat packing plant, an Amazon warehouse, or an industrial farm field. Tens of thousands of meat packers tested positive.

Foucault argues that police took the lesson of the plague town and transformed police into a political technology. Before the plague, argues Foucault, police engaged solely in law enforcement or were instruments for the supervision of political enemies. After the plague, police added a disciplinary function. Police is central to Foucault's arguments. It is police that knitted together the disciplinary institutions in order to "[fill] the gaps."[10] So much for that idea.

It is no accident that the SARS-CoV-2-related quarantine efforts of the first wave in cities and counties in the United States were bookended by two police murders. Louisville police killed Breonna Taylor on March 13, 2020, just as cities and states began imposing shelter-in-place orders to stem the spread of the virus. And just as those cities began "opening up," on May 25, 2020, Minneapolis police killed George Floyd. The plague, in other words, is not only SARS-CoV-2 but also police. The experience of our twin plagues—the virus and police—demonstrated that police have fabricated an order that, as Tyler Wall points out in this volume, secures the conditions for the human, and capital, to exist in the first place. This is a category—the "human"—violently defined and delimited by police. Police define and patrol the line between the monstrous and the human in order to defend the conditions necessary for capital to circulate, which means the job of police is to maim and kill in service to an order we know allows the virus to circulate.

Everything police does is a matter of *discretionary choice* designed to serve class interests and patrol racial lines. And so the best way to defeat SARS-CoV-2 is to defeat police. What good is police, our so-called experts at neutralizing threats and hot spots and confronting emergencies, in this world? During "normal" emergencies and crises, the police expansionists, as

Philip V. McHarris calls them in this volume, repair lost faith in police by reminding us that police are not just irreplaceable but essential to civilization. The twin plagues we face makes this lie more ridiculous than ever. The plague mocks the reformist claim that police is essential to good order. There is no new training tactic or hiring standard that police can implement to fight the virus. There is no less-than-lethal weapon in the police arsenal to overcome the virus. There are no bad apples to throw out of the force. Community policing makes everything worse.

Police have enforced social distancing orders in New York almost exclusively against people of color. Between March 16 and May 5, 2020, the NYPD handed out 374 summonses to people, 81 percent of whom were Black or Hispanic. In Brooklyn, out of forty-one total arrests for violating social distancing guidelines, thirty-five were Black people. Even New York mayor Bill de Blasio, enthusiastic defender of police despite what many rank-and-file cops believe, announced that NYPD officers would no longer enforce mask-wearing because, as he put it, "trust and cooperation" between police and community is most important in a pandemic.[11]

But it is not enough to say that police cannot defeat the virus, or that police are engaging in the same violent, racialized tactics as always. Police have also helped fabricate the current catastrophe. This is in part the argument Neil Smith made when he wrote of Hurricane Katrina that there is no such thing as a natural disaster.[12] Andrea Miller makes a similar argument in this volume when she writes about what she calls "environmental policing" at the Savannah River Site nuclear reservation. The toll that SARS-CoV-2 has taken in working-class communities of color appears "natural" but relies on capitalist and colonial networks to do its damage. There is no such thing as a natural pandemic, in other words. SARS-CoV-2 is deadly but worse in a neoliberal world obsessed with capitalist order, in which police and prisons, just-in-time production, and the valorization of want over need have produced what Mike Davis calls an "abyss of inequality" in an "age of pandemics" that requires more, and more intense, policing.[13]

We don't live in a world remade by the plague; we live in a world made by police for the plague. "The need of a constantly expanding market for its products chases the bourgeoisie over the entire surface of the globe. It must nestle everywhere, settle everywhere, establish connections everywhere."[14]

We might say the virus, like the monsters Mark Neocleous writes about in this volume, was "born into the police power." It has been said that the Asian pangolin, commodified for its meat and scales, or the civet cat, hunted and raised for its musk, served as SARS-CoV-2's intermediary host in its spread from bats to humans. This may be how the virus emerged from its damp cave, but it has been the circuits of capital—the connections everywhere—that have allowed the virus to spread to every factory floor, every prison, every nursing home, and every public housing building.

The virus, like police, nestled and settled everywhere, but it is especially lethal for working-class communities of color and to Native peoples in settler colonial societies, the "forever-enemies" of police that Melanie K. Yazzie writes about in this volume. The virus, like the Minneapolis cop Derek Chauvin who killed George Floyd, robs people of their breath. The virus, like police, focuses its lethality along the lines of race and class. As we write this, a majority of all people infected in New Mexico, for example, are Diné or Pueblo; one-third of all people killed by COVID-19 have been nursing home residents or low-wage workers ordered to the factory floor. This mortality-by-class-and-race is not due to the pathogen's biology or that of its victims, but rather to the ruthless practices of colonial and racist violence that constructed the circuits through which capital, and now the virus, travel. The plague hasn't remade bourgeois power, as Foucault imagined. Rather it has amplified its reach and impact because it travels through a world held together by the circuits of capital, brought to you by police. As we write this, Kern County, California, has recorded among the highest infection rates among California counties. This is no accident. The plague has exposed and expanded the cracks and fractures endemic in the structures of capitalist order. Add COVID-19 to Kern County's "matrix of pesticides and chemicals, air pollution, oil spills, police deaths, and water scarcity" that Julie Sze writes about in this volume.

The wage relation itself has been among the most lethal vectors in this pandemic. In our towns, plagued by police and SARS-CoV-2, the police powers have been used to defend the right of corporations to put low-wage "essential" workers in harm's way. If there is anything this pandemic has made clear, it is that the mandate of police is to fabricate a racialized, bourgeois order where capital can freely circulate. And the virus reveals that police can't even do that very well.

SARS-CoV-2 has slowed, even arrested in some places, the circuits of capital. As Travis Linnemann argues in this volume, police power is "the sovereign power over life and death." The police power is nothing if not a power "actively involved in seizing the necessary material of existence and administering if not celebrating everyday domination and death." The plague of police violence does not undermine the institution of police, and this has been because of the fundamental myth—the fantasy of police in the words of Rachel Herzing in the foreword—that police serve as the guarantors of civilization. The virus makes this myth difficult to sustain. As Linnemann argues, "To find refuge and security from the monster, political subjects must submit to the violent monstrosity from above, the sovereign state and its police." But rather than offer protection from this virus, police and the police powers amplify the threat and the emergency against the poor, the working class, communities of color, and Indigenous peoples. The police preside over a world "going up in flames," as Axel González puts it in this volume, and yet authorities at all levels turn to the police powers as a means of fabricating a "postpandemic" order. They hold fast to their language of reform. They still blame enraged communities marching in the streets. They still think police is the solution. They still claim police murders, such as the brutal killings of Breonna Taylor and George Floyd, are merely aberrations.

Police will make all things worse because the nature of our twin plagues reveals the abolitionist truth that police—all carceral institutions—do not seek efficient and productive modes of social organization. The institution of police does not produce genuine safety or even, as Foucault imagined, productive modes of discipline. A violent, cruel status quo is all police produces. This moment of twin plagues, however, reveals the fissures of this police edifice of order. While it is too early to know if these cracks will take down the entire structure, one thing is certain: police cannot respond to the virus with anything other than the violence and threat of violence that police bring to every situation.

The nature of police is not to protect people and communities but to use violence to fabricate and sustain the conditions necessary for racial capitalism, pandemic or no pandemic. While Minneapolis protestors marching against the police wore masks to reduce their and others' risk of infection, the police fired tear gas and arrested hundreds of people, placing more and more at risk of infection. Just as the pandemic has not stopped antipolice violence movements from their demands for racial justice, so, too, has the pandemic not stopped racialized patterns of police violence.

What, then, replaces police? Against the threat of SARS-CoV-2, it has been solidarity, not police and its violence, that has knitted together the torn fabric of social life in our plague towns. This is our political dream of the plague. With food banks shuttered and many school lunch programs suspended, vast mutual aid groups emerged to replace the disciplinary institutions. Mutual aid sustained people and communities ravaged by COVID-19. In Wuhan, the novelist Fang Fang wrote of the self-organized neighborhood groups that spontaneously emerged. Autonomous grocery collectives formed block by block, building by building in order to distribute food and supplies to those in need.[15] There is revolutionary potential in the solidarity of mutual aid because it threatens the order police fabricate and upon which capital depends. This happened nearly everywhere, but it is no accident that many of the most robust COVID-19 mutual aid networks in the United States can be found in communities like Kern County, California, or Minneapolis, Minnesota, or Ferguson, Missouri, or Korryn Gaines's Baltimore neighborhood that David Correia wrote about in this volume. Many of these groups and networks pivoted when the police tear-gas cannisters started flying. These are communities populated by low-wage "essential" workers, the same people Foucault's disciplinary institutions considered expendable. Police caged them in prisons. Bosses ordered them to the factory floor. Corporate farms sentenced them to the fields. The disciplinary institutions abandoned these communities. They offered no relief from the plague to Black, Native, and working-class communities. It was there, in communities long ravaged by police, that we caught a glimpse of solidarity and reciprocity, of cooperation and care, of a world beyond police.[16]

NOTES

FOREWORD: THE FANTASY OF POLICE

1. While the grotesque on-camera murder of George Floyd under the knee of Derek Chauvin is widely referenced as the catalyst for the summer 2020 uprisings, nearly 850 people have been documented as being killed by police in the United States as of the time of this writing. If we include those not reported, the numbers are likely much higher.

2. See Sam Levin, "Minneapolis Lawmakers Vow to Disband Police Department in Historic Move," *Guardian*, June 7, 2020; "Seattle City Council Overrides Mayor Durkan's Vetoes on Police Defunding," *KREM2* (blog), September 21, 2020, https://www.krem.com/article/news/local /seattle/seattle-city-council-will-vote-on-durkans-budget-vetoes/281 -81a364d7-5155-443a-8ad1-e0583ef52959; and K. Rambo, "Defunding the Portland Police: The Local Abolition Movement, Explained," *Oregon Live* (blog), *Oregonian*, June 16, 2020, https://www.msn.com/en-us/news/us /defunding-the-portland-police-the-local-abolition-movement-explained /ar-BB15zlfK.

3. Astead W. Herndon, "How a Pledge to Dismantle the Minneapolis Police Collapsed," *New York Times*, September 26, 2020.

4. Mitch Dudek and Tom Schuba, "Antioch Teen Arrested in Fatal Shooting during Protests in Kenosha," *Chicago Sun-Times*, August 26, 2020.

5. Jeremy Stahl, "Cleveland Police Union Boss Says Awful Thing about Tamir Rice Again," *Slate*, April 25, 2016, https://slate.com/news-and-politics /2016/04/steve-loomis-says-awful-thing-about-tamir-rice-again.html; Sabrina Siddiqui, "Darren Wilson Testimony: Michael Brown Looked Like 'A Demon,'" *HuffPost*, November, 25, 2014, https://www.huffpost.com /entry/darren-wilson-testimony_n_6216620; Greg Botelho, "What Happened the Night Trayvon Martin Died," *CNN*, May 23, 2012, https:// www.cnn.com/2012/05/18/justice/florida-teen-shooting-details/index.html.

INTRODUCTION: ON THE NATURE OF THE POLICE

1.   Michel Foucault, *Power/Knowledge: Selected Interviews and Other Writings, 1972–1977*, ed. Colin Gordon (New York: Pantheon, 1980), 47, punctuation modified. Outside a small, albeit robust, critical literature, police receives little scholarly attention outside of criminology. It's understandable. Why would any self-respecting critical scholar take police seriously as an object of analysis when it is the primary object of analysis of so bankrupt a discipline?

2.   Michel Foucault, *"Society Must Be Defended": Lectures at the Collège de France, 1975–1976*, trans. David Macey (New York: Picador, 2003), 50.

3.   Marlese Durr, "What Is the Difference Between Slave Patrols and Modern Day Policing? Institutional Violence in a Community of Color," *Critical Sociology* 41, no. 6 (2015): 875.

4.   Sherene Razack, *Dying from Improvement: Inquests and Inquiries into Indigenous Deaths in Custody* (Toronto: University of Toronto Press, 2015), 23.

5.   See Mark Neocleous, *The Fabrication of Social Order: A Critical Theory of Police Power* (London: Pluto Press, 2000).

6.   Guy Debord, "The Decline and Fall of the Spectacle-Commodity Economy," in *Situationist International Anthology*, ed. Ken Knabb (Berkeley: Bureau of Public Secrets, 2006), 194–220.

7.   This is another reason why few critical scholars theorize police. Criminology as a discipline has constrained its consideration of police into such a banal and tedious concern that the very consideration of police itself becomes little more than a banal and tedious concern.

8.   Benjamin used this phrase "a beast that goes berserk" to describe the ruthless reaction to any meaningful challenge to bourgeois order. Walter Benjamin, *Selected Writings: Volume 1, 1913–1926*, eds. Marcus Bullock and Michael W. Jennings (Cambridge, MA: Belknap Press of Harvard University Press, 1996), 246.

9.   Jorge Fitz-Gibbon, "Here's Everything We Know About the Death of George Floyd," *New York Post*, March 28, 2020.

10. Markus Dubber, *The Dual Penal State: The Crisis of Criminal Law in Comparative-Historical Perspective* (Oxford: Oxford University Press, 2018).

11. Johann Gottlieb Fichte, *The Science of Rights*, trans. A. E. Kroeger (Philadelphia: J. P. Lippincott, 1869), 377. Thanks to Mark Neocleous for bringing Fichte's use of policing's "peculiar nature" to our attention.

12. Karl Polanyi, *The Great Transformation* (Boston: Beacon Press, 1957), 3.

13. James O'Connor, *Natural Causes: Essays in Ecological Marxism* (New York: Guilford Press, 1998), 164.

14. E. H. Chapin, *Humanity in the City* (New York: De Witt & Davenport, 1854).

15. Rudolph W. Giuliani and William J. Bratton, *Police Strategy No. 5: Reclaiming the Public Spaces of New York* (New York: Police Department, City of New York, 1994).

16. China Miéville, "On Social Sadism: Essence, Excrescence and the Politics of Neoliberal Cruelty," *Salvage* 2 (2015): 49.

17. Mariame Kaba, foreword to *Invisible No More: Police Violence Against Black Women and Women of Color,* by Andrea Ritchie (Boston: Beacon Press, 2017), xv.

18. See, for example, Andrea Ritchie, *Invisible No More: Police Violence Against Black Women and Women of Color* (Boston: Beacon Press, 2017); Mark Neocleous, *The Fabrication of Social Order: A Critical Theory of Police Power* (London: Pluto Press, 2000); and Markus Dirk Dubber, *The Police Power: Patriarchy and the Foundations of American Government* (New York: Columbia University Press, 2005).

CHAPTER ONE: INVENTING HUMANITY

This chapter is a revised version of a previous published essay. See Tyler Wall, "The Police Invention of Humanity: Notes on the 'Thin Blue Line,'" *Crime, Media, Culture* 16, no. 3 (2020): 319–36.

1. See William Parker, *Thin Blue Line: LAPD Annual Report* (Los Angeles: Los Angeles Police Department, 1951). More than any other person, Parker is most associated with the thin blue line (TBL) phrase during the early years of the post–World War II era. In fact, he is still so linked to the maxim that he is often incorrectly credited with coining it. Parker certainly put this melodramatic shorthand to great rhetorical use. Thirteen years before repressive policing practices sparked the Watts riots of 1965, Parker hosted *The Thin Blue Line*, a local television show that gave him and other cops a platform to convey police perspectives to large audiences. On this show and in more general terms, as Alisa Kramer comments, Parker "used his bully pulpit to praise his officers, and warn the public of the communist menace and lax morality which would hasten the downfall of western civilization. Only the police, he argued, could maintain democracy and the social order." See Alisa Kramer, "William H. Parker and the Thin Blue Line: Politics, Public Relations and Policing in Postwar Los Angeles" (PhD diss., American University, 2007). Parker was right about the indispensable role of police in the fabrication of postwar order. This is not to accept this mythology's premise that there is no good life without police. Rather, it is to account for the truth about the police as a coercive instrument of class rule. As Max Felker-Kantor astutely notes in his history of the postwar LAPD, "Police

power was not incidental or supplemental, but constitutive of post-war city politics and authority." See Max Felker-Kantor, *Policing Los Angeles: Race, Resistance, and the Rise of the LAPD* (Chapel Hill: University of North Carolina Press, 2018), 4.

2. See Iris Marion Young, "The Logic of Masculinist Protection: Reflections on the Current Security State," *Signs: Journal of Women in Culture and Society* 29, no. 1 (2003): 1–25; Wendy Brown, *States of Injury: Power and Freedom in Late Modernity* (Princeton: Princeton University Press, 1995).

3. See Dana Boyd, *National Manhood: Capitalist Civilization and the Imagined Fraternity of White Men* (Durham: Duke University Press, 1998); Bonnie Mann, *Sovereign Masculinity: Gender Lessons from the War on Terror* (Oxford: Oxford University Press, 2014).

4. For a useful theorization of this movement, see Nijah Cunningham and Tiana Reed, "Blue Life," *The New Inquiry*, September 24, 2018. For a very helpful discussion of the ways the deaths of police officers are exploited by the police establishment and others, see Justin Turner, "'It All Started with Eddie': Thanatopolitics, Police Power, and the Murder of Edward Byrne," *Crime, Media, Culture: An International Journal* 15, no. 2 (2019): 239–58.

5. *FBI Law Enforcement Bulletin* 43, no. 12 (Washington, DC: FBI, 1974), 14.

6. Niko Georgiades, "Bulletproof Warrior Training Manual Released," *Unicorn Riot*, May 25, 2018. I want to particularly thank Travis Linnemann for pointing out this quotation to me.

7. On the thin blue line as political theology, see Travis Linnemann and Corina Medley, "Fear the Monster! Racialized Violence, Sovereign Power and the Thin Blue Line," in *Routledge International Handbook on Fear of Crime*, eds. M. Lee and G. Mythen (Abingdon: Routledge, 2017), 65–81; on political demonology see Michael Rogin, *Ronald Reagan, the Movie and Other Episodes in Political Demonology* (Berkeley: University of California Press, 1987).

8. On violence as regenerative see Richard Slotkin, *Regeneration through Violence: The Mythology of the American Frontier, 1600–1860* (New York: Harper Perennial, 1973); S. Schillings, *Enemies of All Humankind: Fictions of Legitimate Violence* (Hanover, NH: Dartmouth College Press, 2017); see also Mark Neocleous, *The Universal Adversary: Security, Capital, and "The Enemies of All Mankind"* (New York: Routledge, 2016).

9. Bill Clinton, "Law Enforcement Vigil 5/13/93," May 13, 1993, Clinton Digital Library, https://clinton.presidentiallibraries.us/items/show/32958.

10. Gary Allen, "Ten-Thirteen: Our Local Police Need Help," *American Opinion* (September 1967): 1–18.

11. Christopher Wilson, *Cop Knowledge: Police Power and Cultural Narrative in Twentieth-Century America* (Chicago: University of Chicago Press, 2000), 5.

12. See Mark Neocleous, *War Power, Police Power* (Edinburgh: Edinburgh University Press, 2014).

13. Stuart Schrader, "More than Cosmetic Changes: The Challenges of Experiments with Police Demilitarization in the 1960s and 1970s," *Journal of Urban History* 46, no. 5 (2017): 1002–25.

14. George Jackson, *Soledad Brother: The Prison Letters of George Jackson* (Chicago: Lawrence Hill Books, 1994). Jackson wrote, "You've heard the patronizing shit about the thin blue line that protects property and the owners of property."

15. Ruth Wilson Gilmore and Craig Gilmore, "Beyond Bratton," in *Policing the Planet*, eds. Jordan Camp and Christina Heatherton (London: Verso Books, 2016), 173–99.

16. See Elizabeth Anker, *Orgies of Feeling: Melodrama and the Politics of Freedom* (Durham: Duke University Press, 2014).

17. See Michael Taussig, *Walter Benjamin's Grave* (Chicago: University of Chicago Press, 2010).

18. See Grégoire Chamayou, *Manhunts: A Philosophical History* (Princeton: Princeton University Press, 2012).

19. The phrase is not of so recent origin, seemingly forming in the nineteenth century as a celebration of heroic white manhood via soldiers dying and killing in the name of saving the nation. Conventional wisdom suggests the "thin blue line" takes as its template the "thin red line," a reference to red-coated British soldiers during the Crimean War in the 1850s. The idea of police as a "thin blue line" circulated at least as early as the 1860s in the pages of *London Society*—"a ruck of policeman walk in a 'thin blue line'"—and probably much earlier due to British bobbies, formed in 1829, who notably donned blue uniforms. Given that upstart urban police forces in the northern United States during the late 1830s and early 1840s were influenced by Peele's British experiment, including borrowing the blue uniforms, it likely didn't take long for the slogan to attach to US cops.

20. Sylvia Wynter, "Unsettling the Coloniality of Being/Power/Truth/Freedom: Towards the Human, After Man, its Overrepresentation—An Argument," *CR: The New Centennial Review* 3, no. 3 (2003): 260.

21. Diren Valayden, "Racial Feralization: Targeting Race in the Age of 'Planetary Urbanization,'" *Theory, Culture & Society* 33, nos. 7–8 (2016): 161.

22. See Ruth Wilson Gilmore, "Abolition Geography and the Problem of Innocence," in *Futures of Black Radicalism*, eds. Gaye Theresa Johnson and Alex Lubin (London: Verso Books, 2017), 225–40.

23. See, for instance, Mark Neocleous, *The Fabrication of Social Order: A Critical Theory of Police Power* (London: Pluto Press, 2000); Bryan Wagner,

Disturbing the Peace: Black Culture and the Police Power after Slavery (Cambridge, MA: Harvard University Press, 2013); and Markus Dubber, *The Police Power: Patriarchy and the Foundations of American Government* (New York: Columbia University Press, 2005).

24. On political bestiary and state violence, see Eduardo Mendieta, "Political Bestiary: On the Uses of Violence," *Insights* 3, no. 5 (2010): 14–32.

25. Frantz Fanon, *The Wretched of the Earth*, trans. Richard Philcox (New York: Grove Press, 2005), 7.

26. Fanon, *Wretched of the Earth*, 3.

27. See Taussig, *Walter Benjamin's Grave*, 185.

28. Parker quoted in Felker-Kantor, *Policing Los Angeles*, 5. William H. Parker, "Surveillance by Wiretap or Dictograph: Threat or Protection? A Police Chief's Opinion," *California Law Review* 42, no. 5 (1954): 728.

29. Barry Ryan, *Statebuilding and Police Reform: The Freedom of Security* (London: Routledge, 2011).

30. See Tyler Wall, "Ordinary Emergency: Police, Drones, and Geographies of Legal Terror," *Antipode* 48, no. 4 (2016): 1122–39.

31. Charles Sloane, "Dogs in War, Police Work, and on Patrol," *Police Science* 46 (1955): 395; Tyler Wall, "For the Very Existence of Civilization": The Police Dog and Racial Terror," *American Quarterly* 68, no. 4 (2016): 861–82.

32. The association between TBL and jungle law is quite clear in newspaper archives and other sources like the FBI bulletin. Where TBL is invoked, it is not uncommon for the "jungle" trope to appear as well. Here, I am only highlighting a few examples across different time periods. For a fascinating extended discussion on "jungle discourse" during the Progressive Era see Michael Lundbland, *The Birth of the Jungle: Animality in Progressive Literature and Culture* (Oxford: Oxford University Press, 2013).

33. "The Sidewalks of New York," *Alexandria Daily Town Talk*, October 20, 1925.

34. Reagan quoted in Lee Lescaze, "Reagan Blames Crime on 'Human Predator,'" *Washington Post*, September 29, 1981.

35. Reagan quoted in Lescasze, "Reagan Blames Crime on 'Human Predator.'"

36. See Valayden, "Racial Feralization."

37. Sylvia Wynter, "No Humans Involved: An Open Letter to My Colleagues," *Forum N.H.I.—Knowledge for the 21st Century: Knowledge on Trial* 11 (1994): 44.

38. Wynter, "No Humans Involved," 35.

39. See Allen Feldman, *Archives of the Insensible: Of War, Photopolitics, and Dead Memory* (Chicago: University of Chicago Press, 2015); Jacques Derrida, *The Beast and the Sovereign*, vol. 1, trans. Geoffrey Bennington (Chicago: University of Chicago Press, 2009); the phrase "murderous enthusiasm"

comes from Paul Gilroy, *Postcolonial Melancholia* (New York: Columbia University Press, 2005), 43.

40. See Michel Foucault, *"Society Must Be Defended": Lectures at the Collège de France 1975–1976*, trans. David Macey (New York: Picador, 2003).

41. Gilroy, *Postcolonial Melancholia*, 32; see also Paul Gilroy, "The Black Atlantic and the Re-Enchantment of Humanism," Tanner Lectures on Human Values, Yale University, February 21, 2014.

42. Although not within the immediate purview of this chapter, it is not a stretch to think of the TBL as a fascist, or fascistic, discourse in the ways it celebrates state authoritarianism, executive violence, and racialized hierarchies while also appealing to naturalistic language such as civilization and savagery. The adoption of TBL by overt neo-Nazis helps bring these connections more directly to the surface.

43. Ruth Wilson Gilmore, "Fatal Couplings of Power and Difference: Notes on Racism and Geography," *Professional Geographer* 54, no. 1 (2002): 16.

44. James Baldwin, "A Report from Occupied Territory," *Nation*, July 11, 1966.

45. Anne McClintock, *Imperial Leather: Race, Gender, and Sexuality in the Colonial Context* (New York: Routledge, 1995), 30.

46. Samera Esmeir, *Juridical Humanity: A Colonial History* (Stanford: Stanford University Press, 2012).

47. Denise Ferreira da Silva, "No-Bodies: Law, Raciality and Violence," *Griffith Law Review* 18, no. 2 (2009): 235.

48. See Sara Jaffe, "Trump Already has a Wall. It's the Thin Blue Line," *New Republic*, September 1, 2017.

49. See Mark Neocleous, *Critique of Security* (Montreal: McGill-Queen's University Press, 2008).

50. Walter Benjamin, "Critique of Violence," in *Reflections: Essays, Aphorisms, Autobiographical Writings*, ed. Peter Demetz (New York: Schocken Books, 1978), 277–300.

51. L. Deutsch, "Jurors Heeded Warning of 'Thin Blue Line,'" *News-Messenger*, April 30, 1992.

52. Cedric Robinson, "Race, Capitalism, and the Antidemocracy," in *Reading Rodney King/Reading Urban Uprising*, ed. Robert Gooding-Williams (London: Routledge, 1993), 78.

53. Feldman, *Archives of the Insensible*.

54. Deutsch, "Jurors Heeded Warning of 'Thin Blue Line.'"

55. Thomas Hobbes, *Leviathan* (London: Penguin Books, 1984).

56. Dimitris Vardoulakis, *Sovereignty and Its Other: Toward the Dejustification of Violence* (New York: Fordham University Press, 2013). Vardoulakis doesn't mean these justifications are universal, only that those justifying sovereign

violence naturalize them as universal even if they often signify different things across history.

57. John Locke, *Second Treatise of Government*, ed. C. B. Macpherson (Indianapolis: Hackett, 1980), 14.

58. K-Sue Park, "The Colonial History of Social Contracts," *The Nakba Files*, September 13, 2016, http:// nakbafiles.org/2016/09/13/symposium -the-colonial-history-of-social-contracts/.

59. Christopher La Barbera, *States of Nature: Animality and the Polis* (New York: Peter Lang, 2012).

60. See Charles Mills, *The Racial Contract* (Ithaca, NY: Cornell University Press, 1997).

61. Kay Anderson, *Race and the Crisis of Humanism* (London: Routledge, 2007).

62. On liberalism's exclusion clauses see Domenico Losurdo, *Liberalism: A Counter-History* (London: Verso Books, 2011), for an overview of the race/ species link re humanism and racism see Zakiyyah Iman Jackson, "Animal: New Directions in the Theorization of Race and Posthumanism," *Feminist Studies* 39, no. 3 (2013): 669–85.

63. Carl Schmitt, *The Leviathan in the State Theory of Thomas Hobbes: Meaning and Failure of a Political Symbol*, trans. George Schwab and Erna Hilfstein (Westport, CT, and London: Greenwood Press, 1996), 31.

64. See, for instance, Giorgio Agamben, *Homo Sacer: Sovereign Power and Bare Life*, trans. Daniel Heller-Roazen (Stanford: Stanford University Press, 1998).

65. Mary Nyquist, *Arbitrary Rule: Slavery, Tyranny, and the Power of Life and Death* (Chicago: University of Chicago Press, 2013), 260.

66. See Barry Lopez, *Of Wolves and Men* (New York: Charles Scribner's Sons, 1978).

67. David Hunter, *The Moon Is Always Full* (Nashville: Rutledge Hill Press, 1989).

68. Dave Grossman and Loren Christenson, *On Combat* (Millstadt, IL: Warrior Science Publications, 2008); Dave Grossman, *On Killing* (New York: Back Bay Books, 1995).

69. For a great discussion on the symbolism and political theories of human/ wolf mergers see Carla Freccero, "A Race of Wolves," *Yale French Studies* 127 (2015): 110–23.

70. See Wall, "'For the Very Existence of Civilization.'"

71. Stephanie Rogish and Dave Grossman, *Sheepdogs: Meet Our Nation's Warriors*, illustrated by Joey Karwal (West Bend, WI: Delta Defense, 2013).

72. See Grégoire Chamayou, *Manhunts: A Philosophical History*, trans. Steven Rendall (Princeton: Princeton University Press, 2012).

CHAPTER TWO: DISRUPTING ORDER

1. "Mapping Police Violence," Mapping Police Violence, accessed May 4, 2020, https://mappingpoliceviolence.org.

2. Josiah Bates, "Report: Police Shootings Continue Unabated Despite COVID-19 Shutdowns," *Time*, August 19, 2020.

3. "COVID19 and Policing," COVID-19 Policing Project, Community Resource Hub, accessed September 30, 2020, https://communityresourcehub.org/covid19-policing/.

4. See Frantz Fanon, *The Wretched of the Earth*, trans. Richard Philcox (New York: Grove Atlantic, 2018), 6.

5. Jackie Wang, *Carceral Capitalism* (Cambridge, MA: MIT Press, 2018).

6. Violent Crime Control and Law Enforcement Act of 1994, H.R.3355, 103rd Cong. (1993–94).

7. "INCITE!-Critical Resistance Statement," INCITE! and Critical Resistance, Statement on Gender Violence and the Prison Industrial Complex, 2001, https://incite-national.org/incite-critical-resistance-statement/.

8. "Sexual Victimization Reported by Adult Correctional Authorities, 2012–15," Bureau of Justice Statistics (BJS), accessed October 1, 2020, https://www.bjs.gov/index.cfm?ty=pbdetail&iid=6326.

9. John Kelly and Mark Nichols, "We Found 85,000 Cops Who've Been Investigated for Misconduct. Now You Can Read Their Records," *USA Today*, June 11, 2020.

10. David Weisburd, Clair White, and Alese Wooditch, "Does Collective Efficacy Matter at the Micro Geographic Level? Findings from a Study of Street Segments," *British Journal of Criminology* 60 no. 4 (2020): 873–91. Robert J. Sampson, Stephen W. Raudenbush, and Felton Earls, "Neighborhoods and Violent Crime: A Multilevel Study of Collective Efficacy," *Science* 277, no. 5328 (1997): 918–24.

11. Lorraine Daston, *The Moral Authority of Nature* (Chicago: University of Chicago Press, 2010).

12. Rachel E. Morgan and Jennifer L. Truman, "Criminal Victimization, 2019," Office of Justice Programs, September 14, 2020, https://www.bjs.gov/index.cfm?ty=pbdetail&iid=7046.

13. Stuart Hall, Chas Critcher, Tony Jefferson, John Clarke, and Brian Roberts, *Policing the Crisis: Mugging, the State and Law and Order* (London: Macmillan, 2013).

14. Jeff Asher and Ben Horwitz, "How Do the Police Actually Spend Their Time?" *New York Times*, June 19, 2020. Rebecca Neusteter and Megan O'Toole, "Every Three Seconds: Unlocking Police Data on Arrests," Vera

Institute, January 2019, https://www.vera.org/publications/arrest-trends
-every-three-seconds-landing/arrest-trends-every-three-seconds/overview.

15. "Clearance Rate: Crime by Type in the U.S. 2018," *Statista*, retrieved October 1, 2020, https://www.statista.com/statistics/194213/crime -clearance-rate-by-type-in-the-us/.

16. Naomi Murakawa, *The First Civil Right: How Liberals Built Prison America* (Oxford: Oxford University Press, 2014).

17. Alex S. Vitale, *The End of Policing* (London: Verso Books, 2017), 50.

18. Elizabeth Hinton and DeAnza Cook, "The Mass Criminalization of Black Americans: A Historical Overview," *Annual Review of Criminology* 4, no.1 (2020): 1–26.

19. Hinton and Cook, "Mass Criminalization of Black Americans."

20. Vitale, *End of Policing*, 50.

21. Micol Seigel, *Violence Work: State Power and the Limits of Police* (Durham: Duke University Press, 2018).

22. Julian Go, "The Imperial Origins of American Policing: Militarization and Imperial Feedback in the Early 20th Century," *American Journal of Sociology* 125, no. 5 (2020):1193–1254.

23. Charles Houston Harris and Louis R. Sadler, *The Texas Rangers and the Mexican Revolution: The Bloodiest Decade, 1910–1920* (Albuquerque: University of New Mexico Press, 2007).

24. Christopher P. Wilson, *Cop Knowledge: Police Power and Cultural Narrative in Twentieth-Century America* (Chicago: University of Chicago Press, 2000).

25. Micol Seigel, "Objects of Police History," *Journal of American History* 102, no. 1 (2015): 152–61.

26. See Elizabeth Hinton, *From the War on Poverty to the War on Crime: The Making of Mass Incarceration in America* (Cambridge, MA: Harvard University Press, 2016); Murakawa, *First Civil Right*.

27. Ruth D. Peterson and Lauren J. Krivo, *Divergent Social Worlds: Neighborhood Crime and the Racial-Spatial Divide* (New York: Russell Sage Foundation, 2010).

28. National Advisory Commission on Civil Disorders, *A Report by the Kerner Commission* (US Government Printing Office, 1968).

29. Hinton and Cook, "Mass Criminalization of Black Americans."

30. Alondra Nelson, *Body and Soul: The Black Panther Party and the Fight against Medical Discrimination* (Minneapolis: University of Minnesota Press, 2011).

31. *Law Enforcement Assistance Act of 1965–Hearings Before a Subcommittee of the Senate Committee on the Judiciary*, 89th Cong., 1st Session, (1965), https://www.ncjrs.gov/App/Publications/abstract.aspx?ID=134196.

32. Hinton, *From the War on Poverty to the War on Crime*.

33. See Murakawa, *First Civil Right*; Hinton and Cook, "Mass Criminalization of Black Americans."

34. Communities United, Make the Road New York, Padres & Jóvenes Unidos, and the Right on Justice Alliance, *The $3.4 Trillion Mistake: The Cost of Mass Incarceration and Criminalization, and How Justice Reinvestment Can Build a Better Future for All*, 2016, accessed January 28, 2021, https://maketheroadny .org/pix_reports/Justice%20Reinvestment%20Final%20Report.pdf.

35. Vesla M. Weaver, "Frontlash: Race and the Development of Punitive Crime Policy," *Studies in American Political Development* 21, no. 2 (2007): 230–65.

36. Michelle Alexander, *The New Jim Crow: Mass Incarceration in the Age of Colorblindness* (New York: New Press, 2010).

37. Robert W. Fairlie, "Drug Dealing and Legitimate Self Employment," *Journal of Labor Economics* 20, no. 3 (2002): 538–67.

38. Doris Marie Provine, "Race and Inequality in the War on Drugs," *Annual Review of Law and Social Science* 7 (2011): 41–60.

39. Jon Hurwitz and Mark Peffley, "Playing the Race Card in the Post–Willie Horton Era: The Impact of Racialized Code Words on Support for Punitive Crime Policy," *Public Opinion Quarterly* 69, no. 1 (2005): 99–112.

40. See Murakawa, *First Civil Right*; John L. Worrall and Tomislav V. Kovandzic, "COPS Grants and Crime Revisited," *Criminology* 45, no. 1 (2007): 159–90.

41. Marion Orr, *Black Social Capital: The Politics of School Reform in Baltimore, 1986–1998*, Studies in Government and Public Policy (Lawrence: University Press of Kansas, 1999).

42. Philip Bump, "Over the Past 60 Years, More Spending on Police Hasn't Necessarily Meant Less Crime," *Washington Post*, June 7, 2020.

43. Amanda Geller, Jeffrey Fagan, Tom Tyler, and Bruce G. Link, "Aggressive Policing and the Mental Health of Young Urban Men," *American Journal of Public Health* 104, no. 12 (2014): 2321–27; Christopher M. Sullivan and Zachary P. O'Keeffe, "Evidence that Curtailing Proactive Policing Can Reduce Major Crime," *Nature Human Behaviour* 1, no. 10 (2017): 730–37; Joscha Legewie and Jeffrey Fagan, "Aggressive Policing and the Educational Performance of Minority Youth," *American Sociological Review* 84, no. 2 (2019): 220–47.

44. US Bureau of Economic Analysis, "Government Current Expenditures: State and Local: Public Order and Safety: Police," FRED, Federal Reserve Bank of St. Louis, 1959, https://fred.stlouisfed.org/series/G160851A027NBEA.

45. Joanna C. Schwartz, "How Qualified Immunity Fails," *Yale Law Journal* 127 (2017): 1–245.

46. Aziz Z. Huq and Christopher Muller, "The War on Crime as Precursor to the War on Terror," *International Journal of Law, Crime and Justice* 36, no. 4 (2008): 215–29.

47. See Sarah Brayne, "Big Data Surveillance: The Case of Policing," *American Sociological Review* 82, no. 5 (2017): 977–1008; and Elizabeth E. Joh, "Policing by Numbers: Big Data and the Fourth Amendment," *Washington Law Review* 89 (2014): 35.

48. Elizabeth E. Joh, "The New Surveillance Discretion: Automated Suspicion, Big Data, and Policing," *Harvard Law and Policy Review* 10 (2016): 15.

49. Joh, "Policing by Numbers."

50. Josmar Trujillo and Alex S. Vitale, "Gang Takedowns in the De Blasio Era: The Dangers of 'Precision Policing,'" Policing and Social Justice Project at Brooklyn College, 2019.

51. Jeffrey Lane, "The Digital Street: An Ethnographic Study of Networked Street Life in Harlem," *American Behavioral Scientist* 60, no. 1 (2016): 43–58.

52. See Elizabeth E. Joh, "Police Surveillance Machines: A Short History," *The Law and Political Economy (LPE) Project*, June 13, 2018, https://lpeproject .org/blog/police-surveillance-machines-a-short-history/; Stephen William Smith, "Policing Hoover's Ghost: The Privilege for Law Enforcement Techniques," *American Criminal Law Review* 54 (2017): 233; Anna Gunderson et al., "Counterevidence of Crime-Reduction Effects from Federal Grants of Military Equipment to Local Police," *Nature Human Behaviour*, December 7, 2020, https://doi.org/10.1038/s41562-020-00995- 5; and Radley Balko, *The Rise of the Warrior Cop: The Militarization of America's Police Forces* (New York: PublicAffairs Books, 2013).

53. Philip V. McHarris and Thenjiwe McHarris, "The Police Killed George Floyd: Redirect Their Funding Elsewhere," *New York Times*, May 30, 2020.

54. See Kimberlé Crenshaw, Andrea Ritchie, Rachel Anspach, Rachel Gilmer, and Luke Harris, "Say Her Name: Resisting Police Brutality against Black Women," African American Policy Forum, 2015; and Kelly and Nichols, "We Found 85,000 Cops."

55. Jay Dow, "Newark to Slash Police Budget, Ban Racism on the Job for City Employees," *WPIX*, June, 8, 2020, https://www.pix11.com/news /local-news/new-jersey/newark-to-slash-police-budget-ban-racism-on-the-job -for-city-employees.

56. S. P. Sullivan, "How Should N.J. Reform Police? Lawmakers Eye Host of Changes amid Protests over Killings," *NJ.com*, July 16, 2020, https://www .nj.com/politics/2020/07/how-should-nj-reform-police-lawmakers-eye-host -of-changes-amid-protests-over-killings.html.

57. Brendan McQuade, "The Camden Police Department Is Not a Model for Policing in the Post–George Floyd Era," *The Appeal*, June 12, 2020, https://theappeal.org/camden-police-george-floyd/.

58. See Julianne Cuba, "Campaign to Remove NYPD from Traffic Enforcement Gains Steam," *Streetsblog New York City*, June 25, 2020, https://nyc.streetsblog.org/2020/06/25/campaign-to-remove-nypd-from-traffic-enforcement-gains-steam/; Joel Rubini and Ben Poston, "LAPD Responds to a Million 911 Calls a Year, but Relatively Few for Violent Crimes," *Los Angeles Times*, July 5, 2020.

59. See "People First! An Oakland Power Projects Report on Policing," Critical Resistance, 2018, https://oaklandpowerprojects.org/. See also "Decoupling Policing from Health Services: Empowering Healthworkers as Anti-Policing Organizers," Oakland Power Projects, accessed January 28, 2021, https://static1.squarespace.com/static/59ead8f9692ebee25b72f17f/t/5b6ab5f7352f535083505c5a/1533720057821/TheOakPowerProj_HEALTHreport.pdf.

60. See Peter Hermann, "He Used to Sell Drugs on D.C. Streets. Now He's Paid to Make Them Safer," *Washington Post,* December 14, 2018; and Ashley Southall, "Police Face Backlash Over Virus Rules. Enter 'Violence Interrupters,'" *New York Times*, May 22, 2020.

61. See "Bay Area Transformative Justice Collective: Building Transformative Justice Responses to Child Sexual Abuse," accessed January 28, 2021, https://batjc.wordpress.com/.

62. Daniel W. Webster, Jennifer Mendel Whitehill, Jon S. Vernick, and Elizabeth M. Parker, "Evaluation of Baltimore's Safe Streets Program: Effects on Attitudes, Participants' Experiences, and Gun Violence," Baltimore, MD: Johns Hopkins Center for the Prevention of Youth Violence (2012); Hermann, "He Used to Sell Drugs on D.C. Streets."

63. Patrick Sharkey, Gerard Torrats-Espinosa, and Delaram Takyar, "Community and the Crime Decline: The Causal Effect of Local Nonprofits on Violent Crime," *American Sociological Review* 82, no. 6 (2017): 1214–40.

64. Sara B. Heller, "Summer Jobs Reduce Violence among Disadvantaged Youth," *Science* 346, no. 6214 (2014): 1219–23.

65. Sara B. Heller, Anuj K. Shah, Jonathan Guryan, Jens Ludwig, Sendhil Mullainathan, and Harold A. Pollack, "Thinking, Fast and Slow? Some Field Experiments to Reduce Crime and Dropout in Chicago," *Quarterly Journal of Economics* 132, no. 1 (2017): 1–54.

66. Charles C. Branas, Rose A. Cheney, John M. MacDonald, Vicky W. Tam, Tara D. Jackson, and Thomas R. Ten Have, "A Difference-in-Differences Analysis of Health, Safety, and Greening Vacant Urban Space," *American Journal of Epidemiology* 174, no. 11 (2011): 1296–1306.

67. "#8toAbolition," #8toAbolition, accessed January 28, 2021, https://www.8toabolition.com/.

68. "TransformHarm," TransformHarm, accessed January 28, 2021, https://transformharm.org/.

69. "Defund the Police," The Movement for Black Lives, accessed January 28, 2021, https://m4bl.org/defund-the-police/.

70. The Electoral Justice Project of the Movement for Black Lives, "The Breathe Act," 2020, https://breatheact.org/.

71. Mary Retta, "MPD150, Reclaim the Block, and the Black Visions Collective Have Been Fighting to Abolish Minneapolis Police for Years," *Teen Vogue*, June 12, 2020, https://www.teenvogue.com/story/mpd150-reclaim-the-block-black-visions-collective-abolish-minneapolis-police-organizing.

72. See, for example, Micol Seigel, *Violence Work: State Power and the Limits of Police* (Durham: Duke University Press, 2018).

73. W. E. B. Du Bois, "The Spawn of Slavery," *African American Classics in Criminology and Criminal Justice* (2002): 83–88.

74. W. E.B. Du Bois, ed., *Black Reconstruction in America: Toward a History of the Part Which Black Folk Played in the Attempt to Reconstruct Democracy in America, 1860–1880* (Abingdon: Routledge, 2017).

75. Angela Y. Davis, *Abolition Democracy: Beyond Empire, Prisons, and Torture* (New York: Seven Stories Press, 2011).

76. Rachel Kushner, "Is Prison Necessary? Ruth Wilson Gilmore Might Change Your Mind," *New York Times*, April 17, 2019.

77. Yves Cabannes, "Participatory Budgeting: A Significant Contribution to Participatory Democracy," *Environment and Urbanization* 16, no. 1 (2004): 27–46.

CHAPTER THREE: THE WHITE DOG AND DARK WATER

1. Laura Pulido, "Flint Michigan, Environmental Racism and Racial Capitalism," *Capitalism Nature Socialism* 27, no. 3 (2016): 1–16.

2. Most notoriously by Sheriff Bull Connor in Alabama, although these police actions are not unique to the South. See Tyler Parry, "Police Dogs and Anti-Black Violence," *Black Perspectives* (blog), July 31, 2017, https://www.aaihs.org/police-dogs-and-anti-black-violence/.

3. Colin Dayan, *The Law Is a White Dog: How Legal Rituals Make and Unmake Persons* (Princeton: Princeton University Press, 2011), 218.

4. Bénédicte Boisseron, *Afro-Dog: Blackness and the Animal Question* (New York: Columbia University Press, 2018), xvii.

5. Examples abound, including Jim Crow legacies, KKK infiltration in the

police force, the mob violence against the only thirteen Black people in the town of Taft in 1975. See Michael Eissinger, "Kern County: California's Deep South," paper presented at *Critical Ethnic Studies and the Future of Genocide: Settler Colonialism/Heteropatriarchy/White Supremacy*, the biannual Critical Ethnic Studies Conference, University of California at Riverside, March 10–12, 2011. On Taft's lynch mob, see Joe Jaras, "Violent Return to a Troubled Past," *Sports Illustrated*, June 23, 1975.

6. "Kern County," US Dept. of the Interior: Natural Resources Revenue Data, https://revenuedata.doi.gov/case-studies/kern/; Jay Jones, "Kern County's Rich Oil Field of History," *Los Angeles Times*, November 27, 2011.

7. "Fracking," Water Education Foundation, accessed February 3, 2021, https://www.watereducation.org/aquapedia-background/fracking.

8. Deborah Gordon and Katherine Garner, "Mapping California's Oil-Water Risks," January 15, 2014, https://carnegieendowment.org/2014/01/15/mapping-california-s-oil-water-risks-pub-54205.

9. These include the Noo ah, the Pahkanapil, the Kawaiisu (Noo ah), the Tübatulabal (Pahkanapil, related to the Shoshone language family), the Palagewan, and the Bankalachi (Toloim). "Native American People of the Kern River Valley," Audubon Kern River Preserve, http://www.kern.audubon.org/cultural_resources.htm.

10. Jeff Nickell, "History: Natives of the Valley," *Bakersfield.com*, July 26, 2013, https://www.bakersfield.com/bakersfield_life/history-natives-of-the-valley/article_7b71a47c-046a-55b6-99b2-ab6d27ecf680.html.

11. Nickell, "History: Natives of the Valley."

12. Dayan, *Law Is a White Dog*, 34.

13. Mark Arax and Rick Wartzman, *The King of California: J. G. Boswell and the Making of a Secret American Empire* (New York: Public Affairs, 2003).

14. Gerald Haslam, "Stop: Tulare Dry Lake," *Invisible 5 Audio Project*, accessed January 28, 2021, http://www.invisible5.org/index.php?page=tulare.

15. *Bakersfield Californian*, "The Story of US: 150 years of Kern County History," *Bakersfield.com*, December 1, 2016, https://www.bakersfield.com/special/150-years/timeline-years-of-kern-county-history/article_3b1dbe9c-ece6-50d6-8b44-88fb09a8507a.html.

16. Cecilia Rasmussen, "The Ghost of a Town Emerges from the Past," *Los Angeles Times*, October 24, 2004.

17. Alexander Nazaryan, "California Slaughter: The State-Sanctioned Genocide of Native Americans," *Newsweek*, August 17, 2016.

18. Eve Tuck and C. Ree, "A Glossary of Haunting," in *Handbook of Autoethnography*, eds. Stacy Holmes Jones, Tony E. Adams, and Carolyn Ellis (Walnut Creek, CA: Left Coast Press, 2013), 646.

19.   Raj Patel and Jason Moore, *A History of the World in Seven Cheap Things: A Guide to Capitalism, Nature, and the Future of the Planet* (Oakland: University of California Press, 2018), 47.

20.   American Lung Association in California, "Lung Association 'State of the Air' 2016 Report Finds More Than 80 Percent of Californians Still at Risk From Unhealthy Air," news release, April 20, 2016, https://www.prnewswire.com /news-releases/lung-association-state-of-the-air-2016-report-finds-more-than -80-percent-of-californians-still-at-risk-from-unhealthy-air-300254278.html.

21.   Jon Swaine and Oliver Laughland, "The County: The Story of America's Deadliest Police," *Guardian*, December 1, 2015.

22.   "Attorney General Kamala D. Harris Opens Investigations into the Kern County Sheriff's Office and the Bakersfield Police Department for Potential Civil Rights Violations," Office of the Attorney General, press release, December 22, 2016, https://oag.ca.gov/news/press-releases/attorney-general -kamala-d-harris-opens-investigations-kern-county-sheriff%E2%80%99s; Liam Dillon, "California's New Top Cop Has to Make Some Big Policing Decisions Soon. No One Knows What He'll Do," *Los Angeles Times*, June 6, 2017; "State Attorney General: Probes into BPD, KCSO Contine," *Bakersfield.com*, June 15, 2020, https://www.bakersfield.com/news/state -attorney-general-probes-into-bpd-kcso-continue/article_d4955880-af44 -11ea-89fa-bb0f29f16a25.html.

23.   ACLU California to Xavier Becerra, November 9, 2017, https://www.aclusocal .org/sites/default/files/letter_to_attorney_general_re_kern_county.pdf.

24.   Controversial Rep. Devin Nunes represents a nearby district that covers Tulare and Fresno Counties.

25.   Nate Berg, "Breathless in Bakersfield," *Guardian*, February 14, 2017.

26.   US Department of Justice to City Attorney, City of Bakersfield, April 12, 2004, https://www.justice.gov/sites/default/files/crt/legacy/2011/04/14 /bakersfield_ta_letter.pdf. ACLU of California, *Patterns and Practices of Police Excessive Force in Kern County: Findings and Recommendations*, November 2017, https://www.aclusocal.org/sites/default/files/patterns _practices_police_excessive_force_kern_county_aclu-ca_paper.pdf.

27.   ACLU, *Patterns and Practices*, 3.

28.   Tyler Wall, "Legal Terror and the Police Dog," *Radical Philosophy* (November–December 2014): 5.

29.   These social and environmental ills of the Central Valley and the activism against these problems are the focus of recent research and public outreach projects, specifically Voices from the Valley and Remembering Teresa, two public, online campus-community collaborative research and outreach projects directed by Tracy Perkins that highlight the photos and narratives of

women environmental justice activists in the region (http://www
.voicesfromthevalley.org and https://rememberingteresa.org/).

30. Rob Nixon, *Slow Violence and the Environmentalism of the Poor* (Cambridge, MA: Harvard University Press, 2011), 2.
31. Wall, "Legal Terror and the Police Dog," 2–7, 5, 7, my emphasis.
32. See Boisseron, *Afro-Dog*, and Parry, "Police Dogs and Anti-Black Violence."
33. Jeannie Shinozuka, "Deadly Perils: Japanese Beetles and the Pestilential Immigrant, 1920–1930," *American Quarterly* 65, no. 4 (Winter 2013): 521–42.
34. Claire Jean Kim, *Dangerous Crossing: Race, Species and Nature in a Multicultural Age* (Cambridge: Cambridge University Press, 2015).
35. Joseph Drexler-Dreis and Kristien Justaert, eds., *Beyond the Doctrine of Man: Decolonial Visions of the Human* (New York: Fordham University Press, 2020).
36. Tyler Wall, "'For the Very Existence of Civilization': The Police Dog and Racial Terror," *American Quarterly* 68, no. 4 (December 2016): 861–82.
37. According to the *Guardian* report by Swaine and Laughland, "The centrepiece of the KCSO website is a photograph of Sheriff Youngblood on a horse. A brilliant white stetson sits atop his head; a golden star rests over his heart. A ceremonial saddle stands at the entrance to his office in Bakersfield."
38. Reyna Harvey, "Sheriff Youngblood: We Are Not a Sanctuary County, We Are a Law-Abiding County," *Bakersfield Now*, April 21, 2017, https://bakersfieldnow.com/news/local/sheriff-youngblood-sayswe-are-not-a-sanctuary-county-we-are-a-law-abiding-county.
39. Eissinger, "Kern County," 1.
40. ACLU, *Patterns and Practices*, 4.
41. Swaine and Laughland, "The County."
42. ACLU, *Patterns and Practices*, 11.
43. Swaine and Laughland, "The County."
44. Swaine and Laughland, "The County."
45. *Guardian* reports the demographics in Bakersfield as follows: 46 percent of residents are Hispanic, 38 percent white, and 8 percent African American. Yet internal statistics show 74 percent of the roughly 390 sworn officers of Bakersfield Police Department are white, and only 21 percent are Hispanic and less than 5 percent are African American.
46. Swaine and Laughland, "The County."
47. Jose Jasper, "Sheriff's Estranged Wife Mauled by Bakersfield Police K9," *Bakersfield Now*, April 10, 2012, https://bakersfieldnow.com/news/local/sheriffs-estranged-wife-mauled-by-bakersfield-police-k-9.
48. Richard Winton, "Kern County Sheriff Is Caught on Tape Saying It Costs Less to Kill Suspects Than to Wound Them," *Los Angeles Times*, April 10, 2018.

49. "Committee for a Better Arvin et al. v. County of Kern," Center for Race, Poverty and Environment, https://crpe-ej.org/resources/legal /committee-for-a-better-arvin-et-al-v-county-of-kern/.

50. James Burger, "Judge Rules in Favor of Kern County in Suit Against County Oil and Gas Permitting Plan," *Bakersfield.com*, March 15, 2018, https:// www.bakersfield.com/news/judge-rules-in-favor-of-kern-county-in-suit -against/article_ffb3d00c-28a8-11e8-b387-3b3a26079f4c.html.

51. Carolina Balazs, Rachel Morello-Frosch, Alan Hubbard, and Isha Ray, "Social Disparities in Nitrate Contaminated Drinking Water in the San Joaquin Valley," *Environmental Health Perspectives* 119, no. 9 (2011): 1272–78.

52. Dayan, *Law Is a White Dog*, 252.

53. Dayan, *Law Is a White Dog*, 252.

54. W. E. B. Du Bois, "The Soul of White Folk," *Verso* (blog), https://www .versobooks.com/blogs/4770-the-souls-of-white-folk.

55. Pankaj Mirsa, "The Religion of Whiteness Becomes a Suicide Cult," *New York Times*, August 30, 2018, my emphasis.

56. W. E. B. Du Bois, *Darkwater: Voices from Within the Veil* (New York: Harcourt, Brace and Howe, 1920), 50–51.

57. Lindgren Johnson, *Race Matters, Animal Matters: Fugitive Humanism in African America, 1840–1930* (New York: Routledge, 2018), 21.

58. Malini Ranganathan, "Thinking with Flint: Racial Liberalism and the Roots of an American Water Tragedy," *Capitalism Nature Socialism* 27, no. 3 (2016): 17–33.

59. Johnson, *Race Matters, Animal Matters*, 21.

60. Johnson, *Race Matters, Animal Matters*, 25.

61. Alison Rowe, "Kern County California: Where Big Oil, Dirty Air, and a Tenacious Community Converge," *Environmental Justice* (blog), May 30, 2016, https://sites.williams.edu/envi-322-s16/ca-by-allie-rowe/kern-county -california-where-big-oil-dirty-air-and-a-tenacious-community-converge/.

62. California does not require buffer zones between active oil and gas wells and homes, schools, or hospitals. Estimates are that 14 percent of the population lives within a mile of a well. It is one of only two states without a production or severance tax on the oil and gas industry, what critics call a "de facto subsidy." Kate Wheeling and Jim Morris, "Big Oil's Black Mark on California's Climate Record," *Pacific Standard*, September 12, 2018, https:// psmag.com/environment/big-oils-black-mark-on-californias-climate-record.

63. Courtney Edelhart, "Tejon Tribe Fought for Recognition throughout Its History," *Bakersfield.com*, March 5, 2012, https://www.bakersfield.com /archives/tejon-tribe-fought-for-recognition-throughout-history/article _079af56f-6d8b-5ce7-bb3f-2b8169a101c6.html.

64. "Man Bites, Injures K9 after Pursuit through Central Bakersfield," *ABC News*, August 21, 2018, https://www.turnto23.com/news/local-news/man -arrested-after-he-led-law-enforcement-on-vehicle-pursuit-through-central -bakersfield.

CHAPTER FOUR: POISONED AND POLICED TO DEATH

1. Paul Rogers, "Environmental Health Exposure—Disease Assessment," Gaines v. Ellison et al., Case 13-25370, April 10, 2014, 6.
2. Gaines v. Ellison et al., "Plaintiff's Memorandum in Support of her Opposition to Defendant Lee Barnstein's Motion for Summary Judgment," Case No. 24-C-12-005655LP, June 2014, 3.
3. Rogers, "Environmental Health Exposure-Disease Assessment."
4. David Correia and Tyler Wall, *Police: A Field Guide* (London: Verso Books, 2018), 39.
5. Carolina Gray et al. v. Stanley Rochkind et al., Baltimore City Circuit Court, Case number, 24C08001821, March 14, 2008.
6. Tamara G. J. Leech et al., "Inequitable Chronic Lead Exposure," *Family and Community Health* 39, no. 3 (2016): 151.
7. Kirsten Schwarz, Richard V. Pouyat, and Ian Yesilonis, "Legacies of Lead in Charm City's Soil: Lessons from the Baltimore Ecosystem Study," *International Journal of Environmental Research and Public Health* 13, no. 2, (2016): 209.
8. Anna Maria Barry-Jester, "Baltimore's Toxic Legacy of Lead Paint," *FiveThirtyEight*, May 7, 2015, https://fivethirtyeight.com/features /baltimores-toxic-legacy-of-lead-paint/.
9. Maryland Department of Environment 2014 Annual Report, "Childhood Lead Surveillance, Baltimore City," 1993–2014.
10. Terrance McCoy, "Freddie Gray's Life a Study in the Effects of Lead Paint on Poor Blacks," *Washington Post*, April 29, 2015.
11. Gaines v. Ellison et al., Rhanda Dormeus deposition, Baltimore City Circuit Court, Case # 24-C-12-005655, July 9, 2013, 76.
12. Dormeus deposition, 32–33.
13. Gaines v. Ellison et al., Ryan Gaines deposition, Baltimore City Circuit Court, Case # 24-C-12-005655, July 9, 2013, 24.
14. Rogers, "Environmental Health Exposure-Disease Assessment," 3.
15. Rogers, "Environmental Health Exposure-Disease Assessment," 7.
16. Barry-Jester, "Baltimore's Toxic Legacy of Lead Paint."
17. On the police fabrication of order, see Mark Neocleous, *A Critical Theory of Police Power: The Fabrication of the Social Order* (London: Verso Books, 2021).

18. Ruth Wilson Gilmore, *Golden Gulag: Prisons, Surplus, Crisis, and Opposition in Globalizing California* (Oakland: University of California Press, 2007), 28.

19. Paul B. Stretsky and Michael J. Lynch, "The Relationship between Lead and Crime," *Journal of Health and Social Behavior* 45, no. 2 (2004): 214.

20. Leech et al., "Inequitable Chronic Lead Exposure," 151.

21. McCoy, "Freddie Gray's Life."

22. German Lopez, "Korryn Gaines Believed She Had Lead Poisoning. In Black Communities, It's Very Common," *Vox*, August 4, 2016, https://www.vox.com/2016/8/4/12373306/korryn-gaines-lead-exposure-police-shooting.

23. It's also inexcusably bad journalism that draws on bad scholarship. Consider: what evidence could any scholar or journalist point to that Gray couldn't "think" or "self-regulate"? He was walking down the street when Baltimore police stopped him, violently arrested him, and then killed him. And what is the claim that lead poisoning cost Gaines her life if not a textbook example of a leap of logic? It is a leap that sends us soaring past the one variable we ought to consider most of all: the police who killed them.

24. US Department of Justice, Civil Rights Division, "Investigation of the Baltimore City Police Department," August 10, 2016, 14.

25. Rogers, "Environmental Health Exposure-Disease Assessment," 6.

26. Rogers, "Environmental Health Exposure-Disease Assessment," 7.

27. Sherene Razack, *Dying from Improvement: Inquests and Inquiries into Indigenous Deaths in Custody* (Toronto: University of Toronto Press, 2015), 141.

28. "Coast Police Chief Accused of Racism," *New York Times*, May 13, 1982.

29. "K-12 Education: Discipline Disparities for Black Students, Boys, and Students with Disabilities," report of the US Congress GAO, March 22, 2018; Shoshana N. Jarvis and Jason A. Okonofua, "School Deferred: When Bias Affects School Leaders," *Social Psychological and Personality Science* 11, no. 4 (2020): 492–98.

30. Andrea J. Ritchie, *Invisible No More: Police Violence Against Black Women and Women of Color* (Boston: Beacon Press, 2017), 77.

31. Tom Jackman, "Did Lead Poisoning, and Outrage over Police Violence, Set the Stage for Korryn Gaines's Death?" *Washington Post*, August 3, 2016.

32. Barbara Ransby, *Making All Black Lives Matter: Reimagining Freedom in the Twenty-First Century* (Oakland: University of California Press, 2018), 87–90.

33. LaShonda Carter and Tiffany Willoughby-Herard, "What Kind of Mother Is She? From Margaret Garner to Rosa Lee Ingram to Mamie Till to the Murder of Korryn Gaines," *Theory & Event* 21, no. 1 (2018): 92.

34. Carter and Willoughby-Herard, "What Kind of Mother Is She?," 99.

35.   Carter and Willoughby-Herard, "What Kind of Mother Is She?," 100.

36.   Keeanga-Yamahtta Taylor, *From #BlackLivesMatter to Black Liberation* (Chicago: Haymarket Books, 2016), 130.

CHAPTER FIVE: POLICING, PIPELINES, AND THE CAPILLARIES OF CAPITAL IN A WARMING WORLD

1.   Nafeez Ahmed, "This Is How UN Scientists Are Preparing for the End of Capitalism," *Independent*, September 12, 2018; Nafeez Ahmed, "The Inevitable Demise of the Fossil Fuel Empire," *Guardian*, June 10, 2014. For an excellent, nuanced critique of peak oil narratives (as well as a critique of some problematic critiques of peak oil), see Mazen Labban, "Oil in Parallax: Scarcity, Markets, and the Financialization of Accumulation," *Geoforum* 41, no. 4 (July 2010).

2.   Paul Mason, "The End of Capitalism Has Begun," *Guardian*, July 17, 2015. Also, see Paul Mason, *Postcapitalism: A Guide to Our Future* (New York: Farrar, Straus and Giroux, 2017).

3.   See David Harvey, *The Enigma of Capital: And the Crises of Capitalism* (Oxford: Oxford University Press, 2010), for a good account of the contradictions of capital accumulation in Marx.

4.   David Correia, "Climate Revanchism," *Capitalism Nature Socialism* 27, no. 1 (January 2, 2016). For a critique of cap-and-trade and other similar carbon mitigation schemes, see Ashley Dawson, "Climate Justice: The Emerging Movement against Green Capitalism," *South Atlantic Quarterly* 109, no. 2 (April 1, 2010): 313–38.

5.   Steven Mufson, Brady Dennis, and Chris Mooney, "Clean up Climate Change? It's Just Good for Business," *Washington Post*, October 12, 2018. See "Summary for Policymakers of IPCC Special Report on Global Warming of 1.5° C Approved by Governments—IPCC," https://www.ipcc .ch/2018/10/08/summary-for-policymakers-of-ipcc-special-report-on-global -warming-of-1-5c-approved-by-governments/.

6.   Geoff Mann and Joel Wainwright, *Climate Leviathan* (London: Verso Books, 2018), 15.

7.   James O'Connor, "Capitalism, Nature, Socialism a Theoretical Introduction," *Capitalism Nature Socialism* 1, no. 1 (January 1, 1988): 22.

8.   Emphasis added. O'Connor, "Capitalism, Nature, Socialism," 22–23.

9.   John Bellamy Foster and Paul Burkett, *Marx and the Earth: An Anti-Critique* (Chicago: Haymarket Books, 2017), 6. To be clear, Foster and Burkett don't accuse O'Connor of Malthusianism. While they find

O'Connor's analysis insightful, they find it lacking in its overestimation of how ecological crises lead to economic crises.

10. O'Connor, "Capitalism, Nature, Socialism," 28.

11. This is a political formation that Mann and Wainright call Climate Behemoth. They see Climate Behemoth as one political possibility among several, though one that is unlikely to win over what they see as the most likely kind of politics to dominate under conditions of climate crisis: Climate Leviathan.

12. This is what Mann and Wainright call Climate Leviathan.

13. For a brilliant critique of how geoengineering projects are the "best excuse for continuing business-as-usual," see Linda Schneider, "Geoengineering and Environmental Capitalism: Extractive Industries in the Era of Climate Change," *Verso* (blog), August 21, 2018, https://www.versobooks.com/blogs /3962-geoengineering-and-environmental-capitalism-extractive-industries -in-the-era-of-climate-change.

14. Mark Neocleous, *War Power, Police Power* (Edinburgh: Edinburgh University Press, 2014), 11.

15. Nia Williams and Laila Kearney, "Daring U.S. Pipeline Sabotage Spawned by Lobster Boat Coal Protest," *Reuters*, October 14, 2016. For more information on the Valve Turners, see: "Valve Turners: Linked Lists of News and Videos," accessed January 28, 2021, http://thegreatstory.org/valve -turners.html#2018; Shiri Pasternak, "#DeedsNotWords: A National Day of Water Protection Solidarity North of the Medicine Line," *Fieldsights*, December 22, 2016, https://culanth.org/fieldsights/1022-deedsnotwords-a -national-day-of-water-protection-solidarity-north-of-the-medicine-line.

16. Jason W. Moore, *Capitalism in the Web of Life: Ecology and the Accumulation of Capital* (London: Verso Books, 2015).

17. Bayou Bridge Inc. is a subsidiary of Energy Transfer Partners, the company that also owns the more well-known Dakota Access Pipeline.

18. Police harassment and violence have been ongoing throughout the effort to stop the pipeline. The police actions I refer to here were part of several police operations throughout the campaign to violently suppress the movement. See Karen Savage, "Sheriff's Deputies Protect Corporate Interests in Bayou Bridge Case," *Truthout*, December 12, 2018, https://truthout.org/articles /sheriffs-deputies-protect-corporate-interests-in-bayou-bridge-case/; Emma Fiala, "Water Protectors Violently Arrested at Illegal Bayou Bridge Pipeline Construction Site," *MintPress News* (blog), September 6, 2018, https://www .mintpressnews.com/bayou-bridge-pipeline-water-protectors-arrested /248904/; also, see NBB's Facebook page for video coverage of some of the arrests: https://www.facebook.com/LeauEstLaVie/videos /346359729515382/.

19. Alleen Brown, Will Parrish, and Alice Speri, "Leaked Documents Reveal Counterterrorism Tactics Used at Standing Rock to 'Defeat Pipeline Insurgencies,'" *Intercept*, May 27, 2017, https://theintercept.com/2017/05 /27/leaked-documents-reveal-security-firms-counterterrorism-tactics-at -standing-rock-to-defeat-pipeline-insurgencies/.

20. "Louisiana House Bill 727," Pub. L. No. 727 (2018), https://legiscan.com /LA/drafts/HB727/2018.

21. · David Naguib Pellow, *Total Liberation: The Power and Promise of Animal Rights and the Radical Earth Movement* (Minneapolis: University of Minnesota Press, 2014).

22. See the NBB website: http://lelvcamp.org/updates/.

23. See NBB's website: http://nobbp.org/about/leau-est-la-vie-camp/. Also see Akiba Solomon, "Inside the Long, Hard Fight to Stop the Bayou Bridge Oil Pipeline," *Colorlines*, January 9, 2019, https://www.colorlines.com/articles /inside-long-hard-fight-stop-bayou-bridge-oil-pipeline.

24. Valerie Volcovici, "Energy Transfer Sues Greenpeace over Dakota Pipeline," *Reuters*, August 22, 2017, https://www.reuters.com/article/us-energy -transf-lawsuit-idUSKCN1B2245.

25. Brown, Parrish, and Speri, "Counterterrorism Tactics Used at Standing Rock."

26. "Dakota Access Pipeline Company Attacks Native American Protesters with Dogs and Pepper Spray," *Democracy Now!*, September 4, 2016, http://www .democracynow.org/2016/9/4/dakota_access_pipeline_company_attacks _native.

27. Andreas Malm, *Fossil Capital: The Rise of Steam Power and the Roots of Global Warming* (London: Verso Books, 2016), 11.

28. Malm, *Fossil Capital*, 226.

29. Malm, *Fossil Capital*, 236.

30. Andreas Malm, *The Progress of This Storm: Nature and Society in a Warming World* (London: Verso Books, 2018), 5; Andreas Malm, "Who Lit This Fire? Approaching the History of the Fossil Economy," *Critical Historical Studies* 3, no. 2 (2016): 221.

31. Malm, *Fossil Capital*, 170. It is impossible to do justice to Malm's important, nuanced argument about the transition to fossil fuels here. See *Fossil Capital* for more on this argument.

32. Malm, "Who Lit This Fire?" 219.

33. Malm, *Fossil Capital*, 235.

34. Fiala, "Water Protectors Violently Arrested."

35. For a brilliant history of the #NoDAPL movement in the context of centuries of Indigenous resistance against the United States, see Nick Estes, *Our History Is the Future: Standing Rock versus the Dakota Access Pipeline,*

and the Long Tradition of Indigenous Resistance (London: Verso Books, 2019).

36. Daniel Wildcat, *Red Alert! Saving the Planet with Indigenous Knowledge* (Golden, CO: Fulcrum Publishing, 2009).

37. Neocleous, *War Power, Police Power*, 13.

38. Malm, *Fossil Capital*, 204.

39. Julie Dermansky, "Louisiana Sheriff Ordered to Release Records on Visit to Standing Rock," *Truthout*, January 6, 2019, https://truthout.org/articles/louisiana-sheriff-ordered-to-releases-records-on-visit-to-standing-rock/.

40. Alleen Brown, "The Infiltrator: How an Undercover Oil Industry Mercenary Tricked Pipeline Opponents into Believing He Was One of Them," *Intercept*, December 30, 2018, https://theintercept.com/2018/12/30/tigerswan-infiltrator-dakota-access-pipeline-standing-rock/.

41. Alleen Brown and Will Parrish, "A TigerSwan Employee Quietly Registered a New Business in Louisiana after the State Denied the Security Firm a License to Operate," *The Intercept*, March 30, 2018, https://theintercept.com/2018/03/30/louisiana-bayou-bridge-pipeline-tigerswan-private-security/.

42. See their website, https://www.hubenterprises.com/.

43. Will Parrish and Sam Levin, "'Treating Protest as Terrorism': US Plans Crackdown on Keystone XL Activists," *Guardian*, September 20, 2018; Julie Dermansky, "Bayou Bridge Pipeline Opponents Say Louisiana Governor's Office Is Surveilling Them," *Truthout,* March 13, 2018, https://truthout.org/articles/bayou-bridge-pipeline-opponents-say-louisiana-governor-s-office-is-surveilling-them; Brown, Parrish, and Speri, "Counterterrorism Tactics Used at Standing Rock."

44. Neocleous, *War Power, Police Power*, 13.

45. Neocleous, *War Power, Police Power*, 14.

46. Savage, "Sheriff's Deputies Protect Corporate Interests."

47. Mark Neocleous, "Security, Commodity, Fetishism," *Critique: Journal of Socialist Theory* 35, no. 3 (December 2007): 341.

48. David Correia and Tyler Wall, "Rent-a-Cop," in *The Police: A Field Guide* (London: Verso Books, 2017).

49. Shiri Pasternak, Katie Mazer, and D. T. Cochrane, "The Financing Problem of Colonialism: How Indigenous Jurisdiction Is Valued in Pipeline Politics," in *Standing with Standing Rock: Voices from the #NoDAPL Movement*, ed. Nick Estes and Jaskiran Dhillon (Minneapolis: University of Minnesota Press, 2019).

50. Patrick Bigger and Morgan Robertson, "Value Is Simple. Valuation Is Complex," *Capitalism Nature Socialism* 28, no. 1 (January 2, 2017).

51. Bigger and Robertson, "Value Is Simple," 71.

52. Bigger and Robertson, "Value Is Simple," 69.

53. Pasternak, Mazer, nd Cochrane, "Financing Problem of Colonialism."

54. Walter Benjamin, "Critique of Violence," in *Reflections: Essays, Aphorisms, Autobiographical Writings*, ed. Peter Demetz, trans. Edmund Jephcott (New York: Schocken Books, 2007).

55. American Legislative Exchange Council, "Critical Infrastructure Protection Act," https://www.alec.org/model-policy/critical-infrastructure -protection-act/.

56. Department of Homeland Security, "Critical Infrastructure Protection Act (CIPA) Passage Out of Homeland Security Committee Is Decisive Step to Protect the Nation," press release, 2015, https://homeland.house.gov/press /critical-infrastructure-protection-act-cipa-passage-out-homeland-security -committee/.

57. Alleen Brown and Will Parrish, "Louisiana and Minnesota Introduce Anti-Protest Bills amid Fights over Bayou Bridge and Enbridge Pipelines," *Intercept*, March 31, 2018, https://theintercept.com/2018/03/31 /louisiana-minnesota-anti-protest-bills-bayou-bridge-enbridge-pipelines/.

58. Underlined sentences are additions/amendments to the law. Emphasis in italics mine.

59. S. 3880 (109th): Animal Enterprise Terrorism Act, https://www.govtrack.us /congress/bills/109/s3880/text.

60. Dermansky, "Bayou Bridge Pipeline Opponents."

61. Pellow, *Total Liberation*, 168.

62. James Jarbow, "The Threat of Eco-Terrorism," testimony before the House Resources Committee, Subcommittee on Forests and Forest Health, 2002, https://archives.fbi.gov/archives/news/testimony/the-threat-of -eco-terrorism.

63. See their website, https://ent.siteintelgroup.com/. I explore SITE's role in the GWOT and in the production of ecoterrorism in another paper.

64. Brown, Parrish, and Speri, "Counterterrorism Tactics Used at Standing Rock."

65. Neocleous, "Security, Commodity, Fetishism," 344.

66. Nexus Media News, "Bayou Bridge Pipeline Protests," September 4, 2018, YouTube video, https://www.youtube.com/watch?v=bA9-iK537jg.

67. L'eau Est La Vie Camp – No Bayou Bridge, "livestream from inside the Energy Transfer Partners (ETP) shareholder meeting," Facebook, October 22, 2018, https://www.facebook.com/LeauEstLaVie/posts/a-must-watch -livestream-from-inside-the-energy-transfer-partners-etp-shareholde r/575717366192827/.

68. See the MOVE Organization's website: http://onamove.com/about/.

69. "25 Years Ago: Philadelphia Police Bombs MOVE Headquarters Killing 11,

Destroying 65 Homes," *Democracy Now!*, May 13, 2010, https://www
.democracynow.org/2010/5/13/25_years_ago_philadelphia_police_bombs.

70. Nexus Media News, "Bayou Bridge Pipeline Protests."

71. Malm, *Progress of This Storm*, 204.

72. Sydney Azari, "IPCC Report: First Thoughts on Next Steps," *System Change
Not Climate Change*, October 19, 2018, https://systemchangenotclimatechange
.org/article/ipcc-report-first-thoughts-next-steps.

73. http://nobbp.org/updates-2/.

CHAPTER SIX: SECURING NATURE'S RETURN

I would like to thank David Correia and Tyler Wall for their thoughtful
feedback and assistance in revising this chapter. I also want to thank Javier
Arbona, Marisol de la Cadena, Caren Kaplan, Ingrid Lagos, and Levi Van
Sant, as well as my interlocutors at SREL.

1. To avoid confusion with the Savannah River Site (SRS) and its previous
name, the Savannah River Plant, I refer to the Savannah River Ecology
Laboratory as the ecology lab or SREL throughout this chapter and the
Savannah River Site as SRS and the site. For clarity, I use the Savannah River
Site and its associated terms to also refer to the site throughout its history,
including the time from its construction until its name changed from the
Savannah River Plant to Savannah River Site in 1989.

2. Eugene P. Odum, *Fundamentals of Ecology*, in collaboration with Howard T.
Odum, 2nd ed. (Philadelphia: W. B. Saunders, 1959), 258.

3. Odum, *Fundamentals of Ecology*, 257.

4. Eugene P. Odum, "The Strategy of Ecosystem Development," *Science* 164, no.
3877 (1969): 269.

5. As Mark Neocleous illustrates, police power is fundamentally about the
generation and maintenance of all manner of "good order." See Mark
Neocleous, *Fabricating Social Order: A Critical Theory of Police Power*
(London: Pluto Press, 2000).

6. Eugene P. Odum, "The Mesocosm," *BioScience* 34, no. 9 (1984): 558–62.

7. See, for instance, Mathew Coleman, "State Power in Blue," *Political
Geography* 51 (2016): 76–86. On practice more generally, see Annemarie
Mol, *The Body Multiple: Ontology in Medical Practice* (Durham: Duke
University Press, 2002).

8. Javier Arbona, "Anti-Memorials and World War II Heritage in the San
Francisco Bay Area: Spaces of the 1942 Black Sailors' Uprising," *Landscape
Journal* 34, no. 2 (2015): 177–92.

9. See Odum, *Fundamentals of Ecology*, 257; Eugene P. Odum, "The Strategy of

Ecosystem Development," *Ekistics* 29, no. 173 (1970): 234.

10. Eugene P. Odum, "Organic Production and Turnover in Old Field Succession," *Ecology* 41, no. 1 (1960): 34.

11. See Odum, *Fundamentals of Ecology*, 487–96; Odum, "Strategy of Ecosystem Development"; Eugene P. Odum, "Energy, Ecosystem Development and Environmental Risk," *Journal of Risk and Insurance* 43, no. 1 (1976): 1–16; Odum, "The Mesocosm"; and Eugene P. Odum, *Ecological Vignettes: Ecological Approaches to Dealing with Human Predicaments* (Athens: University of Georgia Press, 1998).

12. On anachronism, see Anne McClintock, *Imperial Leather: Race, Gender, and Sexuality in the Colonial Context* (New York: Routledge, 1995), 40–41, 244; Shiloh Krupar, *Hot Spotter's Report: Military Fables of Toxic Waste* (Minneapolis: University of Minnesota Press, 2013), 6.

13. Odum, *Fundamentals of Ecology*, 237.

14. Bernard C. Patten, "The Wealth of Ecosystems: How Biodiversity Serves to Maximize Biological and Environmental Fitness in the Economy of Nature," address presented at the Odum School of Ecology 50th Anniversary Reunion and Symposium, University of Georgia, Athens, GA, January 2018, 8.

15. Louise Cassels, *The Unexpected Exodus: How the Cold War Displaced One Southern Town*, with a new introduction by Kari Frederickson (Columbia: University of South Carolina Press, 2007), 11, 13, 87.

16. Cassels, *Unexpected Exodus*, 11, 13, 76. On the "nuclear uncanny," see Joseph Masco, *The Nuclear Borderlands: The Manhattan Project in Post–Cold War New Mexico* (Princeton: Princeton University Press, 2006), 28, 32–34.

17. Cassels, *Unexpected Exodus*, 28.

18. Cassels, *Unexpected Exodus*, 35–36, emphasis added.

19. Cassels, *Unexpected Exodus*, 43. For an analysis of the nonhuman as agent of empire, see Jake Kosek, "Ecologies of Empire: On the New Uses of the Honeybee," *Cultural Anthropology* 25, no. 4 (2010): 650–78.

20. Cassels, *Unexpected Exodus*, 80, 87.

21. Kari Frederickson, *Cold War Dixie: Militarization and Modernization in the American South* (Athens: University of Georgia Press, 2013), 68–69.

22. See Cassels, *Unexpected Exodus*; Tonya A. Browder and Richard D. Brooks, *Memories of Home: Reminiscences of Ellenton* (Columbia: University of South Carolina Press, 1996).

23. Raymond Williams, *The Country and the City* (Oxford: Oxford University Press, 1973), 79.

24. Mark M. Smith, "'All Is Not Quiet in Our Hellish County': Facts, Fiction, Politics, and Race; The Ellenton Riot of 1876," *South Carolina Historical Magazine* 95, no. 2 (1994): 142–55.

25. This narrative is further entrenched when ecological studies at SREL are placed alongside the work conducted by the Savannah River Archaeological Program, whose studies of the SRS extend back to Native prehistory.

26. Odum, "Strategy of Ecosystem Development," 234.

27. As David Correia and Tyler Wall note, "Police logic is the logic of sanitation, the logic of 'polishing' and making 'polite' those 'dirty' populations that threaten order." David Correia and Tyler Wall, *Police: A Field Guide* (London: Verso Books, 2018), 102.

28. Correia and Wall, *Police*, 81–83.

29. Correia and Wall, *Police*, 82.

30. Williams, *Country and the City*, 127.

31. Odum, *Fundamentals of Ecology*, 3–4.

32. See Neocleous, *Fabricating Social Order*, 1–21.

33. Eyal Weizman and Fazal Sheikh, *The Conflict Shoreline: Colonization as Climate Change in the Negev Desert* (New York: Steidl in association with Cabinet Books, 2015), 48.

34. Weizman and Sheikh, *Conflict Shoreline*, 50.

35. Weizman and Sheikh, *Conflict Shoreline*, 30.

36. Frank Benjamin Golley, *A History of the Ecosystem Concept in Ecology: More Than the Sum of the Parts* (New Haven: Yale University Press, 1993), 2–7, 72–75.

37. Golley, *Ecosystem Concept in Ecology*, 5–7

38. Golley, *Ecosystem Concept in Ecology*, 74. See also Sharon E. Kingsland, *The Evolution of American Ecology, 1890–2000* (Baltimore: Johns Hopkins University Press, 2005), 192–95; On ecology at other nuclear sites, see Masco, *Nuclear Borderlands*; Jake Kosek, *Understories: The Political Life of Forests in Northern New Mexico* (Durham: Duke University Press, 2006); Krupar, *Hot Spotter's Report*; Mike Davis, "Dead West: Ecocide in Marlboro County," *New Left Review* I/200 (1993): 49–73; and David G. Havlick, *Bombs Away: Militarization, Conservation, and Ecological Restoration* (Chicago: University of Chicago Press, 2018).

39. Scott Kirsch, "Ecologists and the Experimental Landscape: The Nature of Science at the US Department of Energy's Savannah River Site," *Cultural Geographies* 14 (2007): 501.

40. Odum, *Fundamentals of Ecology*, 7.

41. Odum, *Fundamentals of Ecology*, 257.

42. Odum, *Fundamentals of Ecology*, 258.

43. Odum "Strategy of Ecosystem Development," 269.

44. Odum, *Fundamentals of Ecology*, 258.

45. Odum "Strategy of Ecosystem Development," 262; See also Betty Jean

Craige, *Eugene Odum: Ecosystem Ecologist and Environmentalist* (Athens: University of Georgia Press, 2002), 88–91.

46. Odum, *Fundamentals of Ecology*; Howard T. Odum, *Environment, Power, and Society for the Twenty-First Century: The Hierarchy of Energy* (New York: Columbia University Press, 2007); Bernard Patten and Eugene P. Odum, "The Cybernetic Nature of Ecosystems," *American Naturalist* 118, no. 6 (1981): 886–95; see also Golley, *Ecosystem Concept in Ecology*, 69; Kirsch, "Ecologists and the Experimental Landscape"; Gregg Mittman, *The State of Nature: Ecology, Community, and American Social Thought, 1900–1950* (Chicago: University of Chicago Press, 1992). On Ramón Margalef and cybernetics, see Kingsland, *Evolution of American Ecology*, 210–13.

47. Mittman, *State of Nature*, 209–210; see also Kirsch, "Ecologists and the Experimental Landscape," 500.

48. Odum, *Ecological Vignettes*, 225; see also Golley, *Ecosystem Concept in Ecology*; Craige, *Eugene Odum*, 42–45.

49. Golley, *Ecosystem Concept in Ecology*, 69.

50. Golley, *Ecosystem Concept in Ecology*, 82."

51. Odum, *Fundamentals of Ecology*, 4. See Kingsland, *Evolution of American Ecology*, 202–4.

52. Odum, "Energy, Ecosystem Development," 1.

53. Odum, "Energy, Ecosystem Development," 7.

54. Odum, "Energy, Ecosystem Development," 15.

55. Odum, "Energy, Ecosystem Development," 1.

56. See also Kingsland, *Evolution of American Ecology*, 202–4.

57. Odum, *Fundamentals of Ecology*; Odum "Strategy of Ecosystem Development; Odum, "Energy, Ecosystem Development"; Odum, "The Mesocosm"; Odum, *Ecological Vignettes*.

For a discussion of neo-Malthusian ecology in the western United States, see Nathan Sayre, *The Politics of Scale: A History of Rangeland Science* (Chicago: University of Chicago Press, 2017).

58. Neil Smith, "Giuliani Time: The Revanchist 1990s," *Social Text* 57 (1998): 11; Timothy Mitchell, "Economentality: How the Future Entered Government," *Critical Inquiry* 40 (2014): 479–507; Michelle Murphy, *The Economization of Life* (Durham: Duke University Press, 2017).

59. Murphy, *The Economization of Life*, 6.

60. Odum, "Energy, Ecosystem Development," 8.

61. Markus Dirk Dubber, *The Police Power: Patriarchy and the Foundations of American Government* (New York: Columbia University Press, 2005), 2, 58, 66.

62. Dubber, *The Police Power*, 71. See also Neocleous, *Fabricating Social Order*, 1,

13.

63. See Correia and Wall, *Police*, 129–31; Justin Hansford, "Community Policing Reconsidered: From Ferguson to Baltimore," in *Policing the Planet: Why the Policing Crisis Led to Black Lives Matter*, ed. Jordan T. Camp and Christina Heatherton (London: Verso Books, 2016), 218–23.

64. Neocleous, *Fabricating Social Order*, ix.

65. Odum, "The Mesocosm," 558; Odum, *Fundamentals of Ecology*, 421–22.

66. Kirsch, "Ecologists and the Experimental Landscape," 495; see also Robert Kohler, *Landscapes and Labscapes: Exploring the Lab-Field Border in Biology* (Chicago: University of Chicago Press, 2002). Of interest, Kohler's use of the term *frontier* in his examination of lab-field borders is taken up analogically but uncritically in *Landscapes and Labscapes*, where it appears as a useful, if not loaded, heuristic (Kohler, *Landscapes and Labscapes*, 14–19).

67. Léopold Lambert, *Weaponized Architecture: The Impossibility of Innocence* (New York: dpr-barcelona, 2012).

68. Marisol de la Cadena, *Earth Beings: Ecologies of Practice across Andean Worlds* (Durham: Duke University Press, 2015); Marisol de la Cadena, "Indigenous Cosmopolitics in the Andes: Conceptual Reflections Beyond 'Politics,'" *Cultural Anthropology* 25, no. 2 (2010): 334–70; Kathleen Stewart, "Atmospheric Attunements," *Environment and Planning D: Society and Space* 29 (2011): 445–53; Déborah Danowski and Eduardo Viveiros de Castro, *The Ends of the World*, trans. Rodrigo Nunes (Malden, MA: Polity Press, 2017).

69. This echoes interviews conducted by Kirsch, where ecologists similarly reported that they valued having access to protected field sites safe from human tampering and intervention. See Kirsch, "Ecologists and the Experimental Landscape," 490–91.

70. As two ecologists emeriti I spoke with described, when one underwent the standard medical evaluation required to work at SRS, in the area of the form designated for psychological evaluation, it stated, "Subject wore Bermuda shorts." Ecologists' dress and perceived hippie/antiestablishment leanings were described as often a source of tension between the ecologists and AEC and DuPont officials.

71. For a discussion of inclusion and exclusion at SREL, see Kirsch, "Ecologists and the Experimental Landscape."

72. Mol, *The Body Multiple*; Coleman, "State Power in Blue."

73. On "nuclear time," see Masco, *The Nuclear Borderlands*, 45, 48–49.

74. Kate Brannen, "Blackwater's Descendants Are Doing Just Fine," *Foreign Policy*, July 1, 2014.

75. On the postnuclear and postmilitary environment, see Krupar, *Hot Spotter's*

Report, 2, 125–26, 151, 157, emphasis added.

76. Kirsch, "Ecologists and the Experimental Landscape," 493.

77. Robin Blackburn, *The Making of New World Slavery: From the Baroque to the Modern, 1492–1800* (London: Verso Books, 2010), 515; see also David Harvey, *The Enigma of Capital and the Crises of Capitalism* (London: Profile Books, 2010); Nikhil Pal Singh, "On Race, Violence, and So-Called Primitive Accumulation," *Social Text* 34, no. 3 (128) (2016): 27–50.

78. Karl Marx, *Das Kapital*, vol.1 (New York: International Publishers, 1967), 873.

79. Marx, *Das Kapital*, 874–75.

80. Blackburn, *New World Slavery*, 554.

81. See David Harvey, "The 'New' Imperialism: Accumulation by Dispossession," *Social Register* (2004): 63–87; David Harvey, *A Brief History of Neoliberalism* (Oxford: Oxford University Press, 2005), 159–64.

82. Kirsch, "Ecologists and the Experimental Landscape," 487, emphasis in original.

83. See Kirsch, "Ecologists and the Experimental Landscape."

84. Singh, "On Race, Violence," 37.

85. Krupar, *Hot Spotter's Report*, 6.

86. Krupar, *Hot Spotter's Report*, 6.

87. On the abandonment and misuse of land through historical constructions of "the wasteland," see Vittoria Di Palma, *Wasteland: A History* (New Haven: Yale University Press, 2014).

88. Jacques Rancière, *Disagreement: Politics and Philosophy*, trans. Julie Rose (Minneapolis: University of Minnesota Press, 1999), 29.

89. De la Cadena, *Earth Beings*, 278.

CHAPTER SEVEN: THE ARMED FRIENDLIES OF SETTLED ORDER

1. Elizabeth Cook-Lynn, *New Indians, Old Wars* (Urbana: University of Illinois Press, 2007), 74.

2. Cook-Lynn, *New Indians*, 83.

3. Andrew Curley, "Beyond Environmentalism: #NoDAPL as Assertion of Tribal Sovereignty," in *Standing with Standing Rock: Voices from the #NoDAPL Movement*, eds. Nick Estes and Jaskiran Dhillon (Minneapolis: University of Minnesota Press, 2019), 158–68, 161.

4. Cook-Lynn, *New Indians*, 72.

5. Cook-Lynn, *New Indians*, 71.

6. Cook-Lynn, *New Indians*, 72.

7. Jodi Byrd, *Transit of Empire: Indigenous Critiques of Colonialism*

(Minneapolis: University of Minnesota Press, 2011), 11, 19.

8. Byrd, *Transit of Empire*, 221.

9. Byrd, *Transit of Empire*, 227.

10. Byrd, *Transit of Empire*, 227.

11. See Abraham Riesman, "American Sniper's Comics Homage Is Perfect—and Terrifying," *Vulture*, January 23, 2015, https://www.vulture.com/2015/01/american-sniper-comics-punisher.html.

12. Nate Powell, "About Face: Death and Surrender to Power in the Clothing of Men," *Popula*, February 24, 2019, https://popula.com/2019/02/24/about-face/.

13. Winona LaDuke, *The Winona LaDuke Chronicles: Stories from the Front Lines in the Battle for Environmental Justice* (Black Point, Nova Scotia: Fernwood, 2017), 270.

CHAPTER EIGHT: THE MONSTER AND THE POLICE

This chapter is a slightly revised version of a previously published article. See Mark Neocleous, "The Monster and the Police: Dexter to Hobbes," *Radical Philosophy* 185 (May/June 2014): 8–18.

1. Robert K. Ressler and Tom Shachtman, *Whoever Fights Monsters* (London: Simon and Schuster, 1992); David Bright, *Catching Monsters* (London: John Blake, 2003); Bob Long and Bob McLachlan, *Monsters and Men* (London: Hodder and Stoughton, 2003). See also Richard Tithecott, *Of Men and Monsters: Jeffrey Dahmer and the Construction of the Serial Killer* (Madison: University of Wisconsin Press, 1997), 179.

2. The serial killer David Berkowitz was known by the nickname Son of Sam, but this was in fact a name invented by the media and then adopted by Berkowitz. Prior to adopting it, Berkowitz called himself Mr. Monster. See Ressler and Shachtman, *Whoever Fights Monsters*, 84. In light of the discussion later in this chapter concerning Hobbes's use of "Behemoth," it is worth noting a letter from Berkowitz to the press, written in April 1977, where he says, "I am the 'Son of Sam' . . . I am the 'Monster . . . the chubby Behemoth." Jane Caputi, *The Age of Sex Crime* (London: Women's Press, 1988), 39.

3. "Almost without exception they [serial killers] are always police buffs. They never could make the grade, so they do the next best thing. They may seek an occupation close to the periphery of law enforcement. It could be as a security guard, a private detective, or as a volunteer in a hospital where they would drive an ambulance." *The Federal Role in Investigation of Serial Violent Crime: Hearings Before a Subcommittee of the Committee on Government*

Operations, House of Representatives, 99th Cong., 2nd Session. 20 (1986) (statement of John Douglas, FBI).

4.   See, for example, Bella DePaulo, ed., *The Psychology of Dexter* (Dallas: Benbella Books, 2010); Douglas L. Howard, ed., *Dexter: Investigating Cutting Edge Television* (London: I. B. Tauris, 2010); Richard Greene, George A. Reisch, and Rachel Robison-Greene, eds., *Dexter and Philosophy* (Chicago: Open Court, 2011); Bert Olivier, "When the 'Law' No Longer Suffices: *Dexter*," *South African Journal of Art History* 27, no. 3 (2012): 52–67.

5.   Adam Kotsko, *Why We Love Sociopaths: A Guide to Late Capitalist Television* (Winchester, UK: Zero Books, 2012), 83.

6.   For the themes of monstrosity see Mark Neocleous, *The Monstrous and the Dead: Burke, Marx, Fascism* (Cardiff: University of Wales Press, 2005). For the specific relation between "civilization" and "police" see Mark Neocleous, "The Police of Civilization," *International Political Sociology* 5, no. 2 (2011): 144–59.

7.   Quote cited from Gordon Burn, *Somebody's Husband, Somebody's Son: The Story of Peter Sutcliffe* (London: Faber and Faber, 1984), 334. The nickname appears in the one piece of genuine correspondence from Sutcliffe to the press, a poem sent to the Sheffield newspaper the *Star* taunting the police for being unable to catch him, which he signs off as the Streetcleaner. See Nicole Ward Jouve, *"The Streetcleaner": The Yorkshire Ripper Case on Trial* (London: Marion Boyars, 1986), 214–15.

8.   Mike Brogden, *On the Mersey Beat: Policing Liverpool Between the Wars* (Oxford: Oxford University Press, 1991), 1.

9.   Malcolm Young, *An Inside Job: Policing and Police Culture in Britain* (Oxford: Clarendon Press, 1991), 141.

10. Peter K. Manning, *Police Work: The Social Organization of Policing* (Cambridge, MA: MIT Press, 1977), 112.

11. Bright *Catching Monsters*, 9.

12. Young, *Inside Job*, 388.

13. Young, *Inside Job*, 76.

14. Brogden, *Mersey Beat*, 1.

15. For this paragraph and the next see Mark Neocleous, *The Fabrication of Social Order: A Critical Theory of Police Power* (London: Pluto Press, 2000).

16. Montesquieu, *The Spirit of the Laws*, trans. Anne M. Cohler, Basia Carolyn Miller, and Harold Samuel Stone (Cambridge: Cambridge University Press, 1989), 517.

17. Emer De Vattel, *The Law of Nations*, ed. Joseph Chitty (Philadelphia: T & J. W. Johnson, 1853), 83.

18. Katharine Park and Lorraine J. Daston, "Unnatural Conceptions: The

Study of Monsters in Sixteenth- and Seventeenth-Century England," *Past and Present* 92 (1981): 22; Andrew Gibson, *Towards a Postmodern Theory of Narrative* (Edinburgh: Edinburgh University Press, 1996), 237.

19. Georges Canguilhem, "Monstrosity and the Monstrous," *Diogenes* 40 (1962): 31; Michel Foucault, *Abnormal: Lectures at the Collège de France, 1974–1975*, trans. Graham Burchell (London: Verso Books, 2003), 55, 63–64, 323.

20. Foucault, *Abnormal*, 81.

21. Michel Foucault, *Discipline and Punish: The Birth of the Prison*, trans. Alan Sheridan (London: Penguin, 1977), 101.

22. Foucault, *Abnormal*, 82.

23. Pasquale Pasquino, "Criminology: The Birth of a Special Knowledge," in *The Foucault Effect: Studies in Governmentality*, eds. Graham Burchell, Colin Gordon, and Peter Miller (London: Harvester Wheatsheaf, 1991), 244–45.

24. Andrew N. Sharpe, *Foucault's Monsters and the Challenge of Law* (London: Routledge, 2010). Sharpe mentions police once in passing.

25. "Raped by the state" is the term used by women activists in the environmental movement who have given birth to children whose fathers turn out to have been undercover police officers infiltrating the movement. The House of Commons report into this undercover policing found that there was a "strong framework of statutory regulation" for such undercover actions and that "no authority is ever granted for an undercover officer to engage in a sexual relationship whilst deployed on an authorised police operation." Yet the committee adds that "when we asked him [the Metropolitan Police commissioner] about it, he said that, while it would never be authorised, it 'could almost be inevitable' that it would happen." One undercover police officer said it was "beyond belief" that his superiors did not know that he was exercising his discretion in this way. House of Commons, Home Affairs Committee, "Undercover Policing: Interim Report," Thirteenth Report of Session 2012–13 (HC 837), HMSO, London, 1 (2013), 5–6.

26. Sir Robert Mark. For the citation and a development of the other points in this paragraph, see chapter 5 in Neocleous, *Fabrication*.

27. Foucault, *Abnormal*, 98.

28. Foucault, *Abnormal*, 101.

29. Frances Maseres, preface to *Select Tracts Relating to the Civil Wars in England, in the Reign of King Charles the First*, vol. 1, ed. Frances Maseres (London: R. Bickerstaff, 1815), lxxviii.

30. Thomas Hobbes, *Behemoth, or The Long Parliament*, ed. Ferdinand Tönnies (Chicago: University of Chicago Press, 1990), 204.

31. Franz Neumann, *Behemoth: The Structure and Practice of National Socialism*

(London: Victor Gollanz, 1942), 5.

32. David Williams, *Deformed Discourse: The Function of the Monster in Mediaeval Thought and Literature* (Exeter: University of Exeter Press, 1996), 185–86.

33. Carl Schmitt, *The Leviathan in the State Theory of Thomas Hobbes: Meaning and Failure of a Political Symbol*, trans. George Schwab and Erna Hilfstein (Westport, CT: Greenwood Press, 1996), 21. One should note Schmitt's purpose in using this point as a springboard for some straightforwardly Nazi propaganda.

34. Stephen Holmes, "Introduction to Hobbes," in Hobbes, *Behemoth*, ix.

35. Williams, *Deformed*, 186–87.

36. Howard Jacobson, "The Strange Case of the Hobbesian Man," *Representations* 63 (1998): 1.

37. Francis Bacon, "Of Seditions and Troubles," in *Essays* (London: Dent, 1972), 44.

38. Cited in Jacobson, "Strange Case," 8.

39. Thomas Hobbes, *De Cive: Philosophical Rudiments Concerning Government and Society*, in *Man and Citizen* (Indianapolis: Hackett, 1991), 89.

40. Jacobson, "Strange Case," 9.

41. Jack Henry Abbott, *Inside the Belly of the Beast: Letters from Prison* (New York: Random House, 1981), 37; Stefan Aust, *Baader-Meinhof: The Inside Story of the RAF*, trans. Anthea Bell (London: Bodley Head, 2008), xi, 192–95. The Weathermen once commented that "we began life as Jonah . . . inside the great whale that devours us all"—cited in Jeremy Varon, *Bringing the War Back Home: The Weather Underground, the Red Army Faction, and Revolutionary Violence in the Sixties* (Berkeley: University of California Press, 2004), 177.

42. Friedrich Nietzsche, *Thus Spoke Zarathustra*, trans. R. J. Hollingdale (Harmondsworth, UK: Penguin, 1969), 75.

43. Mark Neocleous, *Imagining the State* (Maidenhead, UK: Open University Press, 2003), 20.

44. My argument here is reinforced by Hobbes's comment in response to Bishop Bramhall's criticisms of his work: "Now this *Leviathan* he calleth '*Monstrum horrendum, informe, ingens, cui lumen ademptum.*' Words not farre fetcht, nor more applicable to my *Leviathan*, than to any other writing that should offend him. For allowing him the word *Monstrum*, (because it seems he takes it for a monstrous great fish) he can neither say it is *informe*; for even they that approve not the doctrine, allow for the method." *The Questions Concerning Liberty, Necessity, and Chance*, in *The English Works of Thomas Hobbes*, vol. 5, ed. Sir William Molesworth (London: John Bohn, 1841), 24.

45. John M. Steadman, "Leviathan and Renaissance Etymology," *Journal of the History of Ideas* 28, no. 4 (1967): 575–76. Also see Noel Malcolm, "The Name and Nature of Leviathan: Political Symbolism and Biblical Exegesis," *Intellectual History Review* 17, no. 1 (2007): 21–39, 34; Patricia Springborg, "Hobbes and Schmitt on the Name and Nature of Leviathan Revisited," *Critical Review of International Social and Political Philosophy* 13, nos. 2–3 (2010): 301.

46. Patricia Springborg, "Hobbes's Biblical Beasts: *Leviathan* and *Behemoth*," *Political Theory* 23, no. 2 (1995): 361; Robert E. Stillman, "Hobbes's *Leviathan*: Monsters, Metaphors, and Magic," *English Literary History* 62, no. 4 (1995): 795.

47. See Karl Marx, "On the Jewish Question" in Karl Marx and Frederick Engels, *Collected Works*, vol. 3 (London: Lawrence and Wishart, 1975), 163.

48. "And in saying that, I am but saying in other words that we are in an epoch of anarchy. Anarchy plus a constable!" Thomas Carlyle, "Inaugural Address at Edinburgh," in *Selected Essays*, ed. T. Nelson (1866), 473. Schmitt's tweaking of this is at *Leviathan*, 22.

49. Hobbes, *Leviathan*, 219, 230.

50. Hobbes, *Leviathan*, 153.

51. Jacques Derrida, *The Beast and the Sovereign*, vol. 1, trans. Geoffrey Bennington (Chicago: University of Chicago Press, 2009), 42, and *The Beast and the Sovereign*, vol. 2, trans. Geoffrey Bennington (Chicago: University of Chicago Press, 2011), 267.

52. James Fitzjames Stephen, "Hobbes's Minor Works," in *Horae Sabbaticae: Reprint of Articles Contributed to the Saturday Review*, 2nd Series (London: Macmillan, 1892), 39; Samuel I. Mintz, "Leviathan as Metaphor," *Hobbes Studies* 2 (1989): 3–9, 4.

53. Peter Linebaugh and Markus Rediker, *The Many-Headed Hydra: The Hidden History of the Revolutionary Atlantic* (London: Verso Books, 2000), 2–3.

54. Karl Marx, *Capital: A Critique of Political Economy*, vol. 1, trans. B. Fowkes (Harmondsworth, UK: Penguin, 1976), 549.

55. Antony Ascham, *Of the Confusions and Revolutions of Governments* (London, 1649), 49, 108.

56. Hobbes, *Leviathan*, 241.

57. Linebaugh and Rediker, *Many-Headed*, 329.

58. Hobbes, *Behemoth*, 72.

59. Linebaugh and Rediker, *Many-Headed*, 6.

60. Neocleous, *Fabrication*, 82, 92; Mark Neocleous, *War Power, Police Power* (Edinburgh: Edinburgh University Press, 2014), 14, 74–82; Klaus Mladek, "Exception Rules: Contemporary Political Theory and the Police," in *Police*

Forces: A Cultural History of an Institution, ed. Klaus Mladek (Basingstoke, UK: Palgrave, 2007), 227.

61. Every item on this list of keepings could be applied to the process of kettling being perfected by the state to deal with protests. And apropos of my earlier point about police discretion and the law, note that kettling was originally introduced purely as a new police tactic, becoming "legalized" after the event, so to speak. On the list of keepings see Hobbes, *Leviathan*, 82, 83, 88, 102, 117, 118, 120, 134, 150, 163, 239, 323–28, 367, 401.

62. The problem with much of the recent work on capitalism as the monster is that it does not really deal with the ways in which monstrosity, and thus capitalism, is policed. In other words, as much as we might need a critical theory of capitalism to understand the power of monstrosity, so we also need a critical theory of police power to understand both capitalism and monstrosity. For such capitalist monstrosity see Rob Latham, *Consuming Youth: Vampires, Cyborgs, and the Culture of Consumption* (Chicago: University of Chicago Press, 2002); Annalee Newitz, *Pretend We're Dead: Capitalist Monsters in American Pop Culture* (Durham: Duke University Press, 2006); Chris Harman, *Zombie Capitalism: Global Crisis and the Relevance of Marx* (London: Bookmarks, 2009); David McNally, *Monsters of the Market: Zombies, Vampires and Global Capitalism* (Leiden, Netherlands: Brill, 2011).

CHAPTER NINE: PROOF OF DEATH

This chapter is a revised version of a previous published essay. See Travis Linnemann, "Proof of Death: Police Power and the Visual Economies of Seizure, Accumulation and Trophy," *Theoretical Criminology* 21, no. 1 (2017): 57–77.

1. Cate Sevilla, "TV Presenter Melissa Bachman Angers Entire Internet after Shooting a Lion," November 15, 2013, *Buzzfeed*, http://www.buzzfeed.com/catesevilla/tv-presenter-melissa-bachman-angers-entire-internet-after-sh.

2. See Deborah Poole, *Vision, Race, and Modernity: A Visual Economy of the Andean Image World* (Princeton: Princeton University Press, 1997). Poole understands visual economies as the many ways in which photographs are exchanged and circulate within contemporary culture. Alan Sekula might also call this the "traffic" in photographs. Alan Sekula, "The Traffic in Photographs," *Art Journal* 41, no. 1 (1981): 15–25.

3. See Allan Feldman, "On Cultural Anesthesia: From Desert Storm to Rodney King," *American Ethnologist* 21, no. 2 (1994): 404–18. Feldman describes cultural anesthesia as a process by which pain and suffering are rendered an object of consumption.

4.   Eamonn Carrabine, "Images of Torture: Culture, Politics and Power," *Crime, Media, Culture* 7, no. 1 (2011): 5–30.

5.   A simple Google search of "police announce major bust" will return a host of articles containing trophy shots, such as Justin L. Mack, "Fishers Police Seize 100 Pounds of Pot, $330,000 Cash in City's 'Largest' Drug Bust," *Indy Star*, July 20, 2015, http://www.indystar.com/story/news/crime/2015/07/20 /fishers-police-announce-major-drug-bust/30423823/.

6.   Jen Chung, "NYPD Gloats about Arresting Graffiti Artist COST," *Gothamist*, October 19, 2014, http://gothamist.com/2014/10/09/nypd _busts_cost_graffiti.php#photo-1.

7.   See "Chicago Police Take 'Trophy' Photo with Arrested University of Pittsburgh Student at G-20 Summit," YouTube video, October 16, 2009, https://www.youtube.com/watch?v=tkwFKf3OcTE.

8.   By the police power, I refer to the broad range of powers extending beyond the uniformed police, which are exercised by a variety of agencies and institutions concerned with the production and maintenance of social order. See Mark Neocleous, *War Power, Police Power* (Edinburgh: Edinburgh University Press, 2014), 11.

9.   Mark Neocleous, *The Fabrication of Social Order: A Critical Theory of Police Power* (London: Pluto Press, 2000).

10.   Jonathan M. Finn, *Capturing the Criminal Image: From Mug Shot to Surveillance Society* (Minneapolis: University of Minnesota Press, 2009).

11.   Grégiore Chamayou, *Manhunts: A Philosophical History* (Princeton: Princeton University Press, 2012). Chamayou argues that hunting or cynegetic power is so seamlessly ingrained in liberal capitalist social order that it largely goes unnoticed.

12.   Travis Linnemann and Tyler Wall, "'This Is Your Face on Meth': The Punitive Spectacle of 'White Trash' in the Rural War on Drugs," *Theoretical Criminology* 17, no. 3 (2013): 315–34.

13.   Christopher Lasch, *The Culture of Narcissism: American Life in an Age of Diminishing Expectations* (New York: Norton, 1991).

14.   It is important to note that while most police trophy shots are probably not true to the selfie form, as narcissistic self-representations they are closely related, regardless of whether subject and photographer are one and the same. For actual selfies taken by police, see the website *Cop Selfies*, accessed January 28, 2021, http://copselfies.tumblr.com.

15.   Jenna Brager, "Selfie Control," *The New Inquiry*, March 17, 2014, https:// thenewinquiry.com/selfie-control/.

16.   In 2013, *selfie* was named the Oxford English Dictionary word of the year, further proving its utility, ubiquity, and perhaps place within a contemporary

culture of narcissism.

17. Brian Merchant, "Selfies with the Homeless, a New Unshareable Low," *Motherboard*, February 10, 2014, https://www.vice.com/en/article/qkv883/selfies-with-the-homeless-a-new-shareable-low.

18. Nicholas Mirzeoff, "In 2014 We Took 1tn Photos: Welcome to Our New Visual Culture," *Guardian*, July 10, 2015, http://www.theguardian.com/books/2015/jul/10/2014-one-trillion-photos-welcome-new-visual-culture.

19. Derek Conrad Murray, "Notes to Self: The Visual Culture of Selfies in the Age of Social Media," *Consumption Markets & Culture* 18, no. 6 (2015): 490–516.

20. Brager, "Selfie Control."

21. Michelle Brown, "Visual Criminology and Carceral Studies: Counter-Images in the Carceral Age," *Theoretical Criminology* 18, no. 2 (2014): 176–97.

22. Majid Yar, "Crime, Media and the Will-to-Representation: Reconsidering Relationships in the New Media Age," *Crime, Media, Culture* 8, no. 3 (2012): 245–60.

23. Yar, "Crime, Media and the Will-to-Representation," 246.

24. Damien Cave, "Eight Teenagers Charged in Internet Beating Have Their Day on the Web," *New York Times*, April 12, 2008.

25. Jack Katz, *Seductions of Crime: Moral and Sensual Attractions in Doing Evil*, (New York: Basic Books, 1988).

26. Willem De Haan and Jaco Vos, "A Crying Shame: The Over-Rationalized Conception of Man in the Rational Choice Perspective," *Theoretical Criminology* 7, no. 1 (2003): 29–54.

27. Simon Cottee and Keith Hayward, "Terrorist (E)motives: The Existential Attractions of Terrorism," *Studies in Conflict & Terrorism* 34, no. 12 (2011): 963–86.

28. Markus Dirk Dubber, "Policing Possession: The War on Crime and the End of Criminal Law," *Journal of Criminal Law and Criminology* 91, no. 4 (2000): 855.

29. *Black's Law Dictionary* defines robbery as "the felonious taking of personal property in the possession of another, from his person or immediate presence, and against his will, accomplished by means of force or fear." "What Is Robbery?," *The Law Dictionary, Featuring Black's Law Dictionary Free Online Legal Dictionary*, 2nd ed., http://thelawdictionary.org/robbery/. And likewise it defines larceny as "the wrongful and fraudulent taking and carrying away by one person of the mere personal goods of another from any place, with a felonious intent to convert them to his (the taker's) use, and make them his property, without the consent of the owner." "What Is Larceny?," *The Law Dictionary, Featuring Black's Law Dictionary Free Online Legal Dictionary*, 2nd ed., http://thelawdictionary.org/larceny.

30. Joseph L. Sax, "Takings and the Police Power," *Yale Law Journal* 74 (1964): 36. According to Sax, police power "is used by the courts to identify those state and local governmental restrictions and prohibitions which are valid and which may be invoked without payment of compensation. In its best known and most traditional uses, the police power is employed to protect the health, safety, and morals of the community in the form of such things as fire regulations, garbage disposal control and restrictions upon prostitution and liquor. But it has never been thought that government authority under the police power was limited to those narrow uses."

31. Sarah Stillman, "Taken," *New Yorker*, August 12, 2013.

32. Christopher Ingraham, "How Philadelphia Seizes Millions in 'Pocket Change' from Some of the City's Poorest Residents," *Washington Post*, June 10, 2015.

33. Curt Anderson, "Fla. Police Cash Force Shows Forfeiture's Growth," *Associated Press*, May 10, 2013, http://www.policeone.com/legal/articles /6229081-Fla-police-cash-force-shows-forfeitures-growth/.

34. The mean seized amount hovered around $192.

35. "Citizens for Justice. Pennies from Heaven, Chief Burton Talks Asset Forfeitures," YouTube video, November 19, 2012, https://www.youtube.com /watch?v=ipHUN-xLLms.

36. Erica Perdue, "Saginaw Sheriff Federspiel Tests Waters on Sale of Mustang Taken from a Local Drug Dealer," *MLive*, April 4, 2012, http://www.mlive .com/news/saginaw/index.ssf/2012/04/saginaw_sheriff_federspiel_tes.html.

37. Trevor Paglen, *I Could Tell You But Then You Would Have to be Destroyed by Me: Emblems from the Pentagon's Black World* (New York: Melville House, 2010).

38. See Christopher Ingram, "How the DEA Took a Young Man's Life Savings without Ever Charging Him with a Crime," *Washington Post*, May 11, 2015.

39. Walter Benjamin, "Critique of Violence," *Reflections* 14, no. 3 (1978): 237.

40. Michael Taussig, *Walter Benjamin's Grave* (Chicago: University of Chicago Press, 2010), 178.

41. Mark Neocleous, "The Monster and the Police: Dexter to Hobbes," *Radical Philosophy* 185 (2014): 8–18.

42. Egon Bittner, *The Functions of the Police in Modern Society* (Chevy Chase, MD: National Institute of Mental Health, 1970), 171.

43. Taussig, *Walter Benjamin's Grave*, 178, emphasis added.

44. Andrew Hawkes, "5 Things Cops and Criminals Have in Common," *Police One*, August 6, 2014, http://www.policeone.com/police-jobs-and-careers /articles/7419138-5-things-cops-and-criminals-have-in-common/.

45. A citizen in Baltimore, Maryland, recently photographed a tremendous example of policing's desire to claim victory and revenge and gloat at the

suffering of state subjects. On the inside door of a police transport van was a warning for prisoners: "Enjoy your ride cuz we sure will!" In the context of the killing of Baltimore resident Freddie Gray, who died in police custody while restrained in a similar van, the victim of a "rough ride," the message is clear. Police are not only unsympathetic but actually delight in the suffering of those under their charge. See Jethro Mullen, "Baltimore Authorities Investigate Photos of 'Enjoy Your Ride' Sign Inside Police Van," *CNN*, July 3, 2015, http://www.cnn.com/2015/07/03/us/baltimore-police-van-sign/.

46. Simon Cottee and Keith Hayward make similar observations of the emotive allure of violent acts of terror. They argue that the existential desire for excitement, meaning, and glory are key and overlooked motivators for those who engage in terrorism. See Cottee and Hayward, "Terrorist (E)motives," 966.

47. Chamayou, *Manhunts*, 87.

48. Tyler Wall, "Unmanning the Police Manhunt: Vertical Security as Pacification," *Socialist Studies / Études Socialistes* 9, no. 2 (2013).

49. Joseph-Achille Mbembé and Libby Meintjes, "Necropolitics," *Public Culture* 15, no. 1 (2003): 11–40.

50. James Axtell and William C. Sturtevant, "The Unkindest Cut, or Who Invented Scalping," *William and Mary Quarterly: A Magazine of Early American History* (1980): 451–72.

51. Donna J. Haraway, *Primate Visions: Gender, Race, and Nature in the World of Modern Science* (Abingdon: Routledge, 2013).

52. Thomas Strychacz, "Trophy-Hunting as a Trope of Manhood in Ernest Hemingway's Green Hills of Africa," *Hemingway Review* 13, no. 1 (1993): 36–47.

53. Jane Desmond, "Displaying Death, Animating Life: Changing Fictions of 'Liveness' from Taxidermy to Animatronics," *Representing Animal* 26 (2002): 159. Matthew Brower, "Trophy Shots: Early North American Photographs of Nonhuman Animals and the Display of Masculine Prowess," *Society & Animals* 13, no. 1 (2005): 13–32.

54. Chamayou argues that in the context of chattel slavery the master and hence hunter is always in a position of supremacy. "Slaveholding domination does not arise from an open struggle but rather from a relationship, which is dissymmetrical from the outset, of manhunting. Here, even before operations begin, the hunter is already in a position to be the master. He knows his power and his material supremacy. The prey, taken by surprise, is not in a position to confront a group of hunters. At first, it has no choice but to flee." Chamayou, *Manhunts*, 108.

55. Linda Kalof and Amy Fitzgerald, "Reading the Trophy: Exploring the Display of Dead Animals in Hunting Magazines," *Visual Studies* 18, no. 2

(2003): 112–22.

56. Elaine Scarry, *The Body in Pain: The Making and Unmaking of the World* (Oxford: Oxford University Press, 1987), 13.

57. Scarry, *The Body in Pain*, 28.

58. Elizabeth Irene Smith, "'The Body in Pain': An Interview with Elaine Scarry," *Concentric: Literary and Cultural Studies* 32, no. 2 (2006): 230.

59. Mark S. Hamm, "'High Crimes and Misdemeanors': George W. Bush and the Sins of Abu Ghraib," *Crime, Media, Culture* 3, no. 3 (2007): 260.

60. James J. Weingartner, "Trophies of War: US Troops and the Mutilation of Japanese War Dead, 1941–1945," *Pacific Historical Review* 61, no. 1 (1992): 53–67.

61. The events of September 11, 2001, saw "terrorist" hunting licenses emerge as an update of this old particularly noxious logic.

62. Mark Boal, "The Kill Team," *Rolling Stone* 27 (2011).

63. Daniel Krier and William J. Swart, "Trophies of Surplus Enjoyment," *Critical Sociology* 42, no. 3 (2016): 371–92.

64. Katz, *Seductions of Crime*.

65. Simon Cottee, "The Pornography of Jihadism," *Atlantic*, September 12, 2014.

66. John Cox, "Mexico's Drug Cartels Love Social Media," *Vice*, November 4, 2013, http://www.vice.com/read/mexicos-drug-cartels-are-using-the -internet-to-get-up-to-mischief.

67. John Tuckman, "Mexican Drug Cartel Massacres Have a Method in Their Brutal Madness," *Guardian*, May 14, 2012, emphasis added.

68. Philip Smith, "Narrating the Guillotine: Punishment Technology as Myth and Symbol," *Theory, Culture & Society* 20, no. 5 (2003): 27–51.

69. Slavoj Žižek, *The Sublime Object of Ideology* (London: Verso Books, 1989), 133–36.

70. Gideon Brough and Alun D. Williams, "Decapitation Strategy," in *The Encyclopedia of War* (Wiley Online Library, 2012).

71. United States Department of Justice, "Statement on the Apprehension of Joaquin 'Chapo' Guzman Loera," February 22, 2014, http://www.justice. gov/opa/pr/statement-apprehension-joaquin-chapo-guzman-loera.

72. See Patrick Keefe, "The Hunt for El Chapo: How the World's Most Notorious Drug Lord Was Captured, *New Yorker*, May 5, 2014. A photo that circulated widely with news of the capture shows the shirtless Guzman sitting or kneeling below his camouflaged captors with a disembodied hand pulling back his head as if to position Guzman for photographic display or perhaps execution.

73. Fred Main and Kim Janssen, "CPD Cops Posed for Photo Standing over Black Man Dressed in Antlers," *Chicago Sun-Times*, May 26, 2015.

74. Guy Debord, *Society of the Spectacle* (Bread and Circuses Publishing, 2012), 34.

75. If we consider the trophy shot featuring Pablo Escobar we might say that this future arrived long ago.

76. Michael Taussig, "Terror as Usual: Walter Benjamin's Theory of History as a State of Siege," *Social Text* 23 (1989): 3–20.

EPILOGUE: THE PLAGUE OF POLICE

1. Michel Foucault, *Discipline and Punish: The Birth of the Prison*, trans. Alan Sheridan (New York Vintage Books, 1995), 197.

2. Foucault, *Discipline and Punish*, 195, 197.

3. Foucault, *Discipline and Punish*, 199.

4. Foucault, *Discipline and Punish*, 196.

5. Foucault, *Discipline and Punish*, 199.

6. Ruth Wilson Gilmore, "What Is to Be Done?" *American Quarterly* 63, no. 2 (June 2011): 257.

7. Sprite Mallapaty, "How Do Children Spread the Coronavirus? The Science Still Isn't Clear," *Nature*, May 7, 2020.

8. David Cyranoski, "Profile of a Killer: The Complex Biology Powering the Coronavirus Pandemic," *Nature*, May 4, 2020.

9. Foucault, *Discipline and Punish*, 218.

10. Foucault, *Discipline and Punish*, 215

11. Ben Kesslen, "NYPD to No Longer Enforce Wearing Masks Absent 'Serious Danger,' Mayor Says," *NBC News*, May 15, 2020, https://www.nbcnews.com /news/us-news/nypd-no-longer-enforce-wearing-masks-absent-serious -danger-mayor-n1207931.

12. Neil Smith, "There's No Such Thing as a Natural Disaster," *Understanding Katrina: Perspectives from the Social Sciences* (Social Science Research Council, 2006).

13. Mike Davis, "C'est La Lutte Finale," *Progressive International*, April 30, 2020, https://progressive.international/blueprint/34da398a-af05 -43bb-9778-c27023932630-la-lutte-finale/en.

14. Karl Marx and Friedrich Engels, *The Communist Manifesto* (New York: Penguin, 2002), 4.

15. Fang Fang, *Wuhan Diary: Dispatches from a Quarantined City* (New York: HarperVia, 2020).

16. See, for example, the Los Angeles COVID-19 Mutual Aid Network, the Baltimore Mutual Aid, STL Mutual Aid, the Mutual Aid Disaster Network, www.covaid.co, and others.

INDEX

Leech, Tamara, 75
Leviathan (Hobbes), 26, 149–54, 156, 167
Life magazine, 172
Linebaugh, Peter, 154–55
Linnemann, Travis, 183
Locke, John, 24, 26
Los Angeles, 46, 55, 141
Los Angeles County, 60
Los Angeles Police Department, 13, 21, 23, 78, 141
Los Angeles Times, 78
Louisiana, 88–90, 92–98
Louisiana Bucket Brigade, 98
Louisville, 5, 180, 180–81
Lynch, Michael, 75

M

Malm, Andreas, 91, 93, 102
Manhunts: A Philosophical History (Chamayou), 170
Mann, Geoff, 86–87
Manning, Peter, 145
The Many-Headed Hydra (Linebaugh and Rediker), 154–55
Marion Correctional Institution, 180
Marshall, John, 129
Marshall Trilogy, 129
Martin, Trayvon, ix
Marxism, 7, 86, 88–89
Marx, Karl, 87, 122–23
Maryland, 99
Mason, Paul, 85
McCarthy, Kevin, 60
McClintock, Anne, 22
McDermott, Timothy, 174
McHarris, Philip V., 181
McLaughlin, Moses A., 59
Medellín Cartel, 174

Mejia, Ramon, 95–96
Mexico, 39, 57, 172–73
Miami Metro Police Department, 143, 151
Michigan, 166
Middle East, 128–29, 134, 136
Miéville, China, 8
militarization of police, 39, 44, 94, 112
Miller, Andrea, 181
Minneapolis, 49, 184
   police in, vii–viii, 5, 45, 180, 182, 183
   protests in, vii–ix, 183
Minnesota, 97, 184
Misra, Pankaj, 66
Mississippian people, 107
Mississippi River, 58
Missouri, 184
Mittman, Gregg, 113
Mixed-Oxide Fuel, 103
Moby-Dick (Melville), 151
Montana, 90
Monterey Shale, 57
Montesquieu, 146, 148
Moore, Jason, 59, 88
MOVE, 101
Movement for Black Lives, 14, 32, 35, 47–48, 132–33, 136–37
MPD 150, viii, 49
Murphy, Michelle, 115

N

Nash, Linda, 58
National Geographic, 159
National Guard, viii, ix
Native nations. *See* Indigenous people
nature, 6, 28
   animalization and, 62
   commodity of, 3–4, 6–8
   domination of, 9

ABOUT THE CONTRIBUTORS

David Correia is a professor of American studies at the University of New Mexico. He is the author of *Properties of Violence: Law and Land Grant Struggle in Northern New Mexico* (2013), coauthor with Tyler Wall of *Police: A Field Guide* (2018), and coauthor with Jennifer Denetdale, Melanie Yazzie, and Nick Estes of *Red Nation Rising: From Bordertown Violence to Native Liberation* (2021).

Axel Gonzalez is a PhD candidate in the department of American studies at the University of New Mexico whose dissertation focuses on the role of the police and the military in the politics of climate change.

Travis Linnemann is associate professor of sociology at Kansas State University. He is the author of *Meth Wars: Police, Media, Power* (2016) and *The Horror of Police* (2022). He is the current coeditor of *Crime, Media, Culture*.

Philip V. McHarris is a presidential postdoctoral fellow in the department of African American studies at Princeton University. He holds a PhD in sociology and African American studies from Yale University.

Andrea Miller is assistant professor of social media and digital cultures in the School of Communication and Multimedia Studies at Florida Atlantic University, where they are also faculty associate in women's, gender, and sexuality studies and Director of the Initiative on Drones, Sensing & Surveillance as part of the FAU Center for the Future Mind. Their work draws from feminist studies, studies of police power and empire and science and technology studies to examine how relationships between technology and sensibilities of security shape racialized life and environments.

Mark Neocleous is professor of the critique of political economy at Brunel University London. His most recent books include *War Power, Police Power* (2014); *The Universal Adversary: Security, Capital, and "The Enemies of All Mankind"* (2016); *A Critical Theory of Police Power* (2021), and *The Politics of Immunity: Security and the Policing of Bodies* (2022).

Julie Sze is a professor of American studies at University of California Davis. She is also the founding director of the Environmental Justice Project for UC Davis' John Muir Institute for the Environment. She is the author of three books, *Noxious New York: The Racial Politics of Urban Health and Environmental Justice* (2006), *Fantasy Islands: Chinese Dreams and Ecological Fears in an Age of Climate Crisis* (2015), and *Environmental Justice in a Moment of Danger* (2000).

Tyler Wall is associate professor of sociology at the University of Tennessee, Knoxville. He is the coauthor with David Correia of *Police: A Field Guide* (2018) and coeditor with Parastou Saberi and Will Jackson of *Destroy, Build, Secure: Readings on Pacification* (2017).

Melanie Yazzie is an assistant professor at the University of New Mexico with a joint appointment in the departments of Native American studies and American studies. She is a coauthor with Jennifer Denetdale, David Correia, and Nick Estes of *Red Nation Rising: From Bordertown Violence to Native Liberation* (2021).

ABOUT HAYMARKET BOOKS

Haymarket Books is a radical, independent, nonprofit book publisher based in Chicago. Our mission is to publish books that contribute to struggles for social and economic justice. We strive to make our books a vibrant and organic part of social movements and the education and development of a critical, engaged, international left.

We take inspiration and courage from our namesakes, the Haymarket martyrs, who gave their lives fighting for a better world. Their 1886 struggle for the eight-hour day—which gave us May Day, the international workers' holiday—reminds workers around the world that ordinary people can organize and struggle for their own liberation. These struggles continue today across the globe—struggles against oppression, exploitation, poverty, and war.

Since our founding in 2001, Haymarket Books has published more than five hundred titles. Radically independent, we seek to drive a wedge into the risk-averse world of corporate book publishing. Our authors include Noam Chomsky, Arundhati Roy, Rebecca Solnit, Angela Y. Davis, Howard Zinn, Amy Goodman, Wallace Shawn, Mike Davis, Winona LaDuke, Ilan Pappé, Richard Wolff, Dave Zirin, Keeanga-Yamahtta Taylor, Nick Turse, Dahr Jamail, David Barsamian, Elizabeth Laird, Amira Hass, Mark Steel, Avi Lewis, Naomi Klein, and Neil Davidson. We are also the trade publishers of the acclaimed Historical Materialism Book Series and of Dispatch Books.

ALSO AVAILABLE FROM HAYMARKET BOOKS

From #BlackLivesMatter to Black Liberation (Expanded Second Edition)
Keeanga-Yamahtta Taylor, foreword by Angela Y. Davis

Policing A Class Society: The Experience of American Cities, 1865–1915
Sidney L. Harring

#SayHerName: Black Women's Stories of State Violence and Public Silence
African American Policy Forum, edited by Kimberlé Crenshaw
Foreword by Janelle Monáe

The Torture Machine: Racism and Police Violence in Chicago
Flint Taylor

Under the Blacklight:
The Intersectional Vulnerabilities that the Twin Pandemics Lay Bare
Edited by Kimberlé Crenshaw and Daniel HoSang

We Do This 'Til We Free Us: Abolitionist Organizing and Transforming Justice
Mariame Kaba, edited by Tamara K. Nopper, foreword by Naomi Murakawa

We Still Here: Pandemic, Policing, Protest, and Possibility
Marc Lamont Hill, edited by Frank Barat
Foreword by Keeanga-Yamahtta Taylor

Who Do You Serve, Who Do You Protect?
Police Violence and Resistance in the United States
Edited by Joe Macaré, Maya Schenwar, and Alana Yu-lan Price
Foreword by Alicia Garza